CLARENDON ARISTOTLE SERIES

General Editors
J. L. ACKRILL AND LINDSAY JUDSON

ARISTOTLE

Topics

Books I and VIII
with excerpts from related texts

Translated
with a Commentary
by

ROBIN SMITH

CLARENDON PRESS · OXFORD

1997

Oxford University Press, Great Clarendon Street, Oxford OX2 6DP

Oxford New York
Athens Auckland Bangkok Bombay
Calcutta Cape Town Dar es Salaam Delhi
Florence Hong Kong Istanbul Karachi
Kuala Lumpur Madras Madrid Melbourne
Mexico City Nairobi Paris Singapore
Taipei Tokyo Toronto
and associated companies in
Berlin Ibadan

Oxford is a trade mark of Oxford University Press

Published in the United States
by Oxford University Press Inc., New York

British Library Cataloguing in Publication Data
Data available

Library of Congress Cataloging in Publication Data
Aristotle.
[Topics. Book 1. English]
Topics. Books I and VIII, with excerpts from related texts /
— (Clarendon Aristotle series)
Includes bibliographical references (p.   ) and indexes.
1. Logic, Ancient. 2. Dialectic. 3. Topic (Philosophy)
I. Smith, Robin, 1946–   . II. Aristotle. Topics. Book 8.
English. III. Title. IV. Series.
B442.A5S55 1996 160—dc20 96-5652
ISBN 0–19–823945–9
ISBN 0–19–823942–4 (Pbk.)

1 3 5 7 9 10 8 6 4 2

Typeset by Best-set Typesetter Ltd., Hong Kong
Printed in Great Britain
on acid-free paper by
Bookcraft (Bath) Ltd
Midsomer Norton, Avon

To
Carolyn

PREFACE

In 1968 G. E. L. Owen noted that the *Topics* was selected as the subject of the third Symposium Aristotelicum because it was 'a work rich in debatable material but relatively poor in commentaries'. Since that time, scholarly debate about Aristotle's conception of dialectic and its relationship to his views on philosophical method has become if anything more intense. However, despite much excellent interpretative work, Brunschwig's Budé edition remains the only commentary in any modern language, and as of this writing even that is still limited to Books I–IV. A new English translation and commentary are very much needed. The present volume scarcely supplies that need, but I hope that it may serve as a stopgap in the interim.

A number of scholars and scholarly audiences have endured my translations and interpretations of one passage or another and kindly ameliorated my errors; I am particularly grateful to Robert Bolton and Charles M. Young. The Editors of the Clarendon Aristotle Series, John Ackrill and Lindsay Judson, were a constant source of help and good advice. I am especially indebted to Professor Ackrill, who provided me with an endless stream of corrections and suggestions: whatever I may have got right in this book should probably be laid to his credit. Finally, I should like to acknowledge the support of a sabbatical leave from Kansas State University, during which much of the commentary was written.

CONTENTS

ABBREVIATED TITLES OF
ARISTOTLE'S WORKS

An. Post.	*Posterior Analytics*
An. Pr.	*Prior Analytics*
Cat.	*Categories*
De An.	*On the Soul (De Anima)*
De Cael.	*On the Heavens (De Caelo)*
De Int.	*On Interpretation (De Interpretatione)*
EE	*Eudemian Ethics*
EN	*Nicomachean Ethics*
GA	*On the Generation of Animals*
GC	*On Coming-to-Be and Passing Away (De Generatione et Corruptione)*
HA	*History of Animals*
Met.	*Metaphysics*
Mete.	*Meteorology*
PA	*On the Parts of Animals*
Phys.	*Physics*
Poet.	*Poetics*
Pol.	*Politics*
Rhet.	*Rhetoric*
SE	*On Sophistical Refutations (De Sophisticis Elenchis)*

INTRODUCTION

The *Topics* is Aristotle's treatise on dialectical argument, that is, argumentation in which two adversaries oppose one another. As such, it has had a long and influential history. Aristotle certainly did not invent adversarial arguments—that practice is perhaps as old as human language—nor did he originate the more narrowly defined types of debates presupposed by much of the *Topics*, especially Book VIII. However, he was, as he tells us himself, the first to offer a dialectical *method*: a systematic art enabling its possessor to construct the most effective possible argument to a given conclusion from the materials available. As a consequence of developing this theory, he initiated the study of logical consequence, that is, *logic*. Aristotle was, in fact, the founder of formal logic; and though the *Topics* lacks the theoretical sophistication of his austere masterpiece in this field, the *Prior Analytics*, it offers us many important insights into his conception of logic. But the *Topics* can also be read for other purposes. It is the richest source among Aristotle's works for evidence about his conception of a definition and the related notions of genus, unique property, differentia, and accident: the so-called *predicables*. This complex of five notions was a part of Aristotle's inheritance from Plato and the Academy, but he subjected it to important modifications and introduced some characteristic doctrines of his own (most notably the doctrine of the categories). We find it reflected throughout his works, and in one form or other it became a commonplace of the ancient philosophical tradition; as codified in a short introductory treatise by Porphyry, usually known by the title *Quinque Voces*, or 'Five Terms', it became part of the basic equipment of every medieval philosopher. Finally, the *Topics* may be studied for insight into Aristotle's conception of the method of philosophical inquiry itself. Even though the treatise disavows any pretensions to scientific precision, there are strong echoes of its procedures in Aristotle's own scientific works, especially his way of working towards his own position by starting with a critical survey of the opinions of his predecessors. Some scholars have gone so far as to maintain that for Aristotle, the conception of philosophical method was fundamentally dialectical; even if we resist this conclusion, it is beyond dispute that an understanding of Aristotle's concept of dialectic sheds light on much that we find in his other works.

What, then, is this dialectical method, and what is its purpose? Here, we must confront a major problem of interpretation. In the last century or two, 'dialectic' has become a word of notoriously pliable meaning: saying that the *Topics* is about dialectic is not very helpful until we know what *Aristotelian* dialectic was. Seeking enlightenment on this point, modern readers like ourselves naturally turn to the *Topics*. In so doing, we are putting his treatise to a different use from the one he intended. Aristotle takes it for granted that his audience already knows what dialectical argument is; he was not concerned to explain its nature to people—for instance, barbarians of a later age like ourselves—for whom that very point is obscure. A cautionary tale can be drawn from the history of interpretation of the *Poetics*. Aristotle defines tragedy as 'the imitation of an action that is serious and also, as having magnitude, complete in itself; in language with pleasurable accessories, each kind brought in separately in the parts of the work; in a dramatic, not a narrative form; with incidents arousing pity and fear, wherewith to accomplish its catharsis of such emotions' (1449^b24–8). As an insightful account of the nature and workings of a certain kind of ancient Greek drama, this may be highly effective. However, it is intended for an audience that already knows what a tragedy is—that is, people who have actually seen tragic performances. It would therefore do little to enlighten a reader who did not know that a tragedy is a kind of *play*—or, worse, who had no idea that there were such things as plays. This was precisely the situation of Averroes and other medieval Islamic commentators on Aristotle. Averroes knew and studied the *Poetics*, but since dramatic presentations formed no part of his own culture it never occurred to him that a tragedy involved actors portraying actions in a story before an audience. Therefore, he took Aristotle to be talking about eulogies: poems in praise of famous men. What Averroes needed was a type of low-level explanation Aristotle had no reason to provide.

We are in much the same situation when it comes to the *Topics*. Time and again, we find Aristotle taking it for granted that his audience understands various technical terms or special practices associated with dialectical argument. He has no reason to offer an account of what dialectical argument is that will be proof against misunderstanding by *us*. To understand the practice for which Aristotle is trying to provide an art, we must first try to determine what he has left unsaid.

Dialectical Art and Dialectical Practice

To begin at the lowest possible level, the activity with which dialectic is concerned, dialectical practice, is *argumentative*: it is an activity in which premisses are advanced and conclusions are drawn from them. We can therefore speak of any dialectical exchange as a dialectical *argument*, and as an argument it will have a conclusion. The point of any argument is to obtain premisses and infer a conclusion from them. Of course, there are many contexts in which conclusions are drawn (forensic speeches and mathematical proofs, for two examples). What differentiates dialectical arguments from other arguments is that they take place by *question and answer*. The person who constructs a dialectical argument does so by asking questions of another person and building an argument out of the responses: the responses serve as premisses from which the questioner draws a conclusion. In its form, then, a dialectical argument differs from other kinds of argument in that its premisses are put forward as *questions*. But this form also entails further characteristics, since the questioner can only use as a premiss that which the answerer has conceded. We can better appreciate these differences, and their implications for Aristotle's dialectical method, if we survey briefly some of the types of dialectical argument historically important in ancient Greece up to the time of Aristotle.

One obvious example of an argumentative practice that fits the above description is Socrates' peculiar style of interrogating people. Socrates asked those he encountered for their opinions on some subject and then undertook to deduce something contradictory, or at least unacceptable to his respondent, from them. As Plato represents him, Socrates insists over and over that he is advancing no opinions himself, only eliciting opinions: it is the answerers who provide the premisses for his arguments. He saw himself as purging people of the false conceit of wisdom by these refutations, showing them that they cannot maintain all the beliefs they profess because those beliefs are inconsistent. If this is to be effective, then the answers Socrates elicits must indeed reflect the opinions of his respondents, and the conclusions he deduces must genuinely follow from them. Socratic dialectic may thus be distinguished from a kind of no-holds-barred verbal combat in which deliberately misleading questions are asked and conclusions deduced using deliberately fallacious arguments: such 'contentious' or 'eristic' argument, portrayed by Plato in the *Euthydemus*, reveals nothing about the answerer's state of knowledge.

Another example, though one we know less about, is the style of argument used by Zeno in support of Parmenides' denial of motion. As Plato tells it, Zeno defended Parmenides by attacking his attackers on the basis of their own opinions, arguing that anyone who asserts there is motion is thereby committed to impossible consequences. Zeno evidently presented his arguments in a written treatise, not (or not only) as a series of questions directed at Parmenides' opponents. Nevertheless, there is a notional kinship with Socratic dialectic as just described, since Zeno argues from what he takes to be his adversaries' opinions. If this is to be an effective defence, then the absurd consequences he deduces must actually follow from those opinions.

Plato's original inspiration in philosophy was Socratic dialectic. As his conception of philosophy matured and developed, his concept of dialectic changed in ways sometimes difficult to follow: it often comes to mean something like 'the method of philosophical investigation'—whatever Plato happens to think that method is at the time. However, dialectic retains its association with argumentation, and probably even with argumentation directed at another person's opinions (see, for instance, the remarks about the risks attached to the education of philosophers in dialectic in *Rep.* VII, 537–9). It appears clear that Plato encouraged some type of argumentative exercises in his Academy in which participants undertook to refute one another's positions. The most important source of information about this activity is in fact Aristotle's *Topics*, especially Book VIII, which presupposes a type of exchange governed by many rules, probably with judges of some kind to oversee individual contests and evaluate them.

I shall return to the details of these latter exchanges below. For the present, what is important is that all these kinds of dialectical argument involve a questioner who secures premises from an answerer and then uses them to deduce—or at least try to deduce—some conclusion which actually follows from them. This is the fundamental purpose of dialectical argument. To show another that his expressed opinions lead to an absurdity, or at least to a proposition he rejects, is to show him something important about his views. But even if an answerer were only pretending to give sincere answers, the dialectical exercise could show that a certain set of opinions, if held by anyone, would be inconsistent. An examination of this sort of the opinions held by other thinkers, or people

xiv

in general, would be a plausible first stage in a philosophical inquiry. As a variant of this, an answerer could undertake to impersonate some well-known sage and answer appropriately; the questioner's arguments then are an examination of that sage's philosophical position. By these and similar measures, dialectical argument becomes a general exploration of the consequences of a set of views, with special emphasis on the detection of inconsistencies.

Carrying out such an exploration in a live exchange between questioner and answerer would have some advantages—for instance, two competitors could do a better job of presenting both sides of a case than one—but a skilled practitioner could dispense with the need for a partner and explore the consequences of a set of views alone. This recalls Aristotle's own practice of beginning his treatments of scientific subjects by first reviewing the 'puzzles,' i.e. the inconsistent conclusions which can be deduced from the received opinions on any subject.

Or we might imagine a development in another direction. Argument persuades by building on what is already accepted: if I wish to convince you of something, I may do so by deducing it from other propositions which you already accept. A dialectical argument, relying on your opinions, is therefore an effective vehicle with which I might persuade you. This holds even if the actual form of presentation is changed. An orator delivering a speech to an audience does not ask questions, but a successful orator will argue from premisses which the audience would accept if put to them as questions. Thus, dialectical skill is an essential component in rhetorical skill. Aristotle takes exactly this position in the *Rhetoric*, describing rhetoric as a kind of grafting together of dialectic and the study of types of character (*Rhet.* I. 1–2, esp. 1356^{a}25–7).

Although dialectical argument is argument by question and answer, not every argument proceeding by question and answer is dialectical. Dialectic has a disreputable cousin: 'contentious' (*eristikos*) or 'sophistical' (*sophistikos*) arguments. Though these resemble dialectical arguments in being presented by a questioner to an answerer, those who present them are not concerned either with whether their conclusions actually follow from their premisses or with whether their answerers really accept their premisses. They are instead a kind of fraud—in fact, they are precisely counterfeit dialectical arguments, that is, arguments by question and answer, resting on premisses *apparently* accepted by the answerer, and *apparently* deducing some conclusion which follows from these.

(For more on just how a premiss can be apparently but not actually accepted, see the Commentary on I. 1, 100ᵇ26–101ᵃ1.)

Contentious argument is of no value for the genuine examination of the consequences of beliefs, since it does not care whether the premisses it extracts really are anyone's beliefs and it does not care whether the conclusions it draws actually follow. It is, instead, a kind of argumentative 'dirty fighting' (*adikomachia*), as Aristotle says in *SE* 11 (Excerpt C). Nevertheless, a study of the devices on which it rests is a useful part of the study of argument, at least as a defence against those very devices. Aristotle provides just such a study in *On Sophistical Refutations*, an addendum to the *Topics*.

Dialectical Arguments, Demonstrations, and Philosophical Method

If dialectic is contrasted on one side with its counterfeit, contentious argument, it is distinguished on the other from proof or demonstration. Aristotle defines a demonstration (*apodeixis*) as a 'scientific argument', that is, an argument which explains and proves its conclusion. For Aristotle, the best examples of demonstrations are mathematical proofs. Such a proof differs formally from a dialectical argument in that its premisses are not offered as questions but rather 'taken' or 'supposed' by the demonstrator. The reason is simple enough: the questioner in a dialectical argument must reason from whatever premisses the answerer accepts, whereas proofs must rest only on true premisses. Thus, the opinions—or indeed the presence—of an answerer are irrelevant. Generally, Aristotle thinks of demonstrative arguments as fitting together into organized systems of proofs, in the style now familiar to us from Greek mathematical works such as Euclid's *Elements* (there is good evidence that some such works were in existence as early as Aristotle's years in Plato's Academy).

Aristotle's principal discussion of demonstrations is contained in the *Posterior Analytics* (a treatise noted for its obscurity), and this present Introduction is not the place for any serious treatment of his views on the subject. A few remarks are in order, however, about the purpose of Aristotelian demonstrations, since this has long been a subject of debate for interpreters. One view, now not widely accepted, is that a demonstration is a vehicle of scientific inquiry or discovery: we discover new truths by deducing them from antecedently known first principles. Such a conception may have some plausibility in mathematics, though even this is limited, but it appears totally inadequate as an account of the procedures of any empirical science; given Aristotle's own strong emphasis on the importance of observation, this is unlikely to be his conception of demonstration. Another view, advocated in recent years by Barnes and others, is that demonstrations are vehicles for teaching bodies of knowledge already established. In my view, this is only part of the truth. Aristotle holds that a demonstration is in effect the embodiment of scientific knowledge of its conclusion: if a proposition is demonstrable, then to know it scientifically just is to possess or grasp its demonstration. Therefore, a demonstration is not merely a device with which a learner can be imparted knowledge, it also represents the form that knowledge itself takes in anyone who possesses it. It follows that scientific inquiry itself must aim at the discovery of demonstrations. Therefore, demonstrations are after all essential to scientific inquiry, but as its end and not its means. For the inquirer, scientific knowledge of a proposition has not been attained until its demonstration has been discovered and grasped. For the student, the demonstration is not mere scaffolding or machinery serving only to bring about conviction with respect to its conclusion; instead, the learner's goal is to grasp the demonstration as a demonstration, coming to see its premises *as* the causes and explanation of its conclusion. Acquiring scientific wisdom, for Aristotle, is as much a matter of conversion as it is a matter of accumulating new information.

A demonstration, for Aristotle, is an argument with a certain epistemic structure: it makes its conclusion known by deducing it from premises which are known. From this, he argues that demonstrative knowledge is possible only if there are some starting-points which are known, but not known as a result of being demonstrated. Since Aristotle does think that demonstrative knowledge is possible, he must also hold that there is some alternative route to the knowledge of the principles or starting-points. Unfortunately, it is far from clear just what he thought this route was. *An. Post.* II. 19, his official statement on the subject, is notoriously difficult to interpret. It has been read as claiming that the starting-points are intuitively self-evident, but this then conflicts with the empiricist sympathies much in evidence in Aristotle's other works. Other scholars instead find an empirical account in the *Posterior Analytics* and suppose that the knowledge of the first principles simply arises from experience through generalization. But it is difficult to reconcile this with Aristotle's claim that the principles must be *better* known than what follows from them, especially given his repeated insistence that what we perceive through our senses is known to a *lesser* degree than the principles and conclusions of demonstrative sciences.

Some have proposed that Aristotle appealed to dialectic to solve this problem. There are several passages (including a crucial text in *Top.* I. 2) which say that dialectical argument, or the art of dialectic, is useful in some way in connection with the first principles on which sciences rest. Perhaps, then, Aristotle supposes that dialectical argument *establishes* these first principles. Such an interpretation is advanced by Irwin (1988), who argues that a modified variety of dialectic ('strong dialectic') was Aristotle's mature concept of the basic method of philosophy. In my opinion, it is difficult to reconcile such views with Aristotle's frequent assertions that dialectical argument cannot establish anything at all. Instead, I see dialectical argument as making more limited, though important, contributions to the acquisition of knowledge of scientific principles through its ability to reveal the contradictions implied by a collection of propositions. What makes this important is that, in Aristotle's view, we begin in a state of considerable ignorance: we do not understand the natures and causes of things. More seriously, we are not aware of this ignorance. We are inclined to take what our senses present to us, and what we have acquired from our upbringing and our society, as the obvious truth about the world. Therefore, we have no inclination even to pursue a better account of things. Like Socrates, Aristotle thinks that the first step in acquiring philosophical wisdom is the realization that our received wisdom is flawed, that there are puzzles and problems implicit in what we took to be most familiar and obvious. Philosophy begins with this puzzlement and is our natural response to this discovery of our ignorance, for we all have a natural desire for knowledge. But the source of puzzlement is just the discovery that we hold views which are inconsistent: and dialectical argument is the tool that reveals these inconsistencies to us. Thus the Aristotelian practice of 'working through the puzzles', exploring the inconsistencies among the received opinions about a subject, is a direct descendant of Socratic refutation.

Dialectical argument is, then, the first mover of philosophical inquiry because it removes us from our intellectual complacency and shows us that there are problems to be solved. Moreover, in revealing just what the puzzles are that must be solved, it sets the agenda for philosophical inquiry and gives a necessary condition for the adequacy of a theory. Occasionally, Aristotle does appear to say that it also provides a sufficient condition. At least in the sphere of ethics, he says that any theoretical account which can solve all the puzzles and nevertheless retain the largest possible number of our received views is sufficient (*EN* VII. 1, 1145^{b}2–7). This suggests a relatively conservative methodology for philosophical inquiry: revise whatever beliefs you have so as to eliminate inconsistencies with the minimum disturbance of other beliefs.

But elsewhere—for instance *Met.* A 1–2—Aristotle contemplates more radical revisions. He tells us that the ultimate truth about things is far removed from common life and that the first principles on which correct theories rest are incomprehensible or repugnant to the ignorant—that is, to ourselves, in our untutored state. Acquiring philosophical wisdom requires a kind of epistemic conversion so that we come to see those first principles as familiar and obvious, rather than strange and absurd, and as the explanations of the ordinary matters of fact we formerly took to be most obvious and least in need of explanation. Conservative adjustments of the fabric of belief to achieve reflective equilibrium with minimum distortion are not likely to bring about this kind of conversion.

There is a role for dialectical argument to play in such a conversion. As in ethics, says Aristotle, so in philosophy our education requires habituation to a new set of feelings. To be virtuous, for Aristotle, is not merely to know the principles of right action and act on them, but also to find enjoyment in right action: those who act rightly but against a contrary inclination are 'continent', not truly good. Likewise, to be wise with theoretical wisdom is not simply to assent to the first principles and work through demonstrations of other truths from them, but also to find those first principles most obvious and most fundamental. As in the moral case, we come to have the right attitude towards the principles through a process of habituation. (See Burnyeat (1980) and Kosman (1973) for discussion of these views.) Dialectical argument may be crucial in this process. If we have worked through the puzzles and contradictions surrounding a subject many times, then the hold of the familiar and received views on our intellect is shaken, and we cease to feel that they are obvious (compare *Met.* A 1–2, *GC* I. 2, 316^{a}5–10). When we have discovered the true account, we will make it our own by working through many arguments from its principles, eventually coming to have the right conviction in the truth of these principles by seeing their role in many different proofs. This is very much what happens in those who learn any theoretical subject: an appreciation of its basic principles only emerges after long experience with their role in explanations.

Gymnastic Dialectic: Argument as a Sport

So far, I have discussed dialectical argument in a relatively general sense as question-and-answer exchange between opponents. *Topics* VIII brings us a picture of something much more specific. Questioner and answerer engage in structured bouts. A single thesis is selected and the two participants take on defined positions about it: the answerer maintains it and the questioner attacks it. The questioner's attack consists of a series of questions that can be answered by a simple 'yes' or 'no' put forward by the questioner for the answerer's acceptance or rejection. The questioner's goal is, ideally, to deduce a contradiction from the thesis and the answerer's concessions; failing that, the questioner may instead try to achieve various lesser types of victory. The answerer, meanwhile, tries to avoid conceding premises to the questioner from which such an argument can be constructed, or at least to keep concessions within various bounds determined by the nature of the exchange (the details are discussed in the Commentary). Much of Book VIII takes for granted a number of rules of the game that permit one or the other party to call foul in certain circumstances; it is also clear that each round is scored and evaluated by judges or some type of audience. This is obviously a kind of sport, a form of dialectic reduced to a competitive game. What connection has it with dialectical argument in general? And what does it tell us about the nature of dialectic?

The best answer, I think, is that these 'gymnastic' arguments have the same relationship to other dialectical arguments as sport-fencing to real and deadly swordplay. In a society in which sword-fighting sometimes takes place in earnest, fencing for sport provides a form of practice that allows participants to improve their skill without danger: judges and formal rules for scoring substitute for the pressures of an actual exchange. Of course, in a real swordfight there are no judges, and rules become valuable only to the extent that they actually serve to keep one from harm. Therefore, we would expect that at least in their origins, the rules for the sport of fencing have some connection with success in deadly swordplay. In the same way, the nominal purpose of gymnastic dialectic is to prepare oneself for the real thing. Consequently, the rules should not be mere arbitrary specifications but instead should encourage good dialectical practice. A survey of the contents of Book VIII generally bears this out: the rules Aristotle cites would generally promote arguments in which the conclusion is in fact supported by the premises and in which the premises are actually accepted by the answerer. For instance, answerers are permitted to complain about invalid inferences, ambiguous language, or deliberately misleading questions, and questioners are sometimes allowed to complain about answerers who refuse to concede obvious consequences of their earlier concessions.

But even though we may invent sport-fencing as a safer substitute for deadly swordplay, the sport soon takes on a life of its own. Victory in sporting contests can then be one's principal reason for fencing; exercise or practice becomes preparation for the sport. We see clear enough evidence in *Topics* VIII that something like this also happened in the case of dialectical argument. The contests Aristotle has in view were highly competitive, and the contestants were eager to win. This no doubt explains why some of Aristotle's advice to competitors borders on the deceptive (e.g. shuffling premises around to make it harder to see where the argument is going, or confusing an answerer by adding irrelevant premises): he is, to some extent, adopting the role of coach. In so doing, he is responding to the needs of an established practice rather than inventing one. We see this most clearly in his assumption that his audience is already familiar with a whole technical vocabulary for dialectical contests, including names for various strategies and fouls.

Some aspects of Book VIII, then, will have been specially relevant to the participants in the kind of sport-argument practised in the Academy. Yet we should not be too quick to dismiss even these details as of no importance to logic or philosophy, for that activity itself was a training in argumentation. However competitive the dialectical sport may have been, Aristotle insists on the difference between it and contentious argument, and the most fundamental point of that difference is that dialectical arguments must be *valid*: one of the rules of the game is that the conclusion must follow from the premises.

The Dialectical Art and the 'Syllogism'

Aristotle tells us that any dialectical argument is either a *deduction* (*sullogismos*) or an *induction* (*epagōgē*). This is in fact his view about all arguments whatever, rhetorical or demonstrative as well as dialectical. However, by far the larger part of his attention in the *Topics* is on deductions. He defines a deduction as 'an argument in which, certain things being conceded, something different from what is conceded results of necessity through them' (100ª25–7). This is a broad definition of logical consequence, applicable to a very wide range of arguments. We find virtually the same definition at the beginning of the *Prior Analytics*, a treatise more closely associated with demonstrative argument. In each place, Aristotle makes it clear that the general notion of deduction transcends the venue in which a deduction takes place: the same deduction can be presented through question and answer, thus making it dialectical, or through the assertion of its premises in monologue, after the manner of demonstration. What *is* essential to a deduction, however, is that it contain premises and a conclusion which necessarily follows from them: deductions are, by definition, *valid arguments*.

This generalized definition of deduction is the basis for Aristotle's claim to the status of founder of logic. Of course, that is not to say that Aristotle was the first to use a deduction or the first person to recognize that some conclusion necessarily followed because of certain premises. On the contrary: the recognition of instances of logical consequence is as old as the use of argument itself, perhaps as old as human language. Aristotle's achievement, reflected in this definition, was to recognize the general phenomenon of logical consequence and make it a subject of theoretical study.

The *Topics*, however, is a practical treatise, and Aristotle's concern is therefore with producing arguments, not only with theorizing about them. In a dialectical situation, a deduction is a means to a certain end, namely, drawing a given conclusion from concessions made by an answerer. To be useful to that end, a deduction will obviously have to have the right conclusion, and therefore a dialectical method will have to include procedures for discovering premises from which a given conclusion can be deduced. However, the dialectical situation imposes a further constraint: the premises are useful only if the answerer accepts them. Briefly stated, then, the objective of Aristotle's dialectical method is to discover premises which satisfy two requirements: (1) the desired conclusion follows from them; (2) the answerer will assent to them.

Collections of Acceptable Premises: Endoxa

We can, of course, determine whether premises satisfy the second requirement simply by putting them forward to the answerer, but that is like determining whether a drug will cure a sick patient by administering it: what we want is a means of determining *in advance* what our answerer will accept. Since art and science, as Aristotle says, deal with universals rather than particulars, the way to accomplish this is by classifying answerers according to a list of general types and associating with each type a list of premises acceptable to persons of that type. Though the evidence is susceptible to more than one interpretation, I think this is just what Aristotle tells us to do. He says that the premises used in dialectic must be *endoxa*, 'acceptable'. Now, 'acceptable' is a relative term: to be acceptable is to be acceptable *to someone*, or to some *type* of person. In several places Aristotle gives us a short list of general types. Some premises are acceptable to everyone; some are acceptable to the majority of people; some are acceptable to 'the wise', others to most of the wise, and others to specific well-known sages (and their schools). The *endoxa*, then, do not form a single list; instead, there are various lists of typical beliefs associated with types of person. (My interpretation here is by no means accepted by all scholars; for further discussion and defence see the Commentary on I. 10.)

To be truly useful, however, these collections should also be organized under subject headings so that those needed for a particular argument can be found readily. This is what Aristotle instructs us to do:

We should construct tables, setting them down separately about each genus, for example about good or about animal, and about every good, beginning with what it is. (I. 14, 105^{b}12–15)

These 'tables' (*diagraphai*: cf. *EE* II. 2, 1228^{a}28), then, will classify the various *endoxa* according to subject-matter, using keywords like 'good'. The classification is hierarchical, starting with very large subjects such as 'good' and 'animal' and moving to subdivisions of these, for instance the various goods ('every good'). Within cach classification, we start with a definition of the subject ('beginning with what it is') and then move to further details. We may speculate that this hierarchical structure is combined with a classification according to type of believer, giving a cross-indexing that would allow ready retrieval of what Heraclitus believed about change or what the mass of humanity think about virtue.

The 'Locations': Argument Forms and their Use

These collections of *endoxa* will be useful for telling us whether our opponent will accept any given premiss, but they will not of themselves tell us which premisses to put forward. This is the job of a second component of the dialectical art, one that is far more significant for the history of philosophy and logic: the collection of *topoi*, 'places' or 'locations'. Aristotle is well aware of the importance of his achievement. In his own evaluation of what he has accomplished in the *Topics* and *On Sophistical Refutations*, he tells us that his predecessors failed to discover a real dialectical art and instead taught argumentation by giving their students set arguments to memorize—as if, he says, one undertook to teach an art of remedying foot problems by giving one's students a collection of shoes of various sizes (see Excerpt D). Aristotle's achievement was to advance from 'This conclusion follows from these premisses' to 'A conclusion of this *form* follows from a set of premisses having this *form*'. And to be able to do this, Aristotle had to develop some concept of *logical form*. With a notion of logical form, whole classes of arguments—in principle, infinite classes— can be grouped together as instances of a single valid form. This is the point at which logical theory begins: when the validity of an argument is seen as resulting from its logical form. Aristotle passes that point in the *Topics*: the *Topics* is the oldest extant logical treatise.

What, then, are these 'locations', these *topoi*, which give the *Topics* its name? Unfortunately, the *Topics* itself does not tell us in so many words. However, Aristotle does say that the internal Books II–VII of the *Topics* consist of *topoi*. Thus, we have plenty of examples, if only we can interpret them properly. There is also a brief definition of a *topos* in the *Rhetoric* as 'that under which many ⟨arguments⟩ fall' (1403ᵃ17–18). This account points to the role of a *topos* as a means of classifying many arguments together. To supplement this evidence, we may appeal to a definition given by

Theophrastus, Aristotle's lifelong associate, and preserved by Alexander of Aphrodisias: a *topos* is

a sort of starting-point or element, by means of which we obtain starting-points for particular cases, definite in outline but indefinite as to the particulars. (Alexander, *In Top.* 126.14–16; cf. 5. 21–6)

Alexander proceeds to illustrate:

For example, 'if a contrary belongs to a contrary, then the contrary belongs to the contrary' is a *topos*. For this statement—that is, this premiss—is definite in outline (for it makes it clear that it is stated about contraries universally), but it is not yet determined in it whether it is stated about these contraries or those contraries. (126. 17–20)

The cryptic sentence Alexander uses as an example is easily interpreted if we turn to *Topics* II. 8, 113^{b}27–8 (see Excerpt A). Roughly, it means: 'If A belongs to B, then the contrary of A belongs to the contrary of B'. Alexander implies that the *topos* is not really a full-fledged statement, though it becomes one with appropriate substitutions for these common terms:

... starting off from [this *topos*], we can make an attack concerning any contrary. If, for example, what is sought is whether the good is beneficial, then starting off from the *topos* presented we will get, as a premiss relevant to the problem, 'if the bad harms, the good benefits'. (126. 20–3)

Let us spell out Alexander's example in more detail. Suppose that our task is to establish something of the form 'A belongs to B', e.g. 'Beneficial belongs to the good' (or, more naturally, 'the good is beneficial'). To recognize a thing as having this form is already to make use of a notion of logical form: our easy substitution of 'A' and 'B' for 'beneficial' and 'good' covers an important intellectual advance. In the example, however, still another element of classification occurs. We must recognize that 'beneficial' and 'good' each fall under the classification 'contrary' (roughly, 'term that has an extreme opposite'). Therefore, our desired conclusion has the form 'A contrary belongs to a contrary', or to be more exact, 'Contrary A belongs to Contrary B'.

The next step in the process appeals to a relationship between logical forms. The 'outline' statement which Theophrastus calls the *topos* itself may be spelled out more explicitly as:

If the contrary of Contrary A belongs to the contrary of Contrary B, then Contrary A belongs to Contrary B

Now 'Contrary A' corresponds to 'Beneficial' in our original conclusion. The contrary of 'beneficial' is 'harmful'. Likewise, if 'Contrary B' corresponds to 'good' in the conclusion, the contrary of Contrary B is 'bad'. The following, then, is *of the form given in the topos*:

> If harmful belongs to bad, then beneficial belongs to good.

The consequent of this conditional is the desired conclusion; its antecedent is a premiss from which we can deduce it. We can take the resultant argument to consist simply of this premiss and conclusion:

> Harmful belongs to bad.
>
> Therefore, beneficial belongs to good.

Alternatively, we may suppose that the condition itself is a premiss of the argument:

> If harmful belongs to bad, then beneficial belongs to good.
> Harmful belongs to bad.
> Therefore, beneficial belongs to good.

It is not easy to say which of these forms Aristotle would prefer. He often treats conditional sentences as if they were arguments, and therefore he might incline towards the first (since the second form would on that understanding be repetitive).

This illustrates the use of a *topos* to establish a conclusion. In many cases, a *topos* can also be used (with appropriate changes) to refute a conclusion. Some *topoi*, however, are useful only for refuting, others only for establishing. In the typical case, Aristotle spells out these details, noting for a given *topos* whether it can be used to refute, to establish, or to do both. (See Excerpts A and B for many examples.)

At the core of a *topos*, then, there is an *argument form*: an abstract or schematic statement of a conclusion-form and corresponding premiss-forms from which it follows. However, the *topos* itself is not just this form, but this form embedded in procedures for its use as part of Aristotle's dialectical method. We can see just how in the way they are presented in the *Topics*. The first formal statement of a *topos* begins:

Now, one *topos* is investigating whether he has given something that belongs in some other manner as an accident. (II. 2, 109ᵃ34–5)

Several features of this are common to statements of *topoi*. To begin with, it is an infinitival phrase ('investigating', *to epiblepein*): for Aristotle, a *topos* is usually described as *doing something*. Frequently, as here, the *topos* is a matter of investigating or inspecting, but that is not always the case: we also find 'showing', 'objecting', 'leading', 'producing'. There is also in this example a reference to the opponent, i.e. the answerer: what is being investigated is what 'he has given'. This is so common that Aristotle never bothers to explain it: as here, we find simply a third-person singular verb, and we must supply its subject. Overall, what the statement describes is an action of probing or testing the answerer's response for a point of weakness. If that point is discovered, then the *topos* provides instructions for mounting an attack on it (in Aristotelian dialectic, 'attack' is virtually synonymous with 'play the role of questioner'). A *topos* is a point at which the answerer's position may be probed for attack.

But there is another dimension to the *topoi* in Aristotle's system. Each *topos* serves as a location at which many arguments may be found by appropriate substitutions in the relevant form. Moreover, the conclusion-form of the *topos* itself serves as a means of finding it when we need it: we know which *topoi* to consult for a given conclusion by determining which forms the conclusion fits under and then going directly to the *topoi* associated with those forms. The *topoi* are thus systematically organized in a way that facilitates timely retrieval, a feature essential to any practical method for live debate: it is no use having a large stock of argument forms in memory unless one can also recall the right one at the right time. Now, there is good evidence that Aristotle's dialectical method drew on mnemonic systems in use during his time. These systems appear to have been based on the memorization of a series of images of actual locations (e.g. houses along a street) in a fixed order; items to be memorized were then superimposed on these images, making it possible to recall them in sequence, in reverse sequence, or directly by position in the series. The term *topos* itself may be intended to recall just such a technique (see the Commentary on VIII. 14, 163^{b}17–33, for further discussion). There are even some indications that Aristotle intended the individual *topoi* to be committed to memory in a fixed order, e.g. the frequent appearance of groups of *topoi* concerning certain general notions, always in the same sequence (see 'A Sampling of *Topoi*' below). It is, as Aristotle is aware, easier to remember a list of items enumerated in fixed order (see VIII. 14, 163^{b}28–9, and Commentary); a dialectician using Aristotle's method could work through the list in sequence, searching for a usable *topos*, rather than casting about at random. A *topos*, therefore, is a location under which a large number of arguments can be stored for ready recall.

An Aristotelian *topos* may then be described in two ways: as a point of attack in an adversary's position, and as a location under which to file arguments. My rendering 'location' is intended to admit both these senses.

These locations and their uses are not yet the whole of Aristotle's dialectical method, since they only yield potentially useful premises. To determine if they are actually useful, i.e. whether the answerer will assent to them, we shall next have to consult the relevant inventory of premises. And if our premises survive this test, we shall then need to couch them in appropriate language and order them for presentation according to a good strategy (see VIII. 1–2). A diagram of the whole process may help:

Desired conclusion ('problem')
↓
1. Match it to a 'common' proposition
↓
Common argument form
↓
2. Make appropriate substitutions in the premisses
↓
Premiss(es) from which desired conclusion follows
↓
3. Check appropriate inventory of acceptable premisses
↓
Acceptable premiss(es) from which desired conclusion follows
↓
4. Put premisses into proper form;
choose a strategic ordering
↓
Dialectical argument

The Forms of Propositions: Predication,
Predicables, and Categories

This is the skeleton of a theory; to flesh it out, we require some theory of logical form, or at least a repertory of forms with which to categorize conclusions. At the most general level, Aristotle does have something approaching a theory. To begin with, he has the notion of a *proposition*, that is, a bearer of a truth-value. It was accepted dialectical terminology to distinguish between 'premisses' (*protaseis*: literally, 'things held out'), which the questioner puts forward for acceptance by the answerer, and the 'problem' (*problēma*: literally, 'thing thrown forward', 'obstacle') about which questioner and answerer are debating. However, Aristotle points out that whatever can be used as a problem can also be used as a premiss, and conversely, just by changing its form of expression (see I. 4). We might express this by saying that premisses and problems are each propositions put to different uses. Thus, even though the *Topics* employs no technical expression for 'proposition' abstracted from premisses and problems, Aristotle is close enough to the general notion of a sentence with a truth-value, abstracted from its use on a particular occasion. (*On Interpretation* does have such an expression: *logos apophantikos*, 'declarative sentence'.)

He also has a general concept of the form of a proposition. He supposes that every premiss or problem concerns whether one *term* is *predicated* of another in some particular way. *Terms* in the *Topics* are general terms: universals such as 'human', 'good', 'animal', 'white', 'colour'. To *predicate* one term of another is to assert that the one is true of, or belongs to, or is an attribute of, the other: 'Animal is true of human', 'Colour belongs to white', 'White is an attribute of animals'. One common way to say that A is predicated of B is to say that B is A, or Bs are As: 'Humans are animals', 'White is a colour'. To put this in more familiar terms, Aristotle takes it for granted that in every premiss or problem there is a subject (which is 'that about which' something is said) and a predicate (which is that which is 'said of', or perhaps denied of, something). Lest this have too much the air of the trivial, we should remember that our words 'subject' and 'predicate', and indeed the basic framework of traditional grammar, descend from Aristotle's usage.

Much more has been written about Aristotle's notion (or notions) of predication than can be discussed in an Introduction. What is important for present purposes is that in the *Topics* Aristotle presents a classification, which purports to be comprehensive, of all predications. In any predication, he says, the predicate must be in one of four relationships to the subject: *definition*, *genus*, *unique property*, or *accident*. He takes some pains to explain these terms in I. 4–5 (see the Commentary for discussion).

There are indications that the predicables are part of Aristotle's inheritance from the Academy, but it also appears that he has modified that legacy in certain ways. In fact, the predicables seem to be closely connected with the business of giving definitions. Plato thought the pursuit of definitions to be an important part of philosophical education as well as philosophy itself, and Academic sport-arguments may have been largely occupied with attacking and defending definitions. From Plato's works and other sources, a certain standard structure for definitions can be inferred: a definition must locate the thing defined in its general class or type (its *genus*) and then specify what differentiates it from other things of that type (its *differentia*). It is also an obvious requirement of correctness for a definition that it apply to all of the thing defined and to nothing else: the *definiens* must therefore be the *unique property* of the *definiendum*. And since a thing's definition must be true of it always or necessarily, it would be important to distinguish definitions from what can both belong and fail to belong to the same thing, as e.g. baldness can both belong and fail to belong to humans: such merely coincidental or concomitant terms are *accidents*.

Aristotle's list differs from this in omitting the differentia (though he sneaks it back in by 'classing it with the genus': 101ᵇ18–19). He also advances the distinction between definition and unique property in a way that suggests it is his innovation (101ᵇ19–23). The predicables serve as the largest classifications both of problems and of *topoi*. The first step in dealing with a problem, then, is to identify which predicable it falls under.

In addition to the predicables, Aristotle classifies predications and the predicates which occur in them in another way: these are the ten *categories* introduced in I. 7 and of much importance in other Aristotelian treatises (see the Commentary on I. 7 for further discussion).

A Sampling of Topoi

The predicables give a highest-level classification of problems or conclusions, and thus a highest-level organization of *topoi*. This is explicitly reflected in the arrangement of Books II–VII, which give *topoi* first concerning accidents (II–III), then genera (IV), then unique properties (V), then definitions (VI–VII). When we look to each of these sections, principles of organization are less obvious:

at first, they appear to be mere listings, with no particular principles of order—just one thing after another, like a bad tragedy, as Aristotle says elsewhere (cf. *Met.* 1090ᵇ19–20). But in fact, there are patterns, and they reveal other categories of classification of conclusions which are actually more important to the *topoi* themselves (and to Aristotle's implicit theory of logical form) than the predicables. In particular, we find a number of closely related *topoi* in each of the four main divisions (i.e. for accidents, for genera, for unique properties, for definitions) which fall under three large classifications: *topoi* involving 'opposites' (*antikeimena*), *topoi* involving 'coordinates' and 'cases' (*sustoicha, ptōseis*), and *topoi* involving 'more and less and equal'. Aristotle generally presents these three groups together and in the same fixed order. An overview of their contents gives a good picture of the nature of an Aristotelian *topos*. (In what follows I refer frequently to Excerpt A for a continuous series of examples of these three groups.)

Opposites

Aristotle distinguishes four varieties of 'oppositions' (*antitheseis*) and 'opposites' (*antikeimena*): contraries (*enantia*), negations (*apophaseis*), privation and possession (*sterēsis kai hexis*), and relatives (*pros ti*). The example from Alexander discussed above illustrates what contraries are and the role they may play in a *topos*. Note that the relation of being a contrary is symmetrical: if A is contrary to B, then B is contrary to A; and each, since it is a contrary *of something*, may also be called a contrary absolutely speaking. Many *topoi* involving contraries are found in the *Topics*, most revolving around the principle that whatever holds of A vis-à-vis B, the same thing holds of the contrary of A vis-à-vis the contrary of B.

The next two forms of opposition show an asymmetry in terminology, that is, the two members of the pair have different designations. A *negation* is a term with 'not' (or some other negative particle) prefixed: 'not good', 'unmarried', 'uninhabited'. It is at least possible that Aristotle supposes every term to have a negation in this sense; however, not every term *is* a negation, since a negation must include some explicit negative particle. The most general *topos* involving negations has some resemblance to what is today called 'contraposition':

If A follows B, then the negation of B follows the negation of A

As an instance:

If animal follows human, then not human follows not animal.

The third kind of opposition is *privation*. A privation is a term that indicates the absence of something, usually the absence of something that should be or would be expected to be present, e.g. 'blind'. To any privation, then, corresponds that of which it is the privation (in the example, 'sighted'); this is called the 'possession' or 'state' (*hexis*). Some, though by no means all, privations are marked as such by a privative particle ('*ir*rational'). Again, Aristotle supposes that however A stands to B, so the privation of A stands to the privation of B.

Finally, *relatives* (*pros ti*) are, as in modern usage, relational predicates like 'double' and 'half', each of which designates one of the members of a two-place relation. Example:

If a triple is a multiple, then a third is a fraction
If knowledge is belief, then what is known is believed

(Compare 114^{a}13–25 in Excerpt A with the above.)

Co-ordinates and Cases

The second subsystem is usually described by Aristotle as 'co-ordinates and cases' (*sustoicha kai ptōseis*). 'Co-ordinates' are terms all of which are derived from some root word, as 'justly' and 'justice' from 'just'. By 'case' Aristotle seems usually to mean adverbial forms in -*ōs* (analogous to the English '-ly'), though sometimes he approaches the later use of 'case' by Greek grammarians to indicate oblique (non-nominative) grammatical cases of a noun. In the main, the *topoi* here rely on straightforward principles of parallel transformation: if you want to establish that the just are virtuous, argue first that whatever is done justly is done virtuously. (See Excerpt A, 114^{a}26–^{b}5.)

More and Less and Equal

The third subsystem, which Aristotle usually calls 'from more and less' or 'from more and less and likewise', is a collection of *topoi* involving the words 'more', 'less', 'equal', 'similarly', and comparative degrees of adjectives and adverbs. In II. 10, we find such representatives as these:

'What is true of one of a group of similar things is true of them all' (114^b25–36).

'If A follows B, then more A follows more B' (114^b37–115^a14)

The type of argument we call *a fortiori*, e.g.: 'If A does not belong to that to which it more likely belongs, then neither does it belong to that to which it less likely belongs', and several similar principles (115^a15–24)

'What makes that to which it is added A is itself A; what makes that to which it is added more A is itself A' (115^a25–$^b2$)

'if something is more A or less A than something, then it is A' (115^b3–10)

From the standpoint of modern logic, some of the *topoi* in these groups share genuine logical connections, while others are only superficially related. This is not surprising, given the practical orientation of the *Topics*: Aristotle's purpose is to provide a convenient scheme for recall, not to explain the theoretical basis of inference. As a result, it would be an overstatement to see a full-fledged logical system underlying the *Topics*. However, it is not an overstatement to say that Aristotle is already focusing on ways to identify the general form of a proposition, and of an argument.

But a logical *theory* is not simply a listing of valid forms but also an articulate explanation *why* those forms are valid. We may therefore ask: how does he suppose the topical rules themselves are established? The *Topics* gives us little evidence about this. We do find instances in which Aristotle establishes the *invalidity* of a form by discovering that it has at least one counter-example: thus he recognizes that a valid form of argument is one no instance of which has true premises and a false conclusion. This is a point which should not be minimized, for the demonstration of invalidity through counter-examples is one of the corner-stones of logical theory. Aristotle himself uses it with great skill in the *Prior Analytics*, where he is unquestionably developing a theoretical account of validity. However, we do not find instances in the *Topics* in which he argues for the *validity* of a rule, nor does he give us any indications that he conceived of a general deductive system with basic rules from which more complex deductions could be derived.

The absence of any theoretical justifications of rules in the *Topics* does not in itself show, of course, that Aristotle did not have any such justifications to offer. The *Topics* is a practical treatise, and practical methods do not need to offer theoretical defences of themselves; indeed, such a theoretical account might very well detract from the practicality of a method. A problem for interpreters, however, does arise in connection with the logical theory of the *Prior Analytics*, for that theory does not appear to rest on exactly the same forms of argument as the *Topics* method. One explanation offered for this is developmental: if the *Topics* reflects an earlier stage of Aristotle's thought than the *Prior Analytics*, then its comparatively crude and unsystematic picture of logical form could have been superseded by the more sophisticated 'analytical' theory. But what then is the relationship of the two? Did the Aristotle of the *Prior Analytics* reject as invalid some forms of argument accepted in the *Topics* as valid? Or did Aristotle suppose instead that the theory of the *Analytics* comprehends all that is in the *Topics*? Aristotle's own testimony seems to favour the latter view, but modern logicians have noted that some valid forms recognized in the *Topics* do not seem reducible to the forms of the *Prior Analytics*. How is this to be explained? These questions, and others equally pressing, about the overall structure and development of Aristotle's logical theories require much more detailed treatment than is possible in this little essay.

The Selections

This volume contains translations of *Topics* I and VIII, with Commentary, and of additional Excerpts from *Topics* II and III, and *On Sophistical Refutations*, without Commentary. These choices are dictated by limitations of space and determined by fairly straightforward matters of content. Books I and VIII describe and discuss Aristotle's dialectical method, while Books II–VII are collections of individual argumentative locations. It is possible to make a good deal of sense of Books I and VIII in separation, and VIII in particular is invaluable for its information about actual dialectical practice. II–VII, by contrast, make very repetitive and tedious reading. However, some sampling of their content is necessary to give a concrete picture of the workings of the dialectical art. The selections from *On Sophistical Refutations* (a treatise which Aristotle intended as the last section of the *Topics*) give Aristotle's perspective on dialectic and on his accomplishments. *SE* 11 (Excerpt C) contains a valuable discussion of the relationship of dialectic to philosophy and its distinction from contentious argument and

INTRODUCTION

sophistry. *SE* 34 (Excerpt D) is really Aristotle's closing chapter for the *Topics*, since it begins with a reference to the project laid out in its opening sentence; it gives Aristotle's own assessment of his achievement and its relationship to what came before.

Since the Commentary is intended to be accessible to the reader with no knowledge of Greek, I have tried to keep it relatively free of philological concerns. However, these sometimes influence the understanding of the text itself. There are also places in which my translation might be regarded as controversial; and, though I generally follow Ross's *Oxford Classical Text* edition of the Greek text (including the marginal lineation), sometimes I do not. In all such cases, the reader deserves to know at least *that* I have taken a position with which others might disagree. Whenever textual matters seem to me to have an important philosophical impact, I have tried to discuss them in the Commentary in a way that will be intelligible to Greekless readers. However, I have appended a series of 'Notes on the Text' with fuller discussions of textual points, as well as explanations of some of my more controversial construals. These Notes also indicate all deviations from Ross's edition; I have frequently been influenced by Jacques Brunschwig's text for Books I–IV (Brunschwig (1967)) and the apparatus for his (at this writing) unpublished version of Books V–VIII, which he graciously allowed me to use. In the main, these divergences are conservative: I have tried to avoid emendations and to make sense of the best-attested text, when I could. Angle brackets (⟨⟩) in the translation mark interpretative additions and, occasionally, emendations of the Greek text; square brackets ([]) mark words that are probably not authentic. Other translations and editions of the *Topics* are cited by author's name alone, books and articles by author's name and year. References for both are found in the Bibliography. A two-way Glossary lists important terms in Greek and in English.

TRANSLATION

BOOK ONE

CHAPTER I

The goal of this study is to find a method with which we shall be 100ᵃ
able to construct deductions from acceptable premises concerning
any problem that is proposed and—when submitting to argument
ourselves—will not say anything inconsistent. First, then, we must
say what a deduction is and what its different varieties are, so that
the dialectical deduction may be grasped (for that is the one we
seek in the present study).

A *deduction*, then, is an argument in which, certain things being 25
supposed, something different from the suppositions results of necessity through them. It is a *demonstration* if the deduction is from
things which either are themselves true and primary or have attained the starting-point of knowledge about themselves through
some primary and true premises. A *dialectical* deduction, on the 30
other hand, is one which deduces from what is acceptable.

Those things are *true and primary* which get their trustworthi- 100ᵇ
ness through themselves rather than through other things (for
when it comes to scientific starting-points, one should not search 20
further for the reason why, but instead each of the starting-points
ought to be trustworthy in and of itself). Those are *acceptable*, on
the other hand, which seem so to everyone, or to most people, or to
the wise—to all of them, or to most, or to the most famous and
esteemed.

A *contentious* deduction is one from what appears to be acceptable but is not, or an apparent deduction from what is actually or 25
only apparently acceptable. For not everything which appears to be
acceptable actually is so: for none of the acceptable things mentioned has this appearance purely on its surface, as actually *does*
happen in connection with the starting-points of contentious arguments (for in their case, the nature of the mistake is usually quite 30
obvious at once to those capable of even modest discernment). Let 101ᵃ
us say, then, that the first of the contentious deductions mentioned
really is a deduction but that the remaining one is a contentious
deduction, not a deduction, since it appears to deduce but does not
do so.

5   Next, apart from all the deductions that have been mentioned, there are the fallacies based on what is appropriate to specific sciences, as we find in the case of geometry and its kindred sciences. For this type does seem to be different from the deductions mentioned; for the person who draws fake diagrams does not deduce
10 from true and primary things, nor from acceptable ones either (for they do not fall within the definition: he does not take what everyone thinks, or most people, or the wise—not all, nor most, nor the most esteemed of them). Instead, he makes his deduction from premisses which are appropriate to the science but not true: for he
15 fakes a diagram by describing semicircles improperly, or by extending certain lines in ways in which they cannot be extended.

So then, we may let the aforementioned be the species of deductions, for the purpose of capturing them in an outline. And as a general comment on all we have said or are going to say later, we
20 may let this be the extent to which we make our distinctions, inasmuch as it is not our intent to give the exact account of any of them; what we want to do instead is develop the account as far as an outline, since we deem it fully sufficient, for the purposes of the present method, to be able to recognize each of them in some way or other.

CHAPTER 2

25 Next in order after what we have said would be to state the number and kinds of things our study is useful for. There are, then, three of these: exercise, encounters, and the philosophical sciences. Now, that it is useful in relation to exercise is obvious at once, for if we have a method we shall be able more easily to attack whatever is
30 proposed. And it is useful in relation to encounters because, once we have reckoned up the opinions of the public, we shall speak to them, not from the beliefs of others, but from their own beliefs, changing their minds about anything they may seem to us not to have stated well. It is useful in relation to the philosophical sciences
35 because if we have the ability to go through the difficulties on either side we shall more readily discern the true as well as the false in any subject.

Furthermore, it is useful in connection with the first of the starting-points about any individual science. For if we reason from the starting-points appropriate to the science in question, it is impossible to make any statement about these (since these starting-points
101ᵇ are the first of them all), and it is by means of what is acceptable

2

about each that it is necessary to discuss them. But this is unique, or at any rate most appropriate, to dialectic: for since its ability to examine applies to the starting-points of all studies, it has a way to proceed.

CHAPTER 3

We shall have a complete grasp of our method when we are in the 5 same condition as in the case of rhetoric, medicine, and other such abilities. [And that is: to do what we choose with what is available.] For the rhetorician will not convince under all circumstances, nor the physician heal; however, if he leaves out nothing that is possible, then we shall say that he has a sufficient grasp of his craft. 10

First, then, we must consider what our method consists of. Now, if we understood the number and kinds of things that arguments are about, what they are made of, and how we are to be equipped to deal with these, then we would have a sufficient grasp of our proposed subject. But the things arguments are made of are equal in number to, and the same as, the things which deductions are 15 about. For arguments are made from premisses, while the things deductions concern are problems: and every premiss, as well as every problem, exhibits either a *unique property*, a *genus* or an *accident* (the differentia, since it is genus-like, should be classified together with the genus).

But since one sort of unique property signifies what it is to be 20 something and another sort does not, let us divide unique properties into both the parts stated, and let us call the sort that signifies what it is to be something a *definition*, while the remaining sort may be referred to as a unique property, in accordance with the common designation given to them. Clearly, then, from what has been said, it turns out that according to the present division they are four in all: either definition, unique property, genus, or accident. No one 25 should take us to mean that each one of these, uttered by itself, is a premiss or a problem, but instead that it is out of these that both premisses and problems arise.

A problem is different from a premiss in its form. For stated in 30 this way: 'Is it the case that two-footed terrestrial animal is the definition of man?' or, 'Is it the case that animal is the genus of man?' it is a premiss; but stated in this way: 'Whether two-footed

terrestrial animal is the definition of man or not', it becomes a
problem (and similarly in other cases). Consequently, it stands to
35 reason that problems and premisses are equal in number, since you
may make a problem out of any premiss by changing its form.

CHAPTER 5

We must say what a definition is, what a unique property is, what a
genus is, and what an accident is. A *definition* is a phrase which
102ª signifies the what-it-is-to-be. It is given either as a phrase in place of
a word or as a phrase in place of a phrase (for it is also possible to
define something signified by a phrase). But as for those who
answer with a word (however they do so), it is clear that these
5 people are not giving the definition of the subject, since every
definition is a phrase. We should, however, class as *definitory* something like 'the beautiful is the fitting', and similarly the question
whether perception and knowledge are the same or different. For
indeed, in connection with definitions, the better part of our time is
10 taken up with whether things are the same or different. To put it
simply, let us call all those things definitory which fall under the
same method as definitions. And that all the cases just mentioned
are of this sort is evident at once. For if we are able to argue that
things are the same or that they are different, then we shall also be
well provided for attacking definitions in the same way (for in
showing that they are not the same we shall also have refuted the
15 definition). But this last statement does not convert: to establish a
definition, it is not sufficient to show that they are the same. However, in order to refute one, it is enough of itself to show that they
are not the same.

A *unique property* is what does not exhibit what it is to be for
some subject but belongs only to it and counterpredicates with it.
20 For example, it is a unique property of a human to be capable of
becoming literate: for if something is human, then it is capable of
becoming literate, and if it is capable of becoming literate, then it is
human. For no one would call something unique which is capable
of belonging to something else (as for instance being asleep for a
human), not even if it happened for a time to belong to one thing
25 alone. Therefore, if something of this sort were to be called a
unique property, it will not be so called without qualification, but
rather unique at a time or in relation to something: being on the
right is unique at a time, and two-footed is really called unique in
relation to something (for instance, of a human in relation to a

4

horse or a dog). But it is clear that nothing which can possibly belong to something else counterpredicates: for it is not necessary 30 for something to be human if it is asleep.

A *genus* is what is predicated in the what-it-is of many things which are different in species. (Let us say that those sorts of things are 'predicated in the what-it-is' which it would be appropriate to give as answers when asked what the thing in question is, as it is appropriate in the case of a man, when asked what it is, to say that 35 it is an animal.) The question whether one thing is in the same genus as another, or in a different one, is also genus-like, since this sort of thing also falls under the same method as a genus: for if we have argued that animal is the genus of man, and also of the ox, then we shall have argued that they are in the same genus, while if **102ᵇ** we show that it is the genus of one and that it is not the genus of the other then we shall have argued that they are not in the same genus.

An *accident* is something which is none of these—not a defini- 5 tion, a unique property, or a genus—but yet belongs to the subject; or, what can possibly belong and not belong to one and the same thing, whatever it may be. For instance, it is possible for 'being seated' to belong and not belong to the same thing. Similarly, also, for 'white', for nothing prevents the same thing from being now white, now not white. The second of these definitions of 'accident' 10 is better. For when the first definition is stated, anyone who is going to understand it must already know what a definition, a unique property, and a genus are; the second definition, on the other hand, is sufficient on its own for recognizing what the thing meant is in and of itself.

We may also include under the heading 'accident' the compari- 15 sons of things with one another which are stated in some way involving what goes with what, for example whether the noble or the expedient is to be preferred, or whether the life according to virtue or the life according to enjoyment is more pleasant, or any- thing else that might be stated in a way resembling these. For in all such cases, the inquiry arises about which one it is the predicate 20 goes with more.

It is clear at once that nothing prevents an accident from becom- ing a unique property at a time or with relation to something: sitting down, for instance, which is an accident, will be a unique property at a time when only one person is sitting, and when it is not only one person who is sitting it will be a unique property with relation to those who are not sitting. Consequently, nothing pre- vents an accident from becoming a unique property either with 25 relation to something or at a time; however, it cannot be a unique property without qualification.

CHAPTER 6

We should not forget that all arguments about unique properties, genera, and accidents are also appropriate to use in connection with definitions. For if we have shown that something fails to
30 belong uniquely to what falls under the definition (as we do in the case of a unique property), or that what is given as such in the definition is not the genus, or that something stated in the formula does not belong (as might also be said in the case of an accident), then we shall have refuted the definition. So, according to the account given previously, all the things we have enumerated would
35 in a way be definitory. But we should not for this reason seek a single universal method for all cases: for, in the first place, it would not be easy to find it; and besides, if it were found, it would be thoroughly obscure and inconvenient for the study at hand. On the other hand, if we were to give a unique method proper to each
103^a genus we have defined, a detailed treatment of our project would readily develop out of what falls appropriately under each of them. Consequently, we should divide them up in outline, as was said earlier, and as for what is left over, we should assign whatever is most appropriate to each division and call them 'definitory' or
5 'genus-like'. The aforementioned have largely been assigned to each of the divisions.

CHAPTER 7

First of all, we must determine the number of ways that 'same' is used. We may regard the same as being divided, in outline, into three parts, for we are accustomed to describe what is the same as 'in number' or 'in species' or 'in genus'. Those are the same in
10 number which have several names though there is one thing, for example a cloak and a coat. Those are the same in species which, though many, are indistinguishable with respect to species, for instance as a human ⟨is the same in species⟩ as a human or a horse the same as a horse (for those things are said to be the same in species which fall under the same species). Similarly, those are the same in genus which fall under the same genus (as a horse ⟨is the same in genus⟩ as a human).
15   One might think that 'same' as it applies to water from the same

6

spring has some differentia apart from those mentioned. But never-theless, let this too be classified in the same group as things called the same with reference in some way to a single species, for all these sorts of cases appear to be of the same kind and comparable to one another. For all water is said to be the same in species as any 20 other water because it has a certain likeness, and water from the same spring only differs in that the likeness is stronger. That is why we do not separate this case from those which are called the same with reference in some way to a single species.

What is one in number is most uncontroversially called the same in everyone's judgement. But even this is customarily indicated 25 in several ways. The strictest case, ⟨where it is indicated in⟩ the primary way, is when that which is the same is indicated by means of a word or a definition, e.g. a coat is the same as a cloak or a two-footed terrestrial animal as a human. The second way is when it is indicated by means of a unique property, e.g. what is receptive of knowledge is the same as a human or what is carried upwards by nature the same as fire. The third way is when it is ⟨indicated⟩ with 30 an accident, e.g. the one sitting (or the musical one) is the same as Socrates. For all these are intended to signify what is one in number.

(One might most readily come to see that this last remark is true from the case of people who change their way of calling someone. Sometimes we give an order, using a name, to call some person who is seated, and when the one we give the order to turns out not to 35 understand it, we change it—thinking he will understand it better from an accident of the person—and tell him to call to us 'the one sitting' or 'the one talking', obviously believing the same thing to be signified by the name as by the accident).

CHAPTER 8

Let 'same', then, be divided in three as has been said.   103ᵇ

One proof that arguments are made from and through the things mentioned previously, and are about them, is by means of induc-tion. For if someone were to examine each premiss or problem, then it would be clear that it had arisen either about a definition, or 5 about a unique property, or about a genus, or about an accident.

Another proof is through deduction. For necessarily, whenever one thing is predicated of another, it either conterpredicates with the subject or it does not. And if it does counterpredicate, then it must be a definition or a unique property (for if it signifies what it 10

7

is to be something it is a definition, while if it does not it is a unique property—that is what we said a unique property was, something which counterpredicates but does not signify what it is to be). But if it does not counterpredicate with the subject, then either it is among the things stated in the definition of the subject or it is not. If it is among the things stated in the definition, then it must be a
15 genus or a differentia, since a definition is composed of a genus and differentiae. On the other hand, if it is not among the things stated in the definition, then it is clear that it must be an accident, for an accident was said to be what is neither a definition nor a unique property nor a genus but still belongs to the subject.

CHAPTER 9

20 Now then, next after this we must distinguish the categories of predications in which the four ⟨types of⟩ predications mentioned are found. These are ten in number: what-it-is, quantity, quality, relation, location, time, position, possession, doing, undergoing. An accident, a genus, a unique property, and a definition will
25 always be in one of these categories, for all the premisses ⟨produced⟩ by means of them signify either a what-it-is, or a quantity, or a quality, or some one of the other categories.

It is clear at once that an ⟨expression⟩ signifying the what-it-is will sometimes signify a substance, sometimes a quantity, sometimes a quality, and sometimes one of the other categories. For,
30 supposing the example under consideration is a man, if it says that the example is a human or an animal, then it says what it is and signifies a substance. On the other hand, supposing the example under consideration is a white colour, if it says that the subject is a white or a colour, then it says what it is and signifies a quality. Similarly, supposing that the example under consideration is a foot-long length, if it says that the example is a foot-long length, then it
35 says what it is and signifies a quantity. And likewise with the other ⟨categories⟩. For any of these, both in the case in which the same thing is said about itself and in the case in which its genus is said about it, signifies what it is. But when it is said about another ⟨category⟩, then it does not signify what it is, but how much or what sort or one of the other categories.

These, then, are the number and variety of things arguments are about and are made from. How we are to obtain them, and the
104ᵃ means by which we are to be equipped to deal with them, must be explained next.

CHAPTER 10

First, then, it should be determined what a dialectical premiss and a dialectical problem are. For not every premiss or every 5 problem should be counted as dialectical: no one in his right mind would hold out as a premiss what nobody thinks or make a problem of what is evident to everyone or to most people, since the latter contains no puzzle while nobody would concede the former.

A *dialectical premiss* is the asking of something acceptable to everyone, most people, or the wise (that is, either all of them, most 10 of them, or the most famous), provided it is not contrary to opinion (for anyone would concede what the wise think, so long as it is not contrary to the opinions of the many). Dialectical premisses also include: things which are similar to what is acceptable; the contraries of things which appear to be acceptable, put forward by negation; and such opinions as are derived from any established 15 arts.

For if it is acceptable that the knowledge of contraries is the same, then it would also appear to be acceptable that the perception of contraries is the same; and if the skill of reading is numerically one, then the skill of flute-playing is numerically one, while if there are several skills of reading, then there are several skills of flute-playing. For all these seem to be similar and 20 related.

And similarly also whatever is contrary to what is acceptable, put forward as a negation, will appear to be acceptable. For if it is acceptable that one must do good to one's friends, then it is also acceptable that one must not do them ill. It is contrary that one 25 must do one's friends ill, but as a negation it is that one must not do them ill. And similarly also, if ⟨it is acceptable that⟩ one must do one's friends good, then it is also ⟨acceptable that⟩ one must not do one's enemies good. This is also in accordance with the negations of contraries, for the contrary is that one must do one's enemies good. Likewise in other cases.

But the contrary applied to the contrary will also appear, in parallel, to be acceptable. For instance, if ⟨it is acceptable that⟩ one must do one's friends good, then ⟨it will be acceptable 30 that⟩ one must do one's enemies ill. (Doing one's friends good might also appear to be contrary to doing one's enemies ill, but whether this is truly so or not will be explained in what we say about contraries.)

9

It is also clear that such opinions as are derived from arts are
35 dialectical premisses. For anyone would concede what those who
have examined these subjects think, e.g. what a doctor thinks about
medical questions, or what a geometer thinks about geometrical
questions, and likewise in other cases.

CHAPTER 11

104ᵇ A *dialectical problem* is a point of speculation, directed either to
choice and avoidance or to truth and knowledge (either on its own
or as working in conjunction with something else of this sort),
about which people either have no opinion, or the public think the
5 opposite of the wise, or the wise think the opposite of the public, or
each of these groups has opposed opinions within itself.

For it is useful to know ⟨the answers to⟩ some problems only for
the sake of choosing or avoiding something (for instance whether
pleasure is to be chosen or not), while it is useful to know others
only for the sake of knowing (for instance whether the universe is
eternal or not). Others are, in and of themselves, of no use for
10 either of these but work in conjunction with other things of this
sort. For there are many things which we do not wish to know in
and of themselves, but for the sake of other things, in such wise
that, because of them, we will come to know something further.

Those are also ⟨dialectical⟩ problems concerning which there are
contrary deductions (for there is a puzzle whether it is so or not,
because there are persuasive arguments about both sides), as well
15 as those about which, because they are vast, we have no arguments,
thinking that it is difficult to give the reason why (e.g. whether the
universe is eternal or not). For one could also pursue an inquiry
about such problems.

Let problems and premisses, then, be defined as has been said. A
20 *thesis* is: a belief contrary to opinion held by someone famous for
philosophy, e.g. that contradiction is impossible (as Antisthenes
used to say), or that everything moves (according to Heraclitus), or
that what is is one (as Melissus says). (For to take things contrary to
our opinions seriously when just any person declares them is silly.)
Or: something about which we possess an argument contrary to our
25 opinions, e.g. that not everything that is either has come to be or is
eternal, as the sophists say of the musician who is literate without
either having become so or always being so (for even someone who
does not think this might ⟨come to⟩ think it because there is an
argument).

10

A thesis, then, is also a problem, but not every problem is a 30
thesis, since some problems are the sort of thing about which we
think nothing either way. But that a thesis is a problem is clear. For
it is necessary from what has been said either that the public disagrees with the wise about the position, or that one or the other
group disagrees among themselves, since a thesis is some belief
contrary to opinion. In practice, all dialectical problems are prob- 35
ably called theses. But let it make no difference whatever it is
called. For it is not because we want to coin terms that we have
distinguished them in this way, but so that we should not overlook
whatever differences there actually are among them.   **105ᵃ**

One ought not to inquire into every problem or every thesis, but
only those which someone might be puzzled about who was in need
of arguments, not punishment or perception. For those who puzzle 5
about whether one must honour the gods and care for one's parents
or not need punishment, while those who puzzle about whether
snow is white or not need perception. Nor ought one to inquire into
that the demonstration of which is near to hand, or those the
demonstration of which is excessively remote. For the former
present no difficulty, while the latter present too much for
exercises.

CHAPTER 12

With these things defined, then, we need to distinguish how many 10
kinds of dialectical argument there are. One kind is *induction*,
another is *deduction*. Now, what a deduction is was explained earlier. Induction, however, is proceeding from particulars up to a
universal. For instance, if the pilot who has knowledge is the best
pilot, and so with a charioteer, then generally the person who has 15
knowledge about anything is the best. Induction is more persuasive, clearer, more intelligible in the way perception is, and commonly used by the public; deduction is more coercive and more
effective with those skilled in contradicting.

CHAPTER 13

Let the classes of things which arguments are about and from be 20
defined as we have said above. The tools by means of which we may
be well equipped with deductions are four: one is obtaining
premisses, the second is being able to distinguish how many ways a
word is said, the third is finding differences, and the fourth is the

25 examination of likeness. In a way, the last three of these are also
premisses, since it is possible to make a premiss about any of them,
e.g. that either the noble, the pleasant, or the useful is choiceworthy; or, that perception differs from knowledge in that it is
possible to get the one back after losing it, but this is impossible for
30 the other; or, that the healthful is in the same relationship to health
as what part of a training program is to being in training. The first
is a premiss about what is said in many ways, the second is a premiss
about differences, and the third is a premiss about similar things.

CHAPTER 14

Now, premisses are to be collected in as many ways as were defined
35 in connection with premisses: making ready for use the opinions
either of everyone, or of the majority, or of the wise (and of the
latter, the opinions of all, or the majority, or the most famous), or
105^b the contraries of opinions which appear to be so, and whatever
opinions are derived from the arts. (One must put forward the
contraries of things which appear to be acceptable as negations, as
was said earlier.)

It is a useful thing, as well, to produce these premisses while
collecting—not only premisses which are actually acceptable, but
5 also premisses which are similar to these, e.g. that the same perception has contraries as its object (for the same science does also), or
that we see by receiving something into ourselves, not sending
something out (for it is also this way in the case of the other senses:
we hear by receiving something, not sending something out, we
10 taste in the same way, and similarly also in the case of the other
⟨senses⟩). Moreover, whatever seems to be so in all or most cases
should be taken as a starting-point or apparent concession, for
those who have not seen it not to hold in a particular instance
concede it.

One should also collect premisses from written works, and make
up tables, listing them separately about each genus, e.g. about good
15 or about animal (and about every ⟨sense of⟩ good), beginning with
what it is. One should also make marginal notes on the opinions of
particular people, e.g. that it was Empedocles who said that there
are four elements of bodies (for someone might concede what was
said by a famous person).

20   In outline, there are three classes of premisses and problems.
Some premisses are ethical, some are scientific, and some are logical. Premisses such as these, then, are ethical: whether one must

12

obey one's parents rather than the laws, if they disagree. Logical premises are such as whether or not the same knowledge has contraries as its object; scientific premises are such as whether or not the universe is eternal. And similarly also with problems. As for 25 what each of the aforesaid kinds is like, it is not easy to state that in definitions about them, and one must try to recognize each of them with the familiarity which comes through induction, studying them in light of the examples given. For the purposes of philosophy, they should be dealt with in accordance with truth, but dialectically in 30 accordance with opinion.

All premises should be obtained in the most universal form possible, and a single premiss should be made into many (e.g. ⟨the premiss⟩ that the knowledge of opposites is the same ⟨should be made⟩ next ⟨into the premises⟩ that ⟨the knowledge⟩ of contraries is, and that ⟨the knowledge⟩ of relatives is). Then these premises are in turn to be divided in the same way, as far as it is possible to 35 divide them (e.g. that ⟨the knowledge of⟩ good and evil, and of white and black, and of cold and hot ⟨are the same⟩). And similarly for the rest.

CHAPTER 15

Concerning premises, then, what has been said is enough. But as **106ᵃ** for the number of ways ⟨something is said⟩, our investigation should not only study which things are called something in different ways but should also try to give definitions for them. For instance, we should say, not only that justice and courage are called goods in 5 one way while that which produces fitness and the healthful are so called in another way, but also that the former are so called in virtue of themselves being of a certain sort, whereas the latter are so called in virtue of being productive of something, and not in virtue of themselves being of a certain sort. And likewise also in the other cases.

Whether the ways in which things are called something are many or one in species should be investigated by means of the following: 10

First is to examine the contrary to see if it is said in several ways and if they disagree either in species or in name. For sometimes, there is a difference right in the very names, e.g. the contrary of 'sharp' is 'flat' in a sound but 'blunt' in a body. It is clear, then, that the contrary of 'sharp' is said in many ways. But if that is, then so is 'sharp'. For in each of these cases, the contrary will be different— 15 the same 'sharp' will not be contrary to 'blunt' and 'flat'—but

13

'sharp' is contrary to each. Again, the contrary of 'flat' is 'sharp' in sound but 'round' in body. Therefore, 'flat' is said in several ways, since its contrary is also. And similarly, also, in the case of a picture
20 the contrary of 'fine' is 'ugly', but in the case of a lineage it is 'base', so that 'fine' is equivocal.

In some cases, there is no disagreement at all in the names, but in the species the difference between them is obvious at once, as in the case of 'bright' and 'dark': for a sound is called bright or
25 dark, and similarly a colour. Now in names, these do not disagree; in the species, however, the difference between them is obvious at once, for the colour and the sound are not called bright in the same way.

This is also clear through sensory perception. For the same sense
30 perceives things which are the same in species. But we do not discern white in the case of a sound and a colour by means of the same sense: rather, we discern one by sight and the other by hearing. The same holds for 'rough' and 'smooth' in tastes and in bodies (except that we discern one with touch and the other with taste):
35 these too do not disagree in names—either those which apply to them or those which apply to their contraries—for 'smooth' is in fact the contrary of each.

Next, if there is something contrary to one but nothing at all contrary to the other. For example, to the pleasure which comes from drinking, the pain which comes from being thirsty is contrary, but to ⟨the pleasure⟩ which comes from contemplating the fact that the diagonal ⟨of a square⟩ is incommensurable with its side
106[b] nothing is ⟨contrary⟩. Thus, pleasure is said in many ways. And to the loving that is a matter of thought, hating is contrary, but to that which is a bodily activity, nothing is: it is clear, then, that loving is equivocal.

Next, turning to the intermediates, if there is something intermediate for one ⟨pair of contraries⟩ but nothing for the other, or if
5 there is something for both but not the same thing. For instance, between bright and dark in colour there is 'grey', but in sound there is none—or, if indeed there is one, it is 'nasal', as some people say that a nasal voice is intermediate. So, 'bright' is equivocal, and likewise also 'dark'. Next, if there are several intermediates for one
10 pair but one for the other, as in the case of bright and dark: for in the case of colours the intermediates are many, while in the case of sound there is the single one 'nasal'.

Next is examining the contradictory opposite to see if it is said in multiple ways. For if this is said in multiple ways, then that which is

opposite to it will also be said in multiple ways. For instance, 'not to 15
see' is said in multiple ways, one being 'not to possess sight' and the
other 'not to exercise one's sight'. But if this is said in multiple
ways, then 'to see' must be also: for to each 'not seeing' something
is opposed, i.e. having sight to not having it, or exercising one's
sight to not exercising it.   20

Next is examining things which are expressed as privation
and state. For if one of these is said in multiple ways, then the
remaining one is also. For instance, if 'sensation' is said in multiple
ways of the soul and of the body, then 'insensible' will also be said
in multiple ways of the soul and of the body. (And that it is as 25
privation and state that the things just mentioned are opposed
is clear, since it is natural for animals to have each kind of
sensation, both that with respect to the soul and that with respect to
the body.)

Next, inflected forms should be examined. For if 'justly' is said in 30
multiple ways, then 'just' will also be said in multiple ways (for
there is a 'just' in accordance with each 'justly'). For instance, if
'justly' means both judging in accordance with one's own opinion
and ⟨judging⟩ as one ought, then so also 'just'. Likewise, if
'healthful' is said in multiple ways, then 'healthfully' will also be 35
said in multiple ways. For instance, if what produces health, what
preserves it, and what indicates it are healthful, then 'healthfully'
will mean 'productively' or 'preservatively' or 'indicatingly' ⟨of
health⟩. And similarly also in other cases: whenever a term itself is
said in multiple ways, then the inflected form derived from it will 107^a
also be said in multiple ways; and if the inflected form is, then so is
the term itself.

There is also examining the categories of predication of the word
to see if these are the same in all cases. For if they are not the same,
it is clear that the expression is equivocal. For instance, the good in 5
foods is what produces pleasure, in medicine what produces health;
but in the case of the soul, it is being of a certain sort (e.g. temperate, courageous, or just) and similarly in the case of a person.
Sometimes, it is a time, e.g. what is opportune ⟨is good⟩ (for that
which is opportune is called good). Often, it is a quantity, as in the 10
case of what is proportionate (for the proportionate is also called
good). Consequently, 'good' is equivocal.

Likewise, bright is a colour in the case of a body, but in the case
of a sound it is the easy to hear. Sharp is much like this, for likewise
the same thing is not meant in all cases. For it is the rapid sound 15
which is sharp (as those who do numerical harmonics say), but it is

the angle less than a right one which is sharp, or the sharp-angled knife.

And there is examining the genera of the things under the same word to see if these are different and not subordinate to one another. Take 'donkey' as an example (both the animal and the
20 machine). For the definition of the word is different for these: the one will be given as 'an animal of a certain sort', the other as 'a machine of a certain sort'. But if the genera are subordinate to one another, then it is not necessary for the definitions to be different. For instance, animal and bird are both a genus of raven. When we say, then, that a raven is a bird, we also say that
25 it is a certain kind of animal, so that both genera are predicated of it. And similarly, also, when we call a raven a flying biped animal, we say that it is a bird. Also in this way, then, both genera, as well as their definitions, are predicated of the raven. But in the case of genera which are not subordinate to one another, this
30 does not happen. For when we call something a machine, we do not call it an animal; nor, when we call it an animal, do we call it a machine.

And there is examining not only the term under consideration to see if the genera are different and not subordinate to each other, but also its contrary (for if its contrary is said in many ways, then it
35 is clear that what is under consideration is also).

It is also useful to examine the definition we have of a complex, e.g. of a white body or a white sound: for if what is unique ⟨to each⟩ is subtracted, the same definition must remain. But this does
107ᵇ not happen in the case of equivocals, e.g. in the cases just mentioned: for one is 'a body having such and such a colour', but the other is 'a sound easy to hear'. When we subtract 'body' and 'sound', then, what remains in each case is not the same: but it
5 would have to be, if the 'white' said in each case were univocal.

But frequently something equivocal tags along unnoticed in the definitions themselves, and for this reason you should also examine the definitions. For instance, if someone says that what indicates and what produces health is what is commensurately related to
10 health, we should not give up but instead should examine what he has meant by 'commensurately' in each case, e.g. if one is 'of such an amount as to produce health' and the other is 'such as to signify of what sort one's condition is'.

Next, if they fail to be comparable with respect to 'more' or 'equally', as for instance a white sound and a white coat, or a sharp
15 taste and a sharp sound. For these are not called equally white or

sharp, nor is one called more so than the other. So 'white' and 'sharp' are equivocal. For everything univocal is comparable: either they will be equally so called, or one will be more so.

Since the differentiae of things from different genera that are not subordinate to one another are also different in kind (take for 20 example animal and knowledge: the differentiae of these are different), there is examining whether the things falling under the same word are differentiae of different genera that are not subordinate to one another, like 'sharp' of a sound and of a body: for one sound differs from another by being sharp, and similarly one body from 25 another, so that 'sharp' is equivocal (for these are differentiae of different genera that are not subordinate to one another).

Next, if the differentiae of the actual things the same name applies to are different, as colour in the case of bodies and colour in melodies. For the differentiae of colour in the case of bodies are 'distending the sight' and 'compressing the sight', but the differen- 30 tiae of colour in the case of melodies are not the same. So, 'colour' is equivocal, for the same things have the same differentiae.

Next, since the species is not a differentia of anything, there is examining the things falling under the same word to see if one is a species and the other a differentia. For instance, white in the case of 35 bodies is a species of colour, but white in the case of sounds is a differentia (for one sound differs from another in virtue of being white).

CHAPTER 16

One should investigate ⟨being said in⟩ many ways, then, by means of these and the like. As for differences, one should study both things within the same genera, in comparison to each other (e.g. in **108ᵃ** virtue of what does justice differ from courage, or wisdom from moderation: all of these are from the same genus), and things from a different genus, in comparison to something else that does not differ too very much (e.g. in virtue of what does perception ⟨differ from⟩ knowledge). For in the case of things very different, the 5 differences are completely obvious.

CHAPTER 17

As for similarity, this should be examined, first, in the case of things in different genera: as the one is to the one, so the other is to the other (e.g. as knowledge is to the known, so is perception to the

perceptible); and, as one thing is in one, so is another in another
10   (e.g. as sight is in the eye, so intelligence in the soul, or as a calm is
in the sea, so is a stillness in the air). We should practice above all
with things that are greatly different, for we shall more readily be
able to discern similar things in the remaining cases. Next, things in
15   the same genus should be examined to see if anything the same
belongs to all of them, e.g. to a human, a horse, and a dog (for to the
extent that something the same belongs to them, to that extent are
they similar).

CHAPTER 18

It is useful to have examined in how many ways a word is said
both for the sake of clarity (for someone would better know
20   what it is he is conceding once it had been brought to light in how
many ways ⟨the term⟩ is applied) and in order to make our
deductions concern the thing itself rather than being about a word.
For when it is unclear in how many ways something is said, it is
possible that the answerer and the questioner are not thinking
25   about the same thing; but once it has been brought to light in
how many ways it is applied and which ⟨of these⟩ ⟨the answerer⟩ is
thinking about in conceding ⟨the premiss⟩, the questioner would
appear ridiculous if he did not make his argument about this.

It can also be used both for resisting fallacies and for producing
fallacies. For if we know in how many ways something is said, we
shall not be taken in by fallacies ourselves but instead will know if
the questioner fails to make the argument about the same thing.
30   And when we are ourselves questioning, we will be able to argue
fallaciously, if the answerer should happen not to know in how
many ways something is said. (This is not possible in all cases, but
only when some of the things said in many ways are true and others
false.) But this type of argument is not appropriate to dialectic, and
35   for this reason one must absolutely avoid this kind of thing, arguing
about a word, in dialectical arguments, unless one is utterly unable
to argue otherwise about the subject proposed.

Finding differences is useful both for deductions about ⟨what is⟩
the same or different and for recognizing what any particular thing
108ᵇ   is. That it is useful for the deductions about ⟨what is⟩ the same or
different is clear: for when we have found any difference whatever
between the things proposed, we shall have shown that they are not
the same thing. But ⟨it is useful⟩ for recognizing what something is

because we usually separate the unique account of the being of 5
anything by means of the differences appropriate to it.

The study of what is similar is useful for inductive arguments, for
deductions from an assumption, and for giving definitions. It is
useful for inductive arguments because it is by means of bringing in
particular ⟨premisses⟩ about similar cases that we claim a right to 10
bring in the universal ⟨premiss⟩ (for it is not easy to perform an
induction if we do not know what the similar cases are).

⟨It is useful⟩ for deductions from an assumption because it is
accepted that however matters stand with one of a group of similar
things, so they also stand with the rest. So, whichever of these we
may be in a good position to argue about, we shall establish an 15
agreement in advance that however matters stand with these, so
they also stand with what is proposed. And when we have shown
the former, then we shall also have shown what was proposed from
an assumption (for it was by assuming that however matters stand
with these, so they stand with the thing proposed, that we made our
demonstration).

⟨The study of similarity is useful⟩ for giving definitions because if 20
we can discern what is the same in any case, we shall not be at a loss
as to what genus we must put the thing proposed into when we are
defining it (for that one of the things common ⟨to the thing proposed and other things as well⟩ which is predicated most in the
what-it-is must be the genus). And similarly, the study of the similar in things greatly differing is also useful for definitions, e.g. that 25
a calm in the sea and a stillness in the air are the same (for each is
a quietness), or a point in a line and a unit in a number (for each is
a beginning). Consequently, if we give what is common to them all
as the genus, we shall not seem to be defining strangely. Those who
define are in fact accustomed to give definitions in this way: they
say that a unit is the beginning of a number and a point the begin- 30
ning of a line. It is clear, then, that they put ⟨the thing defined⟩ in
what is common for both as the genus.

These, then, are the tools by means of which deductions are
made. The attack-locations against which the aforementioned are
useful are as follows.

BOOK EIGHT

CHAPTER I

155ᵇ After this we should discuss arrangement, that is, how one should ask questions. First, then, the person who is going to be devising questions must find the location from which to attack; second, he
5 must devise the questions, and arrange them individually, to himself; and only third and last does he ask these of someone else. Now, up to the point of finding the location, the philosopher's inquiry and the dialectician's proceed alike, but actually arranging these things and devising questions is unique to the dialectician.
10 For all of that is directed at someone else. But the philosopher, or someone searching by himself, does not care if the ⟨premisses⟩ through which his deduction comes about are true and intelligible but the answerer does not concede them because they are close to the initial goal and he foresees what is going to result; rather, the
15 philosopher would in fact probably be eager for his claims to be as intelligible and as close ⟨to the initial goal⟩ as possible, for it is from such that scientific deductions proceed.

The attack-locations from which one should get ⟨premisses⟩, then, were discussed earlier. We must discuss arrangement and devising questions, determining which premisses are to be obtained
20 besides those necessary. The premisses through which the deduction comes about are called necessary; those obtained besides these are of four kinds. They are either for the sake of induction and giving the universal, or to give bulk to the argument, or for the concealment of the conclusion, or to make the argument clearer.
25 Apart from these, you should not obtain any other premisses, but instead it is through them that you should try to build up your argument and devise questions. (Premisses for concealment are for the sake of the contest: but since this entire sort of business is directed at someone else, it is necessary to use these too.)

Now, as for the necessary premisses through which the deduc-
30 tions come about, you should not put these forward right away, but instead you should stand off as far above them as possible. For example, do not expect to get that the same science applies to contraries, should that be what you want, but rather that it applies to opposites. For if he concedes this, it can be deduced that the science applying to contraries is also the same, since contraries are opposites. If, however, he does not concede this, then get ⟨the

20

premiss you need⟩ through induction by putting forward premisses
about particular contraries. For you should get the necessary 35
premisses either through deduction or through induction, or some
by induction and others by deduction. (But if they are extremely
obvious, the premisses themselves may also be put forward.) For in 156ᵃ
either standing off or induction, it is always less clear what is going
to result; at the same time, it is still open to you to put forward the
actual premisses to be used, if you are unable to get them in the
former ways. But the additional premisses we mentioned should be
obtained for these purposes, and each should be used in that way:
when you are arguing inductively, ⟨argue⟩ from particulars to uni- 5
versal and from the familiar to the unfamiliar (it is premisses based
on perception that are more familiar, either unconditionally or to
most people), and when you are concealing give preliminary deductions of the premisses from which the deduction of the initial
thesis is going to come about. And get as many of these as possible.
This would result if you were to deduce not just the necessary 10
premisses but even some of the ones useful for getting them. Next,
do not state the conclusions, but instead deduce them all together
later on (for in so doing, you would stand furthest off from the
initial thesis).

Speaking generally, the person who is getting answers in a
concealed manner must ask in such a way that when the whole
argument has been presented in questions and he has stated his 15
conclusion, the reason why is to be sought. But this will best come
about if we argue in the way just stated. For if only the last conclusion is stated, it will not be clear how it follows, because the answerer will not foresee what premisses it follows from if the
deductions were not spelt out previously. And the deduction of 20
the conclusion would be spelt out to the least degree if we set
down, not the premisses of that deduction, but rather those of ⟨the
deductions of the premisses⟩ through which that deduction comes
about.

It is also useful to avoid obtaining the claims the deductions are
made from in an orderly fashion but instead to obtain premisses for
this and that conclusion in alternation. For if appropriate premisses 25
are put next to one another, what is going to result from them will
immediately be too obvious.

Also, in those cases in which it is possible, you should get the
universal premiss by means of a definition that applies, not to terms
themselves, but to their co-ordinates. For people fallaciously conclude that they are not agreeing to the universal when the defini- 30

tion of the co-ordinate has been obtained. For example, if what has to be got is 'the angry desire retribution because of an apparent slight' and it could be obtained that anger is a desire for retribution because of an apparent slight (for it is clear that once the latter were obtained, we should have the universal we are aiming at). It often happens to those who put forward ⟨a premiss⟩ involving the
35 actual terms that the answerer refuses because he is more ready with an objection to it, e.g. 'those who are angry do not desire revenge since we get angry with our parents but do not desire retribution from them.' Now, his objection is probably not correct, for in the case of some people it is retribution enough to hurt them
156ᵇ and make them regret; nevertheless, he does have something plausible so as not to appear to be rejecting the premiss proposed without reason. But with the definition of anger, it is not equally easy to find an objection.

Next, propose a premiss as if proposing it not on its own but
5 for the sake of something else: for people are cautious about things which are useful towards the thesis. And in a word, make it unclear, as much as possible, whether you want to get what you put forward or its opposite. For if it is unclear which one is useful for the argument, then people will more often concede what they think.

10 Next, get answers through similarity. For not only is this convincing, but in addition the universal gets by more readily. For instance, 'Just as the knowledge and ignorance of contraries are the same, so also the perception of contraries is the same.' Or in the other direction: 'Since the perception is the same, the knowledge is too.' This is similar to induction, but actually not the same thing. For in
15 that procedure, the universal is obtained from the particulars, but in the case of similar things what is obtained is not the universal which all the similar things fall under.

You should also bring an objection against yourself occasionally. For answerers relax their guard with those who appear to be
20 playing fair in their attack. It is also useful to note that such-and-such is familiar or an old saying: for people are reluctant to go against custom if they have no objection to it, and at the same time, since they use such things themselves, they guard against upsetting them.

Next, do not be too eager, even if it is something you really need,
25 because people are more likely to oppose those who are eager. And propose things as if they were illustrations, for if something is put forward for some other reason and not useful in itself people will

more readily concede it. Next, do not put forward the thing you actually need to obtain, but rather something which this follows of necessity. For people more readily agree because it is not equally evident what is going to follow from this, and when the latter has been obtained, the former has also.

And ask near the end for the thing you most want to get. For it 30 is the first things that people reject the most, since most questioners say first what they are most eager to get. With some people, however, these are the things to propose first: for cantankerous people agree most readily to the first things, so long as it is not completely obvious what result they are headed for, but become cantankerous 35 towards the end. And similarly also with people who think they are clever in answering: for after they have conceded the first points, towards the end they quibble and say that the conclusion does not follow from what was conceded; but they concede things offhandedly, trusting in their talent and believing that they cannot be convinced of anything.

Next, stretch out your argument and throw in things of no use **157^a** towards it, as those who draw fake diagrams do (for when there are many details, it is not clear in which the error lies). That is also why questioners who proceed surreptitiously sometimes get away with including premisses which, if put forward by themselves, would 5 never be conceded.

For concealment, then, you should use the things stated. But for embellishment, you should use induction and the division of related things. Now, as to induction, it is clear what sort of thing it is. Division, however, is this sort of thing: 'One science is better than another either in being more exact or in being about better things', 10 or 'Some sciences are theoretical, some practical, and others productive.' For any one of these sorts of things embellishes the argument, though it is not necessary to state them in order to get the conclusion.

For clarity, you should bring in examples and illustrations. And the examples should be familiar ones, taken from sources we know 15 ('as Homer says', not 'as Choirilos says'), for in this way what is put forward would be clearer.

CHAPTER 2

When arguing, use deduction with those skilled in debate more than with the public; contrariwise, use induction more with the public. We have also discussed this earlier. 20

23

In some cases, it is possible for a person performing an induction to put the universal as a question. In other cases, however, this is not easy because a common name has not been assigned to all similarities; rather, when people have to obtain the universal, they
25 say 'thus in all such cases'. But this is one of the most difficult of things, to determine which of the cases brought forward are 'such' and which are not. It is also by this means that people often hood-wink one another in arguments, some saying that things are similar when they are really not and others protesting that similar things are not similar. For this reason, you should try in all such cases to
30 make up a name yourself, so that it will not be possible either for the answerer to protest that the case introduced is not similarly designated, nor for the questioner to quibble that it *is* similarly designated—since many things which are not similarly designated still appear to be so.

When it happens that, after you have induced from many cases,
35 someone does not grant the universal, then it is your right to ask him for an objection. However, when you have not stated that it does hold of some cases, you have no right to ask 'of which cases does it not hold?' For you must previously carry out an induction to ask for an objection in this way.

And he is expected not to bring his objections about the very case that was proposed, unless there should be only one such thing
157ᵇ (as two is the only even number that is prime): for the person objecting must bring an objection about a different case or say that this is the only such case.

Against people who object to the universal statement but bring their objection not against the statement itself but against some-
5 thing equivocal, e.g. that someone might have a colour or foot or hand that is not his, since a painter has a colour and a cook has a foot that are not theirs—in such cases, then, you should make distinctions when asking questions, for if the equivocation goes unnoticed he will seem to have objected properly to the premiss proposed.

But if the answerer blocks the question by objecting, not about
10 an equivocal case, but about the thing itself, then you must put forward premisses by subtracting that to which the objection applies and making the remainder the universal, until you have obtained what you need. For example, take the case of forgetting or having forgotten. For people do not agree that a person who has lost knowledge has forgotten, because when the subject changes he
15 has lost his knowledge but has not forgotten it. Subtracting that to

24

which the objection applies, then, you should state the remainder, e.g. that if someone loses his knowledge when the subject persists, it is because he has forgotten. And similarly also with those who object, 'Why is it that to a greater good is opposed a greater evil?' For they bring forward the fact that to health, which is a lesser good than good condition, a greater evil is opposed (for disease is a greater evil than poor condition). In this case too, then, you should subtract that to which the objection applies. For when it is subtracted, the answerer would more readily concede, e.g. that to a greater good is opposed a greater evil unless one of them brings the other with it (as good condition does health).

Do this not only if the answerer has made an objection, but even if he has refused without objecting because he foresees something like this. For when that to which his objection applies is subtracted, he will be forced to concede because he does not foresee in what is left a case of which it does not hold (and if he does not concede, then when he is asked for an objection he will not be able to respond at all). The premisses which are of this type are those that are true about some things and false about others: for it is in these cases that it is possible to subtract and leave behind a true remainder.

But if you put forward a premiss about many cases and he brings no objection, then he is expected to concede it, for a premiss is dialectical if it holds of many cases and there is no objection against it.

When it is possible to deduce the same thing both without and with argument through the impossible, then, although for someone who is demonstrating and not debating it makes no difference whether it is deduced in one way or the other, someone who is debating with another should not use the deduction through the impossible. For against someone who has deduced without the impossible, it is not possible to protest. However, when he has deduced the impossible ⟨result⟩, then unless it is extremely obvious **158ᵃ** that it is false, people will say that it is not impossible, so that questioners do not get what they want.

One ought also to propose those premisses which hold of many cases and for which either an objection is not possible at all or it is not a simple matter to discern it. For if they cannot discern the cases about which it does not hold, they will concede it as being true.

But you must not make the conclusion a question. Otherwise, if he rejects it, it appears that no deduction has occurred. For even

10 when one does not ask the conclusion but introduces it as that which results, people often reject it, and in doing this they do not appear to have been refuted—to those who do not understand what follows from the concessions. So, when you ask it without even saying that it follows and he denies it, it appears quite as though no deduction has occurred.

Not everything that is universal seems to be a dialectical premiss, 15 for example 'What is a human?' or 'In how many ways is "good" said?' For a dialectical premiss is one to which it is possible to answer yes or no, but this is not possible with the premisses mentioned; therefore, such questions are not dialectical unless you give the definition or distinction yourself in stating them, e.g. 'Is it the 20 case that "good" is said either in this way or in that?' For in response to things of this sort, it is easy to answer by either assenting or dissenting, and you must therefore try to put forward such premisses in this way. At the same time, you probably also have a right to inquire of the answerer in how many ways 'good' is used, when you make the determinations yourself and put them forth but he does not agree with any of them.

25 Whoever spends a long time presenting a single argument is doing a bad job of getting answers. For if the person being questioned is answering, then clearly ⟨he is doing a bad job⟩ because he is asking either many questions or the same ones repeatedly, so that he is either rambling or has no deduction (for every deduction is from few premisses). On the other hand, if his respondent is not answering, then ⟨the questioner is clearly doing a 30 bad job⟩ because he does not either criticize him or abandon the argument.

CHAPTER 3

The same assumptions are hard to attack as are easy to maintain. Such propositions include both those first and those last by nature. For the first propositions require definition, while the final propositions are concluded by means of many steps by anyone wanting to get a continuous argument from the first ones (or 35 otherwise the argumentative attempts appear sophistical: for it is impossible to demonstrate anything without beginning from the appropriate starting-points and connecting up all the way to the last things). Now, answerers neither expect definitions to be given nor, if the questioner does give one, do they pay any attention to it. But **158**[b] if it has not been made obvious what the subject proposed is, then it is not easy to make the attack. This sort of thing happens mostly with the starting-points. For the other propositions are proved through them, but it is not possible to prove them through others, and we must instead come to know each of them by means of a definition. Those things which are too close to the beginning are 5 also hard to deal with. For it is not possible to come up with many arguments about them since the intermediates between them and the beginning—by means of which the subsequent propositions must be proved—are few in number.

Among definitions, the hardest of all to deal with are those in which words have been used such that, first of all, it is unclear 10 whether they are said simply or in many ways, and on top of that one cannot even tell whether they have been used by the definer literally or metaphorically. For since they are unclear, there are no arguments for attacking them; and since one does not know whether it is because of metaphorical use that they are like this, no 15 criticism is available.

In general, you should assume that whenever a problem is hard to deal with, either it requires a definition, or something is said in many ways or metaphorically, or it is not far from the starting-points—⟨assume this⟩ because what is not evident to us at first is this very thing: which of the aforementioned ways it is that gives 20 rise to the difficulty. For if it were obvious which way it is, then it would be clear that we must either define, or distinguish, or supply the intermediate premises (for it is by means of these that the last propositions are proved).

And with many theses, if the definition is not given well, it is not 25 easy to argue and deal with them, e.g. whether one thing is contrary to one, or several. But once 'contraries' has been properly defined, it is easy to infer whether it is possible for there to be several contraries for the same thing or not. It is the same way also in other cases requiring definitions.

It also appears that in mathematics, it is not easy to construct 30 proofs of some things because of the deficiency of a definition, for instance that the line cutting a plane figure parallel to its side divides the area and the line similarly. But once the definition has been stated, the proposition is evident at once. For the areas and the lines have the same reciprocal subtraction: and this is the defi- 35 nition of 'same ratio'.

In a word, the first of the elements are easily proved when the definitions are accepted, e.g. what a line is, what a circle is (although there are not actually many things to deal with about each

of these because the intermediates are not many). But if the definitions of the principles are not accepted, then this is difficult, and in
159ᵃ general wellnigh impossible. The situation is also like this in the
case of arguments.

We must not forget, then, that when a thesis is difficult to deal
with, it has one of the properties mentioned. But when it is a bigger
job to argue for the claim (i.e. the premiss) than for the thesis,
5 then one might be puzzled whether such things should be conceded
or not. For if you do not concede it but expect ⟨the questioner⟩
to argue for this too, then you will impose a greater task in place
of the one initially assigned; but if you do concede it, then you
will acquire conviction on the basis of less convincing premisses. So
10 if the problem must not be made more difficult, it should be
conceded; but if deduction must be through what is more familiar,
it should not be conceded. Or: it should not be conceded by a
learner if it is not more familiar, but it should be conceded by
someone practising if it only appears true. Consequently, it is evident that a questioner and a teacher should not expect concessions
in the same way.

CHAPTERS 4 AND 5

15 So, as for the way we ought to devise questions and arrange them,
these remarks are probably enough. But about answering, first
we should determine what is the task of the good answerer, as
well as the good questioner. Now, the job of the questioner is to
lead the argument so as to make the answerer state the most
20 unacceptable of the consequences made necessary as a result of the
thesis, while the job of the answerer is to make it appear that it is
not because of him that anything impossible or contrary to opinion
results, but because of the thesis (for conceding at first what one
should not is probably a different mistake from failing to defend
25 that concession properly). [VIII. 5] But since these points are not
defined for those who engage in arguments for the sake of exercise
and testing—for the goals are not the same for teachers and learners as for competitors, nor for the latter and for those who engage
with one another for the sake of inquiry. For the learner must
30 always concede the opinions—and nobody tries to teach a falsehood—but among competitors, the questioner must at all costs
appear to be inflicting something on the answerer, while the answerer must appear not to be affected. But when it comes to

dialectical meetings among people who engage in arguments not for the sake of competition, but for testing and inquiry, it has never been spelt out what the answerer must aim at, or what sorts of 35 things he must grant and what not in order to ⟨count as⟩ defending his thesis well or not.—To get back to the point, since nothing has been transmitted to us about these things, let us try to say something ourselves.

Now, the answerer must necessarily take up the argument by agreeing to a thesis that is either acceptable, or unacceptable, or **159**[b] neither; and one that is acceptable or unacceptable either without qualification or in a definite way (as to a specific person, to himself, or to someone else). But it makes no difference in what way the thesis is acceptable or unacceptable: for there will be the same way of answering well, of granting or not granting what is asked. If the thesis is unacceptable, then, the conclusion must become accept- 5 able, and if acceptable unacceptable (for the questioner always concludes the opposite of the thesis). And if what is supposed is neither unacceptable nor acceptable, then the conclusion will also be of that sort. Since whoever deduces well deduces the problem assigned from more acceptable and more familiar things, it is evi- dent that if the thing supposed is unacceptable without qualifica- 10 tion, then the answerer should grant neither what does not seem so without qualification, nor what seems so but less than the conclu- sion. For if the thesis is unacceptable, the conclusion is acceptable; consequently, all the premisses obtained must be acceptable, and more acceptable than the conclusion proposed, if it is through things more familiar that the less familiar is to be concluded. Thus, 15 if one of the premisses asked is not of this sort, the answerer should not concede it. But if the thesis is acceptable without qualification, then it is clear that the conclusion is unacceptable without qualifi- cation. He should therefore concede both everything that seems so and anything which does not but is less unacceptable than the conclusion (for it would appear to have been sufficiently argued). 20 Similarly if the thesis is neither acceptable nor unacceptable. For in this case also he should grant both everything apparent and whatever does not seem so but is more acceptable than the conclu- sion: for in this way it will turn out that the arguments are more acceptable.

Now if what is proposed is acceptable or unacceptable without qualification, then it is with respect to what seems so without qualification that he should make the comparison. But if what is 25

proposed is acceptable or unacceptable, not without qualification, but to the answerer, then it is with respect to what he himself thinks or does not think that he should judge what to concede or not concede. And if the answerer is defending someone else's opinion, then clearly it is with an eye to that person's thought that he must
30 concede or refuse anything. This is also why those who are defending the opinions of others—for instance that good and bad are the same thing, according to what Heraclitus says—refuse to grant that contraries cannot be present simultaneously in the same thing: it is not because they do not think this themselves, but because according to Heraclitus this is what you must say. This is also what those
35 who take over theses from each other do, for they aim at what the one who advanced the thesis would say.

CHAPTER 6

It is evident, then, what the answerer should aim at, whether the thing proposed is acceptable without qualification or to a certain person. But since everything asked must be either acceptable, unacceptable, or neither, and what is asked must be either relevant to
160ᵃ the argument or not relevant to the argument, if it is acceptable and is not relevant to the argument he should grant it, saying that it is acceptable; if on the other hand it is not acceptable and is not relevant to the argument, then he should grant it but add the comment that it is not acceptable, so as not to appear simple-minded. If it is relevant to the argument and acceptable, then he
5 should say that it is acceptable but is too close to the initial thesis and that the thesis is refuted if it is conceded. And if the statement is relevant to the argument but too unacceptable, then he should say that the conclusion follows if this is conceded but that the proposal is too simple-minded. If it is neither unacceptable nor acceptable, then if it has nothing to do with the argument he should
10 grant it without making any distinction; if, on the other hand, it is relevant to the argument, he should add the comment that when it is conceded the initial thesis is refuted. For in this way, not only will the answerer appear not to suffer anything through his own fault, if he concedes each premiss foreseeing ⟨what will follow⟩, but also the questioner will get his deduction, since everything more acceptable than the conclusion is conceded to him. But as for those who try to
15 deduce from things more unacceptable than the conclusion, they clearly do not deduce properly; accordingly, one should not concede what they ask.

30

This is also how unclear and ambiguous questions should be met with. For since it is open to the answerer who does not understand to say 'I do not understand', and, if the question is ambiguous, not necessarily to agree or disagree, it is first of all clear that, if what is said is not precise, he should not be reluctant to say he does not understand it: for it often happens that as a result of granting premisses not asked clearly, one is presented with something vexatious. If, on the other hand, it is intelligible but has many senses, then if what is said is true or false in all cases, he should grant or reject it without qualification; but if it is false in one case and true in another, then he should indicate that it has many senses and that this one is false and that one true (for if he makes this distinction later, it will be unclear whether he also discerned the ambiguity in the beginning). But if he failed to see the ambiguity in advance and conceded with one of the senses in mind, then he should tell a questioner who leads the argument towards the other sense, 'I did not grant it with that sense in mind, but with the other one': for if there are numerous things falling under the same word or argument, then dispute is easy. But if the question is both clear and unambiguous, then he should answer either 'yes' or 'no'.

Since every deductive premiss either is among those the deduction is from or is for the sake of one of these (and it is clear when someone is getting premisses for the sake of another, because of his asking for several similar cases—for it is either through induction or through similarity that people generally obtain universal premisses), the answerer should concede all particulars, so long as they are true and acceptable, but should try to bring an objection against the universal. For to impede the argument without either a real or an apparent objection is cantankerousness. So, if he does not grant the universal when it appears so in many cases, though he does not have an objection, it is evident that he is being cantankerous. Next, if he also cannot give any counter-attack showing that it is not true, then all the more will he seem to be cantankerous. (But in fact not even this is sufficient. For we know of many arguments contrary to our opinions which it is difficult to solve—e.g. Zeno's argument that it is not possible to move or to traverse the sta-

dium—but that is no reason why one should not concede their
10 opposites.) Accordingly, if, though not able either to counter-
attack or to object, he does not concede, it is clear that he is being
cantankerous. For cantankerousness in arguments is responding in
a way—other than those mentioned—which is destructive of the
deduction.

CHAPTER 9

To defend either a thesis or a definition, you should first work out
15 an attack on it for yourself. For it is clear that it is those things on
the basis of which questioners refute the thesis that you should
oppose.

Avoid defending an unacceptable thesis. ('Unacceptable' could
have two meanings: it might mean either a thesis from which ab-
surdities follow, e.g. if someone were to say that all things move or
20 that nothing does; or, it might mean what a bad character would
choose and what is contrary to our wishes, e.g. that pleasure is the
good or that doing wrong is better than suffering it.) For people will
take you to be saying what you think, not defending something for
the sake of argument, and hate you.

CHAPTER 10

As for arguments that deduce a falsehood, solve them by rejecting
that because of which the falsehood comes about. For it is not the
25 case that the person who rejects anything whatever has solved it,
not even if what is rejected is false. For an argument might contain
several falsehoods, as for example if someone took as premisses
that the person seated is writing and that Socrates is seated. For it
follows from these that Socrates is writing. Now, when 'Socrates is
seated' is rejected, the argument is no closer to being solved. And
30 yet the claim is false. But it is not as a result of this that the
argument is false. For if someone happened to be sitting down but
not writing, the same solution will no longer be appropriate for
such a case. Consequently, it is not this premiss that should be
rejected, but rather 'the person seated is writing' (for not every
seated person is writing). Now, the person who rejects that because
of which the falsehood comes about has certainly solved the argument, but it is the person who knows that the argument is by means
35 of this who knows the solution (as in the case of fake diagrams). For
it is not enough to object, not even if what is rejected is false, but he

32

must also demonstrate why it is false: this is how it will be evident whether or not he makes his objection with foresight.

There are four ways to hinder an argument from coming to a 161ᵃ conclusion, as follows. An answerer can do so by rejecting that because of which the falsehood comes about, or by stating an objection to the questioner (for often he does not succeed in solving it, but yet the questioner is not able to carry it forward any further). Third is objecting to the questions asked. For it may result 5 that what the questioner intends does not come about from the questions asked because they have been asked poorly, though when something else is added the conclusion does come about. So then, if the questioner can no longer lead the argument forward, then the objection would be against the questioner, whereas if he can, it would be against the questions asked. The fourth and poor- 10 est kind of objection is the one with respect to time: for some people raise the sort of objection that it would take longer to argue against than the present discussion allows. Objections, then, as we have said, come about in four ways. But only the first kind of objection stated is a solution: the remainder are various hindrances 15 and impediments of conclusions.

CHAPTER 11

A criticism of an argument just as an argument in itself is not the same as a criticism of it when it is put as questions. For the person questioned is often at fault for the argument not being argued well, because he will not agree to the premisses from which it would be possible to argue well against the thesis. For it is not in the power 20 of one participant alone to see that their common work is well accomplished. There are times, then, when it is necessary to attack the speaker, not the thesis—when the answerer is particularly abusive and ready to pounce on the questioner with the contrary of whatever he asks for. By being cantankerous, then, these people make discussions competitive and not dialectical. In addition, since 25 such arguments are for the sake of exercise and testing rather than instruction, it is clear that not only true but also false conclusions must be deduced, and not always by means of true premisses but sometimes also false ones. For it is often necessary for the person conducting the argument to refute when a truth has been supposed, so that he must put forward falsehoods as premisses. And some- times, even when a falsehood has been supposed, he must refute it 30 through falsehoods. For nothing prevents things that are not so

33

from seeming more so to someone than the truth, so that if the argument comes about from what seems so to him he will more likely be convinced or benefited. And anyone who is to change minds well must change them dialectically, not contentiously—as

35 the geometer must do so geometrically—no matter whether the conclusion be false or true. (Which deductions are dialectical was stated earlier.) And since it is a poor participant who impedes the common work, so it is clearly also in an argument. For there is also a common project in these (except for competitive ones: in

40 these, it is not possible for both to achieve the same goal, for it is

161ᵇ impossible for more than one to win.) It makes no difference whether one does this through answering or through questioning: for the person who questions contentiously argues poorly, and so does the answerer who will not grant what is evident or will not

5 understand what it is that the questioner means to get. So it is clear from what has been said that criticism should not be directed in the same manner at the argument in itself and at the questioner. For nothing prevents the argument being poor but the questioner having argued as well as possible with the answerer. For with cantan-

10 kerous people, you simply may not be able to produce the deduction you want, but only one that is possible. And since it is not determined when these people are taking contraries and when they are taking the original conclusions—for when making statements on their own, they often state contrary things and, having initially refused something, grant it later on; therefore, when they

15 are asked for contraries or for the initial thesis they often consent— poor arguments are bound to result. The guilty party is the answerer who does not grant something but then grants something else of that sort.

It is evident, then, that questioners and arguments should not be criticized in the same way.

There are five criticisms of an argument in itself. The first criti-
20 cism applies whenever, from the premises asked, neither what was proposed nor anything else at all is concluded (the premises used to get the conclusion being false or unacceptable, either all or most of them), and the conclusion does not come about either when some premises are taken away, or when some are added, or when

25 some are taken away and others added. The second criticism applies if the deduction is not about the thesis (and is from the sorts of premises, and in the same way, as mentioned before). The third criticism applies if a deduction does come about with certain premises added, but these are inferior to the ones asked for and

less acceptable than the conclusion. Again, if one comes about with
certain premises taken away (for sometimes more premises are
taken than those necessary, so that it is not in virtue of their being 30
so that the deduction comes about). Next, if it is from premises
more unacceptable and less convincing than the conclusion. Or, if
it is from premises which are true but require more work to
demonstrate than the problem.

One should not expect the deductions of all problems to be
equally acceptable and convincing. For just by nature, some things 35
sought are easier and others harder, so that if ⟨the questioner⟩ has
brought it to a conclusion from the most acceptable premises
possible, then he has argued well. It is evident, then, that the same
criticism also does not apply to an argument in relation to the
problem under consideration and in itself. For nothing prevents 40
the argument being worthy of blame in itself but praiseworthy in
relation to the problem. Or again, conversely, ⟨it may be⟩ praise- **162**^a
worthy in itself but worthy of blame in relation to the problem—
when it is easy to conclude it from many acceptable premises, and
even from true ones. Sometimes, an argument which comes to a
conclusion might even be worse than an argument which does
not—when the former is concluded from simple-minded premises 5
(though the problem is not of that sort), the latter is in need of
certain premises which are acceptable and true, and the argument
does not lie in these additional premises.

It is not right to criticize arguments which conclude a truth
through falsehoods. For a falsehood must always be deduced
through falsehoods, but it is sometimes also possible to deduce a
truth through falsehoods. This is evident from the *Analytics*. 10

When the argument stated is a demonstration of something, then
if there is something else not related in any way to the conclusion,
it will not be a deduction about that; and if it should appear to be,
then it will be a sophism, not a demonstration.

[A 'philosopheme' is a demonstrative deduction, an 'epichei- 15
reme' is a dialectical deduction, a 'sophism' is a contentious
deduction, and an 'aporeme' is a dialectical deduction of a
contradiction.]

If something is proved from premises both of which appear to
be so, but not to the same degree, then nothing prevents what is
proved from appearing so more than either of the premises. But if 20
one premiss should seem so and the other should be indifferent, or
if one should seem so and the other should seem not so, then if
these are to the same degree, ⟨the conclusion⟩ would be equally

believed as disbelieved; but if one of these is to a greater degree, ⟨the conclusion⟩ will follow the one that is greater.

25   And then there is this error in deductions: when someone proves through longer steps though it could be done through fewer ones which are actually present in the argument. Suppose e.g. that to prove one opinion is more so than another, a questioner were to argue: 'Each thing itself is such to the highest degree; there is a truly opinable itself; thus, it will be so to a higher degree than the particular opinables; that which is so called in relation to the more so is more so; there is a true opinion itself, which will be more

30   precise than the particular opinions.' But he asked for the premisses that there is a true opinion itself and that each thing itself is such to the highest degree. Consequently, this opinion is a more precise opinion. But what is the fault? Surely, that that on which the argument rests makes us overlook the cause.

CHAPTER 12

35   An argument is *obvious* in one sense (the most popular one) if it is brought to a conclusion in such a way that nothing further need be asked. In another way—and this type is most correctly so called—

162ᵇ when the premisses obtained are those from which it is necessary for it to be deduced and it is concluded through conclusions. Next, if something extremely acceptable is missing.

An argument is called 'false' in four ways. One way is when it appears to come to a conclusion though it does not do so (which is

5   called a contentious deduction). Another way is when it comes to a conclusion but not one relevant to what was proposed (which happens most to those leading to the impossible). Or, it comes to a conclusion relevant to what was proposed, but yet not in accordance with the appropriate study (and this is when it appears to be

10   medical though it is not medical, or geometrical though it is not geometrical, or dialectical though it is not dialectical), whether what follows is false or true. In another way, if it is concluded through falsehoods. The conclusion of such an argument will sometimes be false but sometimes true: for a falsehood is always concluded through falsehoods, but it is possible for a truth to

15   be concluded even though not from truths, as was also stated earlier.

Now, for an argument to be false is a fault of the speaker more than of the argument—and it is not even a fault of the speaker in every case, but only when he is not aware of it—since, considering

36

the argument just in itself, we approve it more than many true ones,
if starting with premisses which seem so to the highest degree it
rejects some truth. For if the argument is of this sort, then it is a
demonstration of other truths: for one of the premisses must not be 20
so at all, so that it will be a demonstration of this. But if the
argument were to conclude a truth through false, and extremely
silly, premisses, it would be worse than many which deduce a
falsehood (and it might be like this even if it concluded a falsehood). Consequently, it is clear that the first point of examination 25
of an argument on its own is whether it comes to a conclusion; the
second is whether this is true or false; and the third is from what
sorts of premisses. For if it is from false but acceptable premisses, it
is a logical argument; if from true but unacceptable premisses, it is
a poor one; and if the premisses are both false and extremely
unacceptable, then it is clear that it is a poor argument, either
without qualification or in application to the subject. 30

CHAPTER 13

How it is that the questioner asks for the initial thing and for
contraries has been explained in accordance with the truth in
the *Analytics*; now, this should be explained in accordance with
opinion.

People appear to ask for the initial thing in five ways. The most 35
obvious, and the first, is if someone asks for the very thing which
needs to be proved. In the case of the statement itself, it is not easy
to get by with this, but it is more likely in the case of synonyms and
those cases in which a word and a phrase signify the same thing.
The second is when someone needing to demonstrate a particular **163ᵃ**
asks for a universal, e.g. trying to show that there is a single science
of contraries, he claims the premiss that there is a single knowledge
of opposites. For he appears to be asking for what he needed to
prove by itself, together with other additional things. Third, if 5
someone proposing to prove a universal should ask for a particular,
e.g. if, proposing to prove this about all contraries, he claims it
about these certain contraries. For this person also appears to be
asking for that which—with additional things—he needed to prove,
apart by itself. Next, if someone divides up the problem in asking,
e.g. if, needing to prove that medicine is of the healthy and the 10
diseased, he should claim each of them separately. Or, if someone
should ask for one or the other of premisses which necessarily
follow from each other, e.g. asking for the premiss that the side is

incommensurable with the diagonal when it is required to demonstrate that the diagonal is incommensurable with the side.

People ask for contraries in the same number of ways as they do
15 the initial thing. First, if someone should ask for an opposed assertion and denial; second, contraries according to an opposition, e.g. ⟨calling⟩ the same thing good and evil; third, if someone who has claimed a universal should ask for its contradictory in the case of particulars (e.g. if, having obtained ⟨the premiss⟩ that there is a single knowledge of contraries, he were to claim that there is a different knowledge of the healthy and of the diseased; or if, having
20 asked for the latter, he should attempt to get the contradictory in the case of the universal); next, if someone should ask for the contrary to what results of necessity because of the things supposed; and if someone were not to obtain the opposites themselves but should ask for two ⟨sets of⟩ premisses such that from them the opposing contradiction arises.
25 Getting contraries differs from getting the initial thing in that the error in the latter case is in relation to the conclusion (for that is what we look to in saying that someone asks for the initial thing), whereas in the case of contraries it is within the premisses, in virtue of their being in a certain relationship to one another.

CHAPTER 14

30 For the sake of exercise and practice in such arguments, you should first become accustomed to converting arguments. For in this way we shall be better able to deal with whatever is said, and also in learning a few arguments we shall learn many. Now, to convert is to reject one of the premisses given by taking the reverse of the conclusion along with the other premisses asked. For it is neces-
35 sary, if the conclusion is not so, for some one of the premisses to be rejected, since it was necessary for the conclusion to be so when they were all conceded.

And for every thesis, investigate the means of attack both for showing that it is so and for showing that it is not so; and as soon as
163ᵇ you have found one, at once look for its solution. For in this way, one will simultaneously get exercise both for asking and for answering; and even if we do not have anyone to practice with, we can do this on our own. Also, select the lines of attack concerning the
5 same thesis and set them out alongside each other. For it makes one very adept at giving compelling arguments, and in addition provides a great support in refuting, when one is readily equipped

to argue both that it is so and that it is not so (for in consequence ⟨one's opponent⟩ must be on guard against arguments from contrary directions). And also, when it comes to knowledge and the wisdom that comes from philosophy, being able to discern—or 10 already having discerned—the consequences of either assumption is no small instrument: for it remains to choose one or the other of these rightly. In order to do that, one must be naturally gifted, and this is what it is to be naturally gifted with respect to truth: to be able properly to choose the true and avoid the false. This is just 15 what the naturally good are able to do, for it is by loving and hating in the right way whatever is presented to them that they judge well what is best.

For those problems which arise most often to deal with, you should learn arguments by heart (and especially about the first theses: for in the case of these, answerers often give up in despair). Next, you should be ready with definitions and have both accept- 20 able and primary premises at your fingertips, for it is through these that deductions come about. You should also try to master those ⟨problems⟩ under which other arguments most often fall. For just as in geometry it is useful to have gone through exercises with the elements, or as in arithmetic having the multiplication table at your 25 fingertips makes a great difference when figuring a multiple of some other number, so too in the case of arguments are having things at your fingertips when it comes to the starting-points and learning premises until they are on the tip of your tongue. For just as in the art of remembering, the mere mention of the places instantly makes us recall the things, so these will make us more apt 30 at deductions through looking to these defined premises in order of enumeration. And it is a common premiss rather than an argument which should be committed to memory, for being ready with a starting-point—that is, assumption—is a matter of manageable difficulty.

Next, get accustomed to making one argument into many, like people who are concealing with the greatest of obscurity: an argu- 35 ment would be of that sort if someone stands off as far as possible from things of the same kind as what the argument is about. Those will be powerful arguments that can undergo this to the most universal degree, e.g. that there is not a single science of several **164**^a things: for so stated, it will apply to relatives, contraries, or coordinates.

You should make your memorized accounts of arguments universal, even if they were argued as particulars. For in this way, it

5 will also be possible to make the one argument into many. (The same also holds in the case of rhetoric for enthymemes.) But you should for your part avoid as much as possible letting arguments tend towards a universal. And you should always examine arguments to see whether they are arguing about common things. For all arguments that argue to a particular conclusion also argue uni-

10 versally, and the demonstration of a universal is present in the particular deduction because it is not possible to deduce anything without universals.

Exercise with those apt at induction should be assigned to a beginner; exercise with those apt at deduction to someone experienced. And try to take premisses from those apt at deduction,

15 examples from those apt at induction. For it is in this that each has been exercised. In general, try to bring away from any argumentative exercise session either a deduction about something, or a solution, or an objection, or whether someone said something correctly or incorrectly (whether yourself or someone else), and

164ᵇ the reason why in either case: for these are what the ability comes from, and exercising is for the sake of ability. This especially concerns premisses and objections. For, in a word, the dialectical person is the one who can put forward and object. Putting forward

5 propositions is making many things into one (for in general that one thing must be obtained to which the argument is directed), while objecting is making one thing many (for he either divides or rejects, granting one of the things put forward but not another).

You should not argue with everybody or practise with just anyone you happen to encounter. For with some people, arguments

10 necessarily become bad. For against someone who tries at all costs to make it appear that he is escaping, it is right to try at all costs to deduce, but it is not seemly. This is why you should not lightly enter into contests with just anyone you meet: the level of argument is bound to degenerate, for even people engaged in exercises are

15 unable to resist arguing contentiously.

You should also have arguments already made up for the sorts of problem concerning which, being ready with the smallest number of arguments, we will have those useful for the greatest number (these are the universal arguments). And in addition, ⟨have already made up⟩ those it is too difficult to come up with out of what is available on the spot.

COMMENTARY

BOOK ONE

CHAPTER I

100ª18–21. The *Topics* is a practical treatise: from the beginning, Aristotle tells us that his purpose is to find a 'method' (*methodos*) that will give us a certain capacity. Only the *Rhetoric* and *On Sophistical Refutations* (which is really an appendix to the *Topics*) are comparably oriented towards a practical goal, and neither takes such pains to stress the point. Despite this practical orientation, however, Aristotle's distinctive concerns with theoretical understanding and classification soon manifest themselves. Much of the treatise (especially Book VIII) is concerned with a very specific kind of 'gymnastic' argumentation which appears to have been Aristotle's inheritance rather than his invention. He also received from tradition a substantial vocabulary of technical terms and a significant armory of strategies concerning this practice. However, he continually subjects this inheritance to reworking and revision, sometimes drastic; as in the *Rhetoric*, Aristotle takes what may have been a skill defined by rules of thumb and practical maxims and undertakes to transform it into an art based on a scientific understanding of its subject-matter. Thus, when he proposes as his project the finding of a 'method' which will enable us to construct deductions about 'any problem that is proposed', he is (as it seems to me) making a deliberately grandiose claim, not dissimilar in scope to the vast sweep he sees for the procedures of the *Prior Analytics* in that work (I. 30).

This opening sentence is thick with technical vocabulary. Aristotle defines several of the most important terms later, but a few explanations may be useful here:

'Study': the word is *pragmateia*, which (like 'study') can mean both the activity of investigating a subject and a written work giving the results of such an investigation.

'Method' (*methodos*): our word 'method' not only descends from this term but also translates it well, with certain caveats. *Methodos* is derived from *hodos*, 'road': by its etymology it could mean 'following on the road after', 'pursuit', though this sense does not seem to appear until well after Aristotle. He most commonly uses it interchangeably with *pragmateia* to mean both a subject studied and a written account of such a study. A broadly similar pair of meanings exists in English: a 'piano method' is both a series of lessons teaching one to play the piano and a set of books containing those lessons.

'Deduce' (*sullogizesthai*), 'deduction' (*sullogismos*): these are the ancestors of our words 'syllogize', 'syllogism', but those descendants make bad translations. The problem is this: although Aristotle defines a *sullogismos* both here and elsewhere in rather general terms to mean, approximately, 'valid argument', he also tries to establish (in the *Prior Analytics*) that every valid argument can be analysed into one of a certain number of forms, or perhaps a combination of those forms: these forms are today referred to as 'categorical syllogisms', or simply 'syllogisms' (Aristotle himself usually calls these 'the deductions in the figures'). Thus, to use this as a translation is seriously misleading, since the English term usually suggests this narrower meaning (it also has the unfortunate result, in connection with the *Prior Analytics*, of trivializing Aristotle's claim, argued for at great length, that every valid argument can be 'reduced' to a syllogism). Note that in the argumentative context presupposed by the *Topics*, a *sullogismos* is normally a deduction of the contradictory of one's opponent's position, or a deduction of an outright self-contradiction from one's opponent's premises, in each case put together by asking questions.

'Acceptable' (*endoxos*): translation of this term has been the subject of much scholarly controversy. As I interpret it, it is in fact a relative term: a proposition is *endoxos* with respect to some definite group of persons, whether it be the public generally, or the community of experts, or someone famous. Aristotle discusses it more a few lines later.

'Submit to argument' (*hupechein logon*) is what the person who answers questions in a dialectical exchange is said to do. Translators differ as to what further sense to give it: 'putting forward an argument', 'sustaining an argument'. But like many of Aristotle's terms concerning argument, this one had an established use in law, where it generally meant having to undergo something (a penalty, a trial, a requirement of giving an account). In VIII. 4 we read that the questioner's goal is to 'appear to do something to' the answerer, while the answerer's goal is to 'appear not to suffer anything' (159ᵃ30–2). Thus, to 'submit to argument' is to allow oneself to be put to a kind of test.

'Inconsistent' (*hupenantion*). This often indicates points of conflict in a group of statements of opinion, e.g. apparent inconsistencies in Homer (*Poet.* 1461ᵇ3, etc.) or contradictions among the opinions held by other philosophers on a subject (*De An.* 409ᵇ22, *De Cael.* 280ᵃ6, *GA* 718ᵃ36, *GC* 323ᵃ26). In the latter sense, it is virtually the same as *aporēma*, 'puzzle'. Some translators suppose *hupenantion* to mean 'self-contradictory', but this seems to me inaccurate on two points. First, Aristotle is probably thinking more of a conclusion that is inconsistent with some previously conceded premiss than of a self-contradictory conclusion. Second, as other contexts show, answerers should be worried about intrinsically absurd or implausible conclusions as well as about internal consistency.

According to VIII. 4, the questioner's goal in an exchange is to force out of the answerer the most implausible consequences that can be derived from the answerer's chosen thesis; the answerer's goal is not so much to avoid these consequences as to make it clear that they are the result of the thesis and not his handling of the argument. We do not find that distinction present here. Aristotle may therefore be thinking of the *general* aim of anyone acting as answerer in any sort of dialectical exchange, not just a formal bout of gymnastic dialectic. For that wider context, a dialectical art should teach how to avoid being forced into accepting conclusions that are inconsistent either with one's expressed opinions or with what is generally accepted.

'Different varieties': Aristotle actually says 'differences' (*diaphorai*), but this term also has the technical sense 'differentia'. The sense is 'what the differences of the various species of deductions are'.

100ᵃ25–101ᵃ4. The most important of Aristotle's logical notions is that of the deduction (*sullogismos*). His definition here, like the virtually identical one in the *Prior Analytics* (24ᵇ18–20), comes close to embracing any sort of valid argument (see also *SE* 164ᵇ27–165ᵃ2, 168ᵃ21–2; *Rhet.* 1356ᵇ16–18), though it probably differs in some points from standard modern logical usage. To begin with, Aristotle specifies that 'what results' must be different from any of the premisses; thus, '*p*; *q*; therefore, *p*' would fail to be a deduction. The Greek commentators also say that the plural *tethentōn* ('certain *things* being supposed') rules out deductions with a single premiss. That may be Aristotle's meaning: he says that nothing 'results of necessity' from a single premiss (*An. Pr.* I. 23, 40ᵇ35–6; II. 2, 53ᵇ16–20). On the other hand, the *Prior Analytics* makes important use of conversion inferences (e.g. inferring 'No B is an A' from 'No A is a B'), and these appear to be single-premiss arguments. More significantly here, many of the inference-patterns found in *Top.* II–VII can plausibly be construed as one-premiss arguments (see Introduction). *Top.* I. 12 recognizes only two kinds of dialectical *arguments*, namely, deductions and inductions; Aristotle has no separate term for 'valid arguments that are not *sullogismoi*'.

'Supposed' (*tethentōn, keimenōn*): Aristotle commonly uses the verbs *tithenai* ('put') and *keisthai* (which functions as the perfect passive of *tithenai*) of the premisses of arguments. Perhaps the most accurate account of their meaning here is 'taken as premisses of an argument' or 'considered in order to see what follows of necessity from them', despite its appearance of circularity. It is not easy to give a better explanation without explaining what logical consequence is, that is, without propounding a philosophy of logic. In the context of the *Topics*, *tithenai* most often is used of the answerer in a dialectical exchange, with the meaning 'concede' (i.e. 'reply affirmatively to a premiss advanced by the questioner'). At least for a dialectical deduction, then, we might gloss 'supposed' with 'conceded'. However, it is an important insight of Aristotle's that whether the conclusion of an argument follows of necessity from its premisses does not depend on the form in which the argument is presented or the use to which it is being put (see *An. Pr.* I. 1).

'Results of necessity through them': this is Aristotle's characteristic way of expressing the relation of logical consequence. The first step for any student in logic is to understand the difference between 'X is necessary' and 'X is a necessary consequence of Y': the latter neither asserts Y nor asserts that X is necessary. The phrase 'through them' may serve to restrict the definition to arguments in which the conclusion follows from the premisses *alone*, i.e. arguments in which nothing else is tacitly presupposed (modern usage sometimes calls such arguments 'enthymemes'). (There may be an explicit recognition of this in the remark in *An. Pr.* I. 32 (47ª33–5) that 'the necessary is more extensive than the *sullogismos*'.)

100ª27–ᵇ23. Aristotle now gives brief discussions of three species of arguments: *demonstration* (*apodeixis*), *dialectical deduction* (*sullogismos dialektikos*), and *contentious deduction* (*eristikos sullogismos*). Demonstrations are discussed at great length in the *Posterior Analytics*, while contentious deductions are the subject of *On Sophistical Refutations* (which is an appendix to the *Topics*). It is tempting to say that a demonstration is a deduction which makes its conclusion known by deducing it from known (and therefore true) premisses; likewise, it is tempting to gloss 'contentious' with 'fallacious'. Aristotle's actual characterizations, however, are somewhat more complex. Before considering them, it will be useful to take note of some basic points about arguments and their premisses.

First, there is a connection between validity and truth. If a valid argument has true premisses, then its conclusion must also be true. This connection may be seen as definitional: on most accounts, what it means to say that an argument is valid is that it cannot have true premisses and a false conclusion (thus, whatever follows from true premisses is true). We may call this the *semantic* picture of validity.

Arguments also have a *doxastic* dimension, however, and are frequently offered as vehicles of persuasion. If an argument is to persuade, it must make an appeal of this form: 'You accept these premisses; therefore, you must accept this conclusion'. In such a case, what is important is not the truth of the premisses—at least not directly—but the fact that they are believed. Likewise, the persuasiveness of an argument turns on whether its audience believes its conclusion to follow from its premisses, not whether it actually does follow. False premisses which I believe will be useful in persuading me; true ones I do not believe will not. Similarly, premisses will be useful in getting me to believe a conclusion only if I *believe* that conclusion follows from them. Put briefly: whatever is (believed to be) deduced from believed premisses is believed.

This last generalization says something about how we behave as epistemic subjects, for obviously it must be relative to a particular believer. We often have false beliefs, including false beliefs about what follows from what, and we may think that an argument is valid when it is not. If we consider inferences just as dispositions to assent to certain conclusions after having assented to certain premisses, then perhaps the study of persuasive arguments is ultimately a matter for psychology. However, inferential beliefs are not—or at least need not be—mere blind dispositions to behave. Instead, they presuppose a connection with truth, specifically, the *belief* that if the premisses are true then the conclusion must be true. Validity, semantically defined, is thus what we aim at in our inferential beliefs, and it serves as their normative goal. If an argument is valid, then a disposition to infer its conclusion from its premisses is *rational*; if an argument is invalid, then the analogous disposition is irrational. If we discover that we have dispositions to infer conclusions from premisses which do not really necessitate them, then in order to be rational we must change those dispositions.

This leads to an important connection between deduction and knowledge. Whatever else philosophers might wish to say about knowledge, most have taken it as obvious that what is known must be both true and believed. The fact that truth and belief are both transmitted by valid arguments thus makes validity especially relevant to knowledge: the argument's validity and the truth of its premisses imply the truth of its conclusion, while my beliefs that the premisses are true and that the argument is valid lead to my belief that the conclusion is true. In brief: whatever is known to follow from known premisses is known. An argument which functions in this way, leading to knowledge of its conclusion on the basis of knowledge of its premisses, is a *proof* or *justification*.

In the *Posterior Analytics* Aristotle says that a demonstration is a deduction such that 'we have knowledge in virtue of possessing it' (71^{b}18–19). *An. Post.* I proceeds to discuss in detail the structure of this type of knowledge (for which Aristotle reserves the term *epistēmē*). He enumerates some six properties which the premisses of a deduction must have if it is to be a demonstration: they must be true, 'primary', 'immediate'

45

(*amesoi*), prior to the conclusion, 'better known' than the conclusion, and the cause or explanation of the conclusion's truth. These properties (to which *An. Post*. I. 4 adds necessity) will ensure that the demonstration is a 'deduction producing scientific knowledge', which Aristotle explains as a matter of knowing the cause why the conclusion must be as it is. From this definition, Aristotle then argues that the 'starting-points' (*archai*) on which demonstrations depend must have other properties. In particular, they must themselves be incapable of demonstration and, since Aristotle identifies scientific knowledge (*epistēmē*) with knowledge that results from demonstration, they must be known in some other way that provides even more 'trustworthiness' or 'conviction' (*pistis*) than demonstration (*An. Post*. I. 2, 72ᵃ25–ᵇ4). An Aristotelian demonstration, then, is a proof of a special sort, from premises meeting a series of additional conditions.

Top. 100ᵃ27–9 does reflect some of this: the phrase 'true and primary' corresponds exactly to *An. Post*. I. 2, and Aristotle's later explanation of the phrase in 100ᵃ30–ᵇ21 not only attributes an inherent trustworthiness (*pistis*) to what is true and primary but also calls such premises 'starting-points' (*archai*). We might try to see more by taking the remark that one 'should not seek further the reason why' in connection with these starting-points as an allusion to the causal role of demonstrative premises in the *Posterior Analytics*. However, what the *Topics* says is not that the starting-points must *be* causes, but rather that one must not seek *their* causes.

What is the meaning of the statement that true and primary propositions 'get their trustworthiness through themselves'? In the *Posterior Analytics* Aristotle holds that demonstrations must rest on undemonstrated first premises (or otherwise there is an infinite regress of premises, with no beginning). However, he stops short of saying that these first premises must be self-evident or obvious in some way that transcends proof. The term I translate 'trustworthiness' is *pistis*, which can mean 'trust' (of persons), 'belief', or 'conviction' (of propositions). It is possible that Aristotle uses it to indicate some intrinsic epistemic quality of first premises, for instance a kind of indubitability. However, in rhetoric and in forensic oratory *pistis* had the semi-technical sense 'proof', i.e. argument or evidence used to prove something (*Rhet*. 1354ᵃ13, elsewhere). Aristotle also uses the phrase *lambanein pistin* to mean 'obtain a *proof*' (frequently in *De Cael*. 279ᵇ33, 277ᵇ9, 283ᵇ30, 287ᵃ31; *Met*. 1090ᵃ3; *Mete*. 372ᵃ32). If that is the sense Aristotle has in mind, then he may mean that the premises of demonstrations constitute, on their own, proofs or evidence for *other* propositions.

There is another interpretation worth considering. Aristotle frequently differentiates demonstration and dialectical argument on the grounds that demonstrations 'take' their premises whereas dialectical deductions 'ask' them (see e.g. *An. Pr.* I. 1 and the Commentary on 101ᵇ28–36 below). This difference of form reflects a difference in purpose. Demonstrations take their premisses as established and seek to establish their conclusion from them, whereas dialectical arguments treat them merely as hypothetical and seek to explore what follows from them. Aristotle's point, then, may be just this: 'Unlike a dialectical deduction, a demonstration must take its premisses as established; therefore, they must actually *be* established, either on their own merit or through some other kind of proof.'

Since the main subject of the *Topics* is dialectical argument, not demonstration, it is probably unwise to press comparisons on this point with the *Posterior Analytics* too far.

100ª30–ᵇ19. 'have attained [*eilēphen*: perfect] the starting-point of knowledge about themselves through some primary and true premisses': most interpreters take this to mean 'have previously been demonstrated'. Such an interpretation comports well with the deductive structure presented in Euclid's *Elements* and in the precursors of it which may have existed as early as Aristotle's time in the Academy: a science proves its theorems in systematic order, first establishing the simplest theorems and then using them as premisses from which to prove more complex ones. (But it is curious that Aristotle takes little if any note of this structure in the *Posterior Analytics*, speaking instead as if *every* demonstration must rely on indemonstrable starting-points.) Note that it is the *premisses* of the demonstration which are said to have 'attained the starting-point of knowledge about themselves'. This may reflect a conception of a demonstration as providing a foundation for its conclusion by linking that conclusion up with its explanatory principles: it is the conclusion demonstrated which 'reaches' these starting-points, and the demonstration is the means through which it does this. (The perfect *eilēphen* could indicate having entered into, and remained in, a certain state: as a result of prior demonstration, these premisses join the ranks of the permanently established.)

100ᵇ23–5. In effect, Aristotle defines a contentious deduction as a counterfeit dialectical deduction, that is, something which appears to be a dialectical deduction but is not. Such a counterfeit can take two forms: either a deduction with merely apparently acceptable premisses or a merely apparent deduction with acceptable premisses. (Of course, a single contentious deduction might exhibit both vices.) As Aristotle notes, the first sort of contentious deduction is a species of deduction, whereas the second sort is not, just as fake pearls are not pearls. In modern terminology, contentious deductions of the second sort are *invalid*. There is no standard modern term describing the vice of the first sort of contentious deduction, but we might see an analogy with those that are valid but *unsound* (i.e. have at least one false premiss). In each case, the vice in question is not a mere lack but an actual counterfeit, deceptively passing for its corresponding virtue.

What is it about contentious arguments that brings about these deceptive appearances? In most cases, it will be a matter of their form. Generally, we recognize valid arguments to be valid by recognizing them to be instances of forms which are valid, that is, which can never be instantiated by true premisses and a false conclusion. However, there are forms of argument which people are often inclined to think valid even though they are not. We usually call these *fallacies*. A contentious argument of the second sort is a fallacy put to a certain deceptive use: the contentious reasoner propounding it will generally know it is invalid, but his victim will not.

The first question to arise about contentious arguments of the first sort, genuine deductions with merely apparently acceptable premisses, is: what is it for a premiss to be *only apparently* acceptable? As we learn in the next sentence, it is again form that causes the misleading appearance.

100ᵇ26–101ᵃ1. 'not everything which appears to be acceptable': these lines, which have proved difficult for interpreters, shed light on the notion of an apparently acceptable premiss, but they do so rather indirectly. The reason, as so often in the *Topics*, is that Aristotle was writing for an audience already familiar with dialectical practices and terminology, not for us. Aristotle's contemporaries were familiar with a whole collection of argumentative puzzles (such as those displayed in Plato's *Euthydemus*) which often turn on getting people to accept trick premisses. Many of these are such that, once the trick has been sprung, it is obvious how it works and equally obvious that the initial premiss should not have been conceded. Consider an example: 'What you have not lost, you have; you have not lost horns; therefore, you have horns.' The problem with this argument is not that it is invalid but that its first premiss is false. To be caught by the trick, I must first concede this premiss, which I might do because it has a certain superficial plausibility; on reflection (or after seeing what follows from it), I realize that I do not believe it after all, even though at first I *thought* I did.

Of course, once I have caught on to the trick, the offending premiss no longer even *appears* to me to be something I accept. Thus, what appears to be acceptable is not only relative to a particular person but also subject to modification. This gives rise to a problem. On any plausible view of acceptability, what is *actually* acceptable could well change in the same way: the wise, and even the many, gradually change their views in the light of experience, fashion, or other influences. Especially for those who engage in dialectical argument, one of those influences can be the discovery that some belief leads to absurdity or contradiction. If, for instance, I am thoroughly persuaded by Zeno's arguments concerning motion, then I will decide that, though I at first inclined to accept the proposition 'There is motion', I now realize that I do not accept it at all. A contentious argument could bring about a change in what I accept in just the same way: the only difference is in how quickly I come to make the required adjustment. To put the point another way, what counts as a contentious argument for the quick-witted might constitute genuine dialectical inquiry for the obtuse. We are thus left without a clear distinction between the dialectical and the contentious.

Aristotle might try to solve this by appealing to another distinction. Contentious argument, as he thinks of it, is *deceptive*. Those who lie differ from those who are sincerely mistaken in that they believe what they say is false; likewise, those who argue contentiously give arguments which they realize are flawed. But this again implies that one and the same argument might be contentious or dialectical, depending on the logical insight of its propounder.

Aristotle does not take note of these issues here because his purpose is to discuss dialectical rather than contentious arguments: he reserves the latter for a more extensive treatment in *On Sophistical Refutations* (see in particular *SE* 8, *SE* 10).

101^{a}5–17. This passage takes note of a problem in Aristotle's classification of arguments. The word I translate 'fallacy' (*paralogismos*) carries an implication of deliberate trickery which 'fallacy' does not: its cognate verb *paralogizesthai* commonly means 'cheat' or 'embezzle' (though Aristotle does occasionaly use it of people who have simply made errors in reasoning, e.g. Melissus and Zeno in *Phys.* I. 3). In *On Sophistical Refutations*, fallacies are contentious deductions of the *second* variety as defined above: invalid arguments that appear to be valid.

Now, Aristotle sees a problem with a particular variety of deceptive reasoning that he describes as 'based on [*ek*, which often indicates the premisses of an argument] what is appropriate to specific sciences'. His illustration is highly specific. A geometrical proof, for the Greeks, was usually closely connected with a diagram, so much so that *graphein*, 'draw', can mean simply 'prove' (i.e. by drawing a diagram). A trick 'proof' for some impossible result can sometimes be constructed by drawing a diagram which is actually impossible, e.g. represents certain lines as intersecting which cannot actually intersect, or cannot intersect as represented (it may help to draw many irrelevant lines so as to make it harder to see what is going on: cf. VIII. 1, 157^{a}1–5). The propounder of such a puzzle is a 'false-drawer' or 'fake-diagrammer' (*pseudographos*). We meet with these characters a few times in the *Topics*, and in *SE* 11 (see Excerpt C), but nowhere else in Aristotle, and there is scarely any mention of them in other sources except Aristotle's commentators. It is therefore impossible to say with certainty who these 'false-drawers' were and what the purpose of their activity might have been—geometers devising puzzles to discomfit their colleagues? Philosophers trying to undermine the pretences of geometry? Mere puzzle-mongers?

For Aristotle, the problem is that, unlike contentious reasoners, these people actually use geometrical principles in their puzzles. This means that their arguments only work within the sphere of geometry, and indeed only for people with at least some geometrical knowledge. Now Aristotle is often at pains to emphasize the complete generality of application of dialectical and contentious argumentation to any subject matter (cf. *SE* 11), and he also holds that for this reason both skills are content-free or topic-neutral: I do not have to know anything at all about a science in order to produce dialectical arguments concerning it. But fake-diagrammers seem instead to rely on the very science they try to undermine.

After raising the question where these arguments fit in his classification, Aristotle does not answer it. For a more complete statement of his view, we must turn to *On Sophistical Refutations*, the principal subject of which is contentious arguments. There, we find Aristotle taking great pains to explain why the *pseudographos* is not a contentious reasoner: see *SE* 9 and *SE* 11 for more on the relationships among the *pseudographos*, the contentious reasoner, and the dialectician.

101ᵃ18–24. 'capturing them in an outline': 'outline' (*tupos*) refers to images stamped on coins or engraved on gems. Such pictures have just enough detail to permit one to recognize their originals; in the same way, Aristotle explains, his present sketch is only supposed to be a superficial one, with just enough detail to permit the user of his method to *recognize* the various types of deduction. The 'exact account' (*akribēs logos*) concerning any subject would be a scientific study that offered causes and explanations. Aristotle explicitly says that he is *not* aiming at an explanatory account of deductions and is only providing a sort of field-guide that will enable its users to classify arguments for practical purposes. This has important consequences for our interpretation of the various definitions in the *Topics*: we cannot assume that Aristotle would regard any of them as truly explanatory. But neither should we take him to mean that the 'outline' account is in any way false: a 'definition' intended to aid in recognizing a thing and a scientific definition intended to capture its essence serve different purposes and may in consequence require different formulations.

In the case of demonstrations, the present 'outline' only says enough to indicate how dialectical arguments differ from them; the 'exact account' of this species of argument is to be found in the *Posterior Analytics*. The other species of deduction Aristotle mentions, apart from the dialectical deductions which are his present subject, are contentious arguments and the class of technical fallacies, each of which is discussed in *On Sophistical Refutations*. Since Aristotle's references elsewhere to it make it clear that he thought of this as part of the *Topics* and not a separate treatise, some scholars conclude that *On Sophistical Refutations* is a later appendix to the *Topics* and not part of its original conception.

There is another sort of 'exact account' of deductions in general in the *Prior Analytics*. Though Aristotle clearly asserts that this theory applies to all arguments, dialectical as well as demonstrative (see *An. Pr.* II. 23, 68ᵇ8–14), the *Topics* shows no awareness of it. This has been taken as evidence that the *Topics* antedates the theories in the *Analytics*; but even if that is the case, we would still need to ask why Aristotle did not care to revise the *Topics* in the light of his later theory. It seems to me that the practical orientation of the *Topics* would be a sufficient explanation for Aristotle's silence about his theory of inference, whether or not it postdates the *Topics*: the art of dialectic is a practical art, whereas the contents of *An. Pr.* I are ill adapted to the practical business of discovering arguments. It is no more to be expected that he should include a discussion of his theory of validity in such a practical manual than that a modern logician should feel compelled to give a full account of first-order theory in a textbook of informal logic.

CHAPTER 2

101ª25–7. 'Exercise' (*gumnasia*): not some general sort of 'mental exercise' for the sharpening of wits, but debating contests of a specific type (the details emerge in Book VIII). To 'attack' (*epicheirein*: literally, 'lay hands on') is, in the technical vocabulary of dialectical disputation, to take the role of the questioner. Since the attacker aims at deducing something unacceptable from the respondent's answers, 'deduce' sometimes has a similar sense (cf. the first sentence of the treatise). On the roles of attacker and defender, see VIII. 3–5.

It is less clear what an 'encounter' (*enteuxis*) is. Some interpreters suppose these to be exchanges, perhaps under more or less formal conditions, with those 'from outside', i.e. (on the assumption that the *Topics* is a manual for Academy members) from outside the Academy; others translate 'casual encounters'. But *Rhet.* I. 1, 1355ª27–9, which appears to refer to this passage, mentions 'encounters with the public' (*hē pros tous pollous enteuxis*). The point Aristotle is making is that his dialectical art is *also* useful for more general argumentative situations in which the formal rules of 'gymnastic' disputation do not apply.

'Changing their minds' (*metabibazontes*): Aristotle has in mind the correction, or conversion, of others' opinions, not 'shifting the ground' in an argument so as to defeat one's opponent. Compare VIII. 11, 161ᵃ29–36, and *EE* I. 6, 1216ᵇ28–35: the latter makes clear the role of this in leading others to philosophical understanding, claiming that we all have some understanding of the truth, on which philosophical education builds.

The 'philosophical sciences' are those pursued for the sake of understanding rather than for a practical end. Aristotle claims that his dialectical method can contribute to the discovery of truth as well as to the winning of arguments. To 'go through the difficulties' (*diaporein*) is to give a survey of the problems which need to be solved in an area of inquiry: Aristotle's treatises frequently begin with such *diaporiai*, which summarize the views of his predecessors and attempt to set the stage for his own position as a resolution of those difficulties.

101ᵃ36–ᵇ4. This second 'philosophical' value is quite different from the preceding three. Several interpreters have seen in this section an adumbration of a much more important use for dialectic, namely, as the fundamental method of philosophical inquiry (see Irwin 1988). Though Aristotle argues that the first premisses of demonstrations must be themselves known without demonstration, many interpreters find the account of the cognition of these first principles in *An. Post.* II. 19 to be very unsatisfactory (Irwin describes it as appealing to an empty 'pseudo-performance'). This has motivated attempts to find a better account in the treatises. In an influential paper, G. E. L. Owen (1961) called attention to the similarities between the approaches Aristotle regularly takes in his scientific treatises, especially his surveys of the opinions of his predecessors and of the contradictions and puzzles which can be derived from them, and dialectical argument. These surveys, as well as collections of empirical data, give the 'appearances' (*phainomena*) from which scientific inquiry must begin. Those *phainomena* which consist of the opinions of others would seem to be very much like the *endoxa* of the *Topics*. Now, a celebrated passage in *EN* VII. 1 appears to indicate that *endoxa* play a crucial role in the establishment of scientific principles: 'We must, as in all other cases, set the phenomena before us and, after first discussing the difficulties, go on to prove, if possible, the truth of all the reputable opinions (*endoxa*) about these affections or, failing this, of the greatest number and the most authoritative; for if we both resolve the difficulties and leave the reputable opinions (*endoxa*) undisturbed, we shall have proved the case sufficiently'

(1145ᵇ2–7, rev. Oxford tr.). From this evidence, some interpreters have concluded that Aristotle believed some form of dialectical argument could establish the first principles of sciences. Perhaps the most fully elaborated view of this sort is given by Irwin (1988), who proposes a developmental account: Aristotle had a largely negative picture of the powers of dialectic when he wrote the *Topics* and other logical works, but he later came to think that a refurbished kind of dialectical argument ('strong dialectic') could establish first principles and, indeed, was the proper method of philosophy.

In this connection, we should note also that Aristotle makes a distinction between the first principles 'peculiar' (*idios*) or 'appropriate' (*oikeios*) to an individual science and certain 'common' principles which apply to all sciences (his standard examples of the latter include the laws of excluded middle and non-contradiction). In the logical works and the *Rhetoric*, he often insists that these common principles (however we identify them) are not the principles of any science, and he does not seem to regard them as the objects of any kind of scientific or philosophical inquiry. In *Met.* B, however, Aristotle raises the question which science is to consider these common principles, and in *Met.* Γ he argues that they are studied by 'first philosophy'. Owen (1960, 1961, 1968) and Irwin (1988) see this as an important break with the *Topics* (and the logical works generally): they suppose that in the *Metaphysics* Aristotle recants an earlier view of dialectic as merely a critical instrument and an earlier rejection of a universal science, now proposing a 'science of being as such' and a methodology for it that is in some way dialectical. The existence of such a break has also been vigorously denied; see Code 1986, Owens 1963; for criticisms of Irwin, see Hamlyn 1990, Bolton 1990, Smith 1993.

These two questions—whether the conception of first philosophy in the *Metaphysics* is a retraction of Aristotle's views in the logical treatises, and whether the *Metaphysics* and other works introduce a strengthened kind of dialectical argument as their basic methodology—are too complex to treat here. However, I do not think that the present passage is strong evidence for a view of dialectic as that which establishes first principles.

Let us first note how this new use for dialectic differs from what was said earlier in 101ª34–36. Aristotle said there only that dialectic is useful for discovering what is true and false, not that it is useful for discovering which *starting-points* are true. The process of 'going through the dif-ficulties' could lead to the simple rejection of many views, as for instance Aristotle rejects the views of Zeno on motion. The present passage, by contrast, does limit itself to starting-points or what is 'first'. However, it says neither that dialectic establishes nor that it discovers these starting-points.

Now Aristotle clearly says that it is not possible to *demonstrate* the starting-points since they are the very things from which demonstrations begin. The phrase 'from the starting-points appropriate to the science in question', which is closely associated with demonstrations in the *Posterior Analytics*, makes this certain. However, it is far from clear that the rest of the passage is intended to offer some alternative to demonstration as the means of *establishing* the starting-points. What he says is that the only possible way of 'discussing' these starting-points is something especially appropriate to dialectic. The term I translate 'discuss' (*dielthein*) literally means 'go through'; in his other treatises, Aristotle uses this word over and over, typically with the preposition *peri* ('about'), to announce the beginning or ending of his treatment of some subject. Thus, Aristotle does not say merely that the starting-points cannot be demonstrated, but that by means of demonstration we cannot say *anything* about them (*adunaton eipein ti peri autōn*). The alternative to having nothing to say is having something to say, and that could fall far short of establishing.

Furthermore, Aristotle's claim for a special usefulness for dialectic in this connection appeals to its 'critical' or 'testing' (*exetastikē*) capacity. This is an uncommon term in Aristotle; Socrates used its cognate verb *exetazein* for the 'examinations' of others through questioning which he took to be his philosophical purpose in life. Socrates' goal was to make clear to others their own unrecognized ignorance, and he accomplished this by deducing consequences—usually contradictory ones—from their admissions. Similarly, examining views, including the views of earlier philosophers and the views of ordinary people, by exploring their consequences and looking for contradictions is an important part of Aristotle's philosophical method. Moreover, he sometimes makes refutation an essential feature of dialectical arguments (e.g. *SE* 2, 165ᵇ3–4), and the connection with Socrates' practice is made explicit in *SE* 34, 183ᵇ6–8. However, all that the present passage says is that such critical examinations are 'useful' in 'discussing' scientific starting-points, and that falls far short of claiming that dialectic either establishes or discovers those starting-points. Finally, given Aristotle's repeated claims in the *Topics* and *On Sophistical Refutations* that dialectical argument cannot establish *anything*, it would be more than a little surprising for him to hold that it can establish what scientific demonstrations cannot.

101ᵇ3–4. I have construed this last sentence differently from other translators, who all take the central phrase '[to] the starting-points of all studies' as modifying 'way': 'since dialectic is [or has] an ability to examine, it has a way to the starting-points of all inquiries.' But the logic of this is not very clear: why should a capacity to examine entail a power of getting to all starting-points? Instead, I take Aristotle to be making the more modest claim that since dialectical methods of examination can be applied to anything, including the starting-points of sciences, they provide us with a way of discussing them.

In a few places, Aristotle speaks of 'making trial' as a feature of dialectic or mentions an 'art of making trial' (*peirastikē*): see VIII. 5, 159ᵃ25–36; VIII. 11, 161ᵃ24–8; *SE* 2, 165ᵇ4–7; *SE* 8, 169ᵇ23–9; *SE* 11 throughout, esp. 171ᵇ3–12, 172ᵃ21–ᵇ4; *SE* 34, 183ᵃ37–ᵇ6. Many of these passages seem to distinguish 'peirastic' from dialectic or to define 'peirastic' arguments as a distinct species of dialectical arguments, but sometimes 'making trial' appears to be a general function of dialectic. *Met.* Γ 2, 1004ᵇ25–6, says that dialectic has (or is) a power of 'making trial' about the things of which philosophy is 'knowledgeable' (*gnōristikē*). The subject in question there is 'first philosophy', which applies in a way to whatever there is and studies the most general principles of all. This seems quite clearly to imply that dialectic does *not* amount to a science of the most general principles; Aristotle says this same thing quite explicitly in *SE* 11, where he is at pains to argue that the universal applicability of dialectic's testing ability does not make it a universal science. (For a very different picture of peirastic argument, see Bolton 1990.)

CHAPTER 3

101ᵇ5–10. I. 3 must be read as continuous with I. 4 if its point is to be understood (note the very close parallel between 101ᵇ10 'has a sufficient grasp of his craft' and 101ᵇ13 'would have a sufficient grasp of our proposed subject'). Since Aristotle is about to expound an art of dialectic, he first wants to make it clear what the goal of that art is. Now one might initially think that dialectical skill would be an ability to deduce *any* desired conclusion from *any* available premisses. However, that would be like defining medical skill as the ability to heal anyone who is ill, or rhetorical skill as the ability to persuade anyone of anything: but such skills do not exist. Aristotle notes elsewhere that medicine, rhetoric, and kindred arts (the commentators call them *stochastikai*, 'aiming') do not, even if practised without error, always succeed: the doctor sometimes just cannot heal, for some patients are incurable, and the orator sometimes just cannot persuade, owing to the nature of the case. Likewise, some positions just cannot be successfully defended or attacked. Therefore, we cannot in these cases do *anything* we choose, and there is no art which provides this ability. The dialectical art should instead provide an ability to find the best argument available for a given conclusion and a given respondent. This is one point in which dialectic differs from sophistry: the sophist seeks only victory in

55

argument, even if that requires fallacious arguments and deceptive premisses.

Given this interpretation, the phrase in brackets in 101ᵇ7 must be, as Brunschwig holds, an incompetent gloss added by a later editor.

CHAPTER 4

101ᵇ11–16. 'what our method consists of': as the close echoes of this sentence in 103ᵇ39–104ᵃ2 show, there are two parts to this method. The first is a matter of *classifying* 'what arguments are about' and 'what arguments are made from'; Aristotle says at the end of I. 9 that he has accomplished this task. The next part of the task is to give the means through which we may be 'equipped to deal with these'. The term I translate 'equipped to deal with' (*euporein*) has as one common meaning 'to have plenty of', and many translators take this passage to mean 'how we may be well supplied with arguments'. But for many of the occurrences of this word in the *Topics*, there is no indication of what it is that we are supposed to have plenty of (cf. 110ᵇ5, 111ᵇ38, 112ᵃ27, 112ᵃ35); 'know how to deal with' or 'be skilled in handling' fit these contexts better. Though this distinction seems minor, it is important. If Aristotle thought of his method as a matter of merely having a *large supply* of arguments, then it begins to resemble the teaching of his unsystematic predecessors who gave their students large collections of potted arguments to memorize (see Excerpt D). An *art* of dialectic instead gives the ability to find the premisses needed for proving the desired conclusion, and this is not a matter of having a *supply* of arguments but of *knowing what to do* when confronted with any particular conclusion. I have translated 'be *equipped to* deal with' in order to retain the suggestion of 'having plenty', though I think it is at most secondary.

'Premiss' (*protasis*) and 'problem' (*problēma*) are central terms in the technical vocabulary of Aristotle's logic. Both are derived from verbs: *protasis* from *proteinein*, literally 'stretch out', 'hold out', 'offer', and *problēma* from *proballein*, 'throw forward', 'put forward'. In ordinary use, *problēma* means 'thing put forward as a defence', 'obstacle', or even 'excuse'. In the context of dialectic, a 'problem' is a subject of argument: as Aristotle explains later (104ᵇ1–5), it is a question which is both important for some purpose and the subject of significant disagreement. But in the context of dialectical debate, this means that a problem is a proposition argued about, i.e. something which the questioner undertakes to attack and the answerer to defend.

The term *protasis* ('premiss') is not found before Aristotle, though his usage suggests that it was an established term of art in dialectical practice and not his coinage. Based on its derivation, a *protasis* should be the act of holding out or offering something (e.g. for approval), or that which is held out in such a way. In the context of dialectic, a premiss is a question offered by the questioner to the respondent. Of course, the purpose of making such an offering is to secure materials with which to construct a deduction (that is, to get premisses for an argument); thus, a premiss contains within it a proposition, to which the answerer is being asked to offer assent or dissent.

At bottom, then, premisses and problems are both propositions, though they are propositions put to different uses: a premiss is a proposition offered to a respondent in the form of a question, while a problem is a proposition that is the subject of disagreement between questioner and answerer. Of course, those uses impose their own requirements of suitability, making some propositions appropriate as premisses, others as problems: a premiss has no chance of being accepted if nobody would ever believe it, and a problem will not make a very good subject of debate if there is no disagreement about it (or if it bears on no interesting issue). Aristotle returns to these points in I. 10 and I. 11: see the Commentary on those chapters and on 101ᵇ28–36.

101ᵇ17–36. In order to be 'equipped to deal with' problems and premisses in a systematic way, we must first *classify* them, then learn methods for dealing with each *class*. A system for classifying propositions is therefore crucial to Aristotle's dialectical art. The one he advocates begins by classifying the relationship asserted to hold between subject and predicate of a proposition: the predicate may be *definition* (*horos*), *genus* (*genos*), *unique property* (*idion*), or *accident* (*sumbebēkos*) of the subject. In fact, as Aristotle mentions in passing, there is a fifth possibility: the predicate may also be the *differentia* (*diaphora*) of the subject. In later antiquity, these five 'predicables', as they were later called, took on considerable importance in metaphysics as well as logic. If we put 'species' in place of 'definition', we have the 'five terms' of Porphyry's *Introduction to Logic* (commonly known under the title *Quinque Voces*), which became one of the most familiar handbooks of logic in the early Middle Ages.

The entire structure of the *Topics* rests on this fourfold division: Books II–III deal with accidents, IV with genera, V with unique properties, and VI and (in part) VII with definitions. But it appears that Aristotle adopts his fourfold classification in full awareness of the fivefold one. For instance, his classification of the difference as 'genus-like' (*genikē*) makes it clear that he expected his audience to understand this term; why then does he seem to wish to suppress it? Furthermore, he actually begins with a *threefold* classification which omits to mention 'definition': but it is likely on several grounds that definitions were both the most venerable and the most important subject of debates (the association of defining with the early Academy is almost proverbial—see, however, the discussion of I. 8). Aristotle's approach is argumentative, not simply expository: he is justifying his more sophisticated approach to an audience who can be assumed already to know the terminology.

Although he says nothing about it in the *Topics*, Aristotle elsewhere (most carefully in *On Interpretation*) distinguishes general predications such as 'The horse is a mammal' (in which both subject and predicate are general terms, or universals) from individual predications such as 'Socrates is a man' (in which the subject is an individual). But although this distinction is not discussed explicitly in the *Topics*, there are times when Aristotle seems to speak of predicable relationships between a predicate and an individual (e.g. 102ᵇ20–6). I return to this point in several places below. (See Geach 1972, Kneale and Kneale 1962, 63–7, on difficulties about the relationship between the predicables and the theories of *On Interpretation* and *An. Pr.* I.)

Here, Aristotle simply asserts that all predicates can be classified according to the predicables. Later, in I. 8, he tries to prove it.

101ᵇ18–19. This proposal somehow to include differentiae under the heading of genera is not reflected in the rest of the *Topics*: there are scattered mentions of differences in Book IV, the treatment of genera, but the most extensive discussion is in VI. 6, as part of the account of definitions.

101ᵇ19–23. This passage should not be taken to imply that 'definition' is a terminological innovation of Aristotle's: the term was already in use in the Academy. Aristotle is instead recommending a new way of understanding definitions, and in particular urging that not just any identifying description that applies uniquely to a thing should count as its definition. It may be that in the Early Academy this was sometimes all that mattered about a definition (there is a story that Diogenes of Sinope lampooned a Platonic definition of humans as 'featherless biped animals' with a plucked chicken).

Aristotle's usual word for definition in the *Topics* is *horos* ('boundary'), although he sometimes uses the word *horismos* ('that which limits', from the verb *horizesthai*, which is in turn closely related to *horos*). There seems to be no difference in meaning between the two, but it is at least worth noting that *horismos* predominates outside the *Topics* and that in the *Analytics* the word *horos* almost always has the different technical sense 'term'.

101ᵇ28–36. We should remember the distinctive argumentative roles of problems and premisses (see Commentary on 101ᵇ13–16) when interpreting Aristotle's claim that the essential difference between them is their verbal form. A premiss is a certain type of question, i.e. one that admits of a yes-or-no answer, asked in the course of a dialectical exchange. A problem, by contrast, is a 'question' which a dialectical exchange undertakes to resolve, either in the affirmative or in the negative. Since a 'question' of this sort has two sides, it can also be put in the form of a yes-or-no question. However, a problem is not something *put as a question* in the course of an argument, but instead something attacked or defended by the entire argument. The difference in form Aristotle has in mind is, in Greek, the difference between an opening interrogative formula (*ara ge*, which I translate 'is it the case that': cf. Boethius' 'putasne') and an expression ('whether') that in effect *names* a question. (Some interpreters take the 'or not' at the end of the two examples here to be the crucial distinction between premiss and problem, but as Alexander points out Aristotle sometimes adds 'or not' to premisses as well.)

In arguing that premisses and problems may be put into one–one correspondence by these syntactical transformations, Aristotle is putting to one side the extra-verbal properties which fit an utterance to serve as a premiss or problem in dialectical debate. Here, the point is that it is possible to extract, from any premiss or any problem, some *proposition*, that is, something which is either true or false: the problem 'Whether virtue is more rewarding than vice' and the premiss 'Is virtue more rewarding than vice' both are constructed from 'Virtue is more rewarding than vice'. This is taken a step further in the *Prior Analytics*, where Aristotle defines a 'deductive premiss' (*protasis sullogistikē*) as 'the affirmation or denial of one thing of another', abstracting this as a common element (much like 'proposition' for us) present in dialectical and demonstrative premisses. A related abstraction from argumentative role occurs in connection with 'problem'. Since the 'problem' in a dialectical exchange is that which one tries to deduce (or deduce the contradictory of) as conclusion, it is a short move to give it the sense 'conclusion'. In the *Prior Analytics* Aristotle is interested in determining what forms of arguments can yield different forms of conclusions, where the forms of conclusions are the four 'categorical sentences' (universal affirmative, particular affirmative, etc.). Thus, 'problem' comes to mean 'type of conclusion', or, at an even higher level of abstraction, 'type of categorical sentence': compare the way in which *katēgoriai*, 'predications', becomes a shorthand for 'kinds of predication' (*ta genē tōn katēgoriōn*), i.e. 'categories' (see I. 9).

59

CHAPTER 5

101ᵇ38–102ᵃ5. Defining, for Aristotle, is not lexicography but an activity of greater philosophical and scientific importance. He does acknowledge definitions that serve simply to explain what a word means (cf. *An. Post.* II. 10, 93ᵇ30–1), but for him a true definition defines, not a word, but the reality behind the word. It is less easy to say what the reality is that is defined. Generally, Aristotle associates definitions with universals rather than particulars. This implies that universals have some kind of reality, if it is possible to give definitions saying what they are.

The phrase 'the what-it-is-to-be' (*to ti èn einai*) is one of the most heavily discussed of Aristotelian expressions. Word by word, it means 'the what it *was* to be', though the commentators assure us that 'was' has no temporal significance and thus amounts to 'is'. The philosophical term 'essence' (or its Latin ancestor) was coined to serve as a translation of this phrase. I have generally avoided it in the translation, though I sometimes resort to 'essence' and 'essential' in the commentary. A what-it-is-to-be or essence is always a what-it-is-to-be *for* something (usually expressed in Greek with the dative). The definition of X tells what it is to be for X, or what it is for X to be. Accordingly, we sometimes find phrases like 'the to-be for a human' (*to anthrōpōi einai: An. Post.* 91ᵇ5–6, *Met.* 1006ᵃ34). Aristotle generally holds that only existing things can have essences, and thus non-existent or imaginary things cannot be defined: there is no definition of 'goat-stag' except in the sense of saying what the word means (*An. Post.* 92ᵇ5–8). Aristotle's answers to the questions 'What is a thing's essence?' and 'What things have essences?' are among the most difficult and disputed of issues in Aristotelian scholarship.

The word I translate 'phrase' is *logos*, a term with a wide range of senses: 'speech', 'account', 'reason', 'ratio', 'understanding'. The contrasting term I translate as 'word' is *onoma*, which in everyday Greek most commonly means 'name'. Aristotle's requirement that a definition always be a *logos*, never an *onoma*, is more than an arbitrary stipulation. The difference between word and phrase here is at bottom a difference of two sorts of signifiers. A word, or name, simply designates; a phrase has a structure and therefore may carry with it an explanation (compare *An. Post.* II. 8–10, where Aristotle suggests that some definitions are a sort of compressed explanation of a thing's cause). The underlying assumption is that defining is a type of analysis, replacing simple signifiers with articulated accounts of their significance. The grammatical division of speech into individual words is therefore a secondary matter, since a phrase can function as an unanalysable semantic unit.

102ª10–17. This passage is one of several notes inserted into the text of I. 5 that try to clean up small details. Aristotle has just discussed two examples of 'definitory' things, and he summarizes with a general account of 'definitory' as 'falling under the same method as definitions'. He then adds this note, showing that the *second* of his examples (arguments about whether things are the same) does indeed fit this account. Following this, there is a note on the note ('what was just said' again), alerting the reader to the fact that there is more to defining than simply showing things to be the same, so that the argumentative strategy indicated is only destructive. Such digressions are not only common in the *Topics*, they are also often clearly later additions, sometimes rejecting what has just been said, or even (in second-order notes) objecting to an objection. We may explain these notes by supposing that Aristotle worked over the treatise repeatedly, inserting comments and corrections; or by supposing that marginal remarks by later editors or commentators have crept into the text; or by supposing that this occasional fondness for digression is simply part of Aristotle's style. Doubtless all three explanations are correct, on different occasions, though I believe the first is generally the most likely.

It seems at first that the *Topics* follows this suggested assimilation of questions about 'same' to 'definition': VII. 1, which immediately follows the discussion of definitions (VI), deals with 'same', and VII. 2 actually refers to our present passage. However, VII. 1 sits rather arbitrarily in its place: it follows a declaration at the end of VI that the discussion of definitions is over, and VII. 2 is clearly transitional.

102ª18–30. Since the first part of this definition of 'unique property' is a purely negative characterization (following the restriction given at 101ᵇ19–23), the clause 'belongs to it alone and counterpredicates with it' indicates what is common to definitions and unique properties. As the present text shows, 'A counterpredicates with B' means 'If anything is A then it is B, and if anything is B then it is A'. In modern terminology, this means that counterpredicating predicates are coextensive with each other. This might suggest a relatively broad interpretation for the undifferentiated notion of unique property, found in 101ᵇ18–23 and embracing definitions as well:

A is a (broad) unique property of B = A counterpredicates with B

But this has unexpected consequences. Counterpredication is symmetrical: if A counterpredicates with B, then B counterpredicates with A. Suppose now that A is the definition of B; then A counterpredicates with B, and therefore B counterpredicates with A, and therefore B is a unique property of A. Moreover, if we assume that 'definition of' is asymmetric, any definiendum is a unique property in the narrow sense of its definiens. In any event, if being a unique property is simply a matter of coextension, then any predicate might have unique properties. I do not think this is Aristotle's intent. He thinks of the four predicables as possible relations between predicate and subject, and he does not generally think of the relation of predication as symmetrical. In order for A to be a unique property of B, it must first be predicated of B.

A number of difficulties can be raised about the interpretation of Aristotelian predications with general terms as their subjects (see above, 101ᵇ17–36 and Commentary). Here, I shall observe that the phrase 'belongs to it alone' makes the relationship 'is a unique property of' asymmetric and rules out definienda as unique properties of their definientia. Aristotle holds that *if* A belongs to B, *then* whatever is B is A; but this is a matter of entailment, not a definition or explication. On the most plausible interpretation, 'A belongs to B alone' means 'A belongs to B and only to B'; where B is a general term, this would imply 'Whatever is B is A, and only what is B is A', and thus that A and B counterpredicate. However, 'counterpredicates with' is a consequence of 'belongs only to', not a definition of it, and therefore counterpredication is merely a necessary condition for being a unique property. In general, A can be a unique property of B only if A is predicated of B in the first place. (Thus, if 'capable of laughing' and 'capable of speaking' are both unique properties of humans and therefore counterpredicate, it still does not follow that either is a unique property of the other.)

The traditional rendering for *idion* is 'property', which in archaic English usage had exactly the right sense. However, its common use in modern philosophical parlance to mean 'attribute' makes this a poor (because confusing) choice. I have opted instead for 'unique', which gets precisely the sense of Aristotle's definition, but I have added 'property' (in the modern sense) in order to get a substantival expression (and also to retain a verbal echo of the traditional rendering). 'Unique' by itself suffices when *idion* is used adjectivally.

102ᵃ20. 'literate': *grammatikē* is not grammatical knowledge but just the ability to read and write (Aristotle defines it himself at 142ᵇ31 as 'knowing how to write down what is dictated and to read it back').

102ᵃ26–7. 'being on the right': unlike Aristotle's other examples, this only seems to make sense as a unique property of an individual, not a kind (cf. 103ᵃ33–9).

102ᵃ31–5. 'Predicated in the what-it-is' (*en tōi ti esti katēgoroumenon*): the explanation of this technical expression offered here is very close to the discussion of 'what-it-is' or 'substance' in I. 9 and is related to the characterization of a definition as 'signifying the what-it-is-to-be'. To judge by

103^b35-7, both a thing's definition and its genus 'say what it is' and are thus predicated of it in the what it is. If the what-it-is of a thing is its essence, then predication in the what-it-is may be called 'essential predication'. Although I believe it is best to preserve something approximating Aristotle's construction in translation, I shall avail myself of this convenient phrase in the commentary.

In *An. Post.* I. 4 and elsewhere, Aristotle uses the closely related concept of *per se*, or 'of-itself', predication. A is predicated of B of-itself if either A is in the definition of B or B is in the definition of A.

The phrase 'which are different in species' introduces the term 'species'. Although it receives no explicit attention in the *Topics*, this term belongs to the same conceptual environment as the other predicables (in Porphyry's *Introduction to Logic*, it replaces 'definition'). In one sense, 'species' is the correlative of 'genus': if A is the genus of B, then B is a species of A. So interpreted, genera and species may be regarded simply as universals in certain relationships, and the same universal may be both genus (of some universals) and species (of another), as mammals are a species of animal and genus of humans. In fact, we might expect that this will be true of most universals, although there will presumably be some 'lowest' species which have no further subspecies and some 'highest' genera which are not species of any further genera. These lowest species, since they are not genera, may be distinguished as species *simpliciter* from the higher species which are also genera. As for the highest genera, which are not themselves species, an ancient tradition identified them with Aristotle's 'categories'. Still more distinctions can be made. If A is a species of B and there is no term C which is genus of A and species of B, then B is the *closest* genus of A and A is an *immediate* species of B. Each of the immediate species of a genus is distinguished from its co-ordinate species by some characteristic which belongs to it uniquely among those species; this is the *specific differentia*, the 'difference which makes the species' (*eidopoios diaphora*: cf. 143^b8).

A basis for this picture can be found scattered through Aristotle's treatises. For the most part, however, he takes it as a given rather than something to be explained—probably because the picture derives from Plato's Academy, where it was associated with the activity of determining definitions through a process of dividing a higher genus into its species, dividing these in turn, etc. Thus in this passage, even though Aristotle is offering definitions of basic technical terminology, he does not bother to explain 'species' at all. The hierarchical structure of genera and species was part of the intellectual common property of Aristotle and his audience.

Perhaps inadvertently, commentators have generally taken Aristotle to be defining 'genus' in an absolute sense here: A is a genus if A is predicated in the what-it-is of several things different in species. But he defines all the other predicables as *relatives*: A is definition, unique property *of B* if A stands in a certain relationship *to B*. The most direct way to put the present definition into this form is as follows:

> A is genus of B = A is predicated in the what-it-is *of B and* of many things different in species *from B*

As spelt out, this definition would require that predication in the what-it-is be a kind of universal, not just general, predication. Such an extension is not difficult to imagine, although it is not clear that Aristotle is aware of the distinction. If A is genus of B, then is it also the genus of individual Bs (e.g. is animal the genus of Socrates and Plato)? Some passages seem to imply this (see *Cat.* 2 and 5 and the discussion of I. 9 below).

If, as the commentators say, the point of adding 'different in species' is to distinguish genera from species, then presumably something like the following would be a definition of 'species' taken absolutely:

> A is a species = A is predicated in the what-it-is of many things, but not things different in species

That is, A is a species if and only if the things it is predicated in the what-it-is of do not differ in species from one another. This will hardly be an illuminating definition, of course, unless we have some other account of what 'different in species' means.

Further problems arise in connection with essential predication and the definition of 'genus': see the Commentary on I. 8.

102ª35–b3. If it is Aristotle's purpose to discuss what is 'genus-like', then it is odd that he does not discuss the differentia, which he has already so characterized at 101b18–19.

102b4–7. The term 'accident' (*sumbebēkos*) is the perfect participle of *sumbainein*, 'happen' or 'accompany'. An accident of something, therefore, is something which merely happens to be true of it, or something which is incidental to it, or something which accompanies it. These are not equivalent; however, they all make appearances at different times in Aristotle's usage. Complicating matters, Aristotle here gives us two definitions of 'accident' and assumes, without argument, that they are equivalent. The first of these—in effect, 'none of the above'—guarantees (in a trivial way) that the four predicables exhaust the possible relations of predicate to subject. However, this definition will be equivalent to the second only on the further supposition that any predicate failing to be a definition, unique property, or genus satisfies it; and that is by no means obvious (see I. 8 below).

What does the second definition mean? If we take 'at one time and not at another' literally, Aristotle would have in mind an individual subject ('one and the same thing') to which the accident now belongs and now does not. An accident would then be a temporary or passing property:

A is an accident of X =   A belongs to X at one time but not at another

However, Aristotle frequently uses temporal language to express modal qualifications (possibility and necessity), so that it may be equivalent to 'contingent property':

A is an accident of X =   A belongs to X, but not necessarily

Alternatively, temporal language can sometimes express mere generalization: 'always' and 'sometimes' may mean 'for every', 'for some'. On this reading, Aristotle may have in mind something like

A is an accident of B =   Some As are Bs and some As are not Bs

It is consistent with this last reading that an accident A might belong necessarily to those Bs to which it does belong and necessarily not belong to those Bs to which it does not belong, so that A would be an accident of B in general but of no individual B. In fact, Aristotle does give us some examples of 'accidents' meeting this description: 'odd' is an accident of number, since some numbers are odd and some are not, even though it is not true of any particular number that it could, while remaining the same number, both be odd and not be odd. (Such accidents are in effect 'necessary accidents'.)

Returning to I. 5, Aristotle's two definitions of 'accident' are obviously not equivalent. If A is not a definition, unique property, or genus of B, then we can conclude that (i) A and B do not counterpredicate; (ii) A is not predicated of B and other things different in species in the what-it-is. If nevertheless 'A belongs to B', then what possibilities remain? At least two can be distinguished:

(i)   A belongs to every B, but not in the what-it-is, and to other things as well
(ii) A belongs to some but not every B

Of these, only (ii) corresponds to a plausible sense of the second definition, and nothing Aristotle says rules out (i) as a possibility. We might still try to save the equivalence of the two by interpreting accidents as contingent predicates. It is plausible enough that definitions and genera are necessarily true of their subjects, and Aristotle makes it fairly clear that A is a unique property of B only if A and B *necessarily* counterpredicate, that is, only if they *must* be true of the same things (cf. 102^{a}28–30). Thus, if A is contingently true of B, then it cannot be its definition, genus, or unique property.

Does the converse hold? No; the obvious counter-example is differentiae. As components of definitions, they must be necessary properties, but they are neither definitions nor unique properties nor genera. Moreover, Aristotle says nothing that would rule out still other examples of necessary properties, e.g. A might be necessarily true of whatever B is true of, and of other things as well, without being B's genus.

The second definition recalls a statement in the *Categories*: 'It seems most distinctive of substance that what is numerically one and the same is able to receive contraries' (4^{a}10–11). Already in the notion of an accident, Aristotle's theory of predication is present. To say that an accident can either belong or not belong 'to one and the same thing' presupposes that it makes sense to talk of that same and single thing persisting, and remaining identical, while its accidents change. Some Greek philosophers before Aristotle had put forward denials of this claim, ranging from the serious and problematic (Parmenides) to the more superficial (the two brothers in Plato's *Euthydemus*).

There are a number of other uses for the term 'accident' and the related phrase 'by accident' (*kata sumbebēkos*) in Aristotle's works. Generally, these get their meanings by negation: an X 'by accident' is something that is called X but somehow fails to be X in some strict sense or in some paradigmatic way. Aristotle's first definition follows this pattern.

See also the Commentary on I. 8.

102^{b}14–20. Since this section depends on a sort of equivocation, it is difficult to translate it smoothly into English: as noted above, the word for 'accident' (*sumbebēkos*) is actually the perfect participle of the verb *sumbainein*, and therefore it may take on any of its meanings, 'happen', 'result', 'go along with'. I have tried to reproduce this (very lamely) with the translation 'accompany'.

Top. III. 1–3 contains a discussion of such comparisons involving what is 'preferable', and since this Book is an extension of II, which concerns accidents, it might seem that Aristotle is following his own suggestion in classifying them under the same head. However, as commentators have generally noticed, the arguments Aristotle is thinking of are almost certainly those he elsewhere calls 'from more and less and likewise', and discussions of these sorts of arguments are found in every Book, in connection with each of the predicables.

102^{b}20–5. Compare 102^{a}22–8, which introduces unique properties at a time or with respect to something rather as a concession, and 103^{a}32–9. The distinction between unique properties without qualification and unique properties with some qualification is not as straightforward as at first appears. Aristotle says: the property of being seated, which *is* an accident, would be a unique property at a time when only one person was seated. Being seated is (presumably) an accident of the one person seated in the sense that it is a temporary property, in accordance with (one interpretation of) Aristotle's earlier definition. Is it a genuine unique property? We cannot apply the counterpredication test, for there is only one predicate. Instead, we have a situation in which a predicate happens, at a certain time, to have an extension with exactly one member. In effect, then, that predicate can be used to construct a *definite description*, in modern terminology, which designates an individual: if there is one and only one person seated, then 'the person seated' succeeds in designating that person.

It may be instructive to compare this with full-fledged unique properties, which may be regarded as alternative ways of designating a species: if 'capable of acquiring science' applies to all and only humans, then it designates the human species. However, the question whether A is or is not a unique property of B is a question about the relationship between the extensions of A and B: if they are not the same, then A fails to be unique to B. By contrast, a definite description like 'the one seated' will fail to designate any individual if more than one person, or no person, is seated. The question whether 'the one seated' is a unique property of Socrates at a time thus contains two subsidiary questions: (i) Is it a unique property of anyone (i.e. is there exactly one person seated)? (ii) Is that person Socrates? In the case of a unique property of a species, it is not clear what would correspond to the first of these questions.

CHAPTER 6

102^b27–103^a5. I. 6 is closely bound up with the remarks about what is 'definitory', etc., scattered through I. 5 (and with the comment about differences in I. 4, 101^b18–19). The content is curious: first, Aristotle argues that we could really call all the 'questions' definitory; next, he says that this is no reason for seeking a single procedure, citing the elusiveness and inconvenience it would have; and then concludes that *for that very reason*, we should, as he said earlier (101^a18–24), use an outline division and assign 'what is left over' to each subdivision, as seems most appropriate,

Now, this is in part a description of what Aristotle does, as indeed the last sentence indicates: those things which do not seem to fit into the fourfold scheme (such as differences, questions about sameness, questions about which of several things is so-and-so, or more so-and-so) should be plugged in to whichever of the four seems most appropriate. But this is an argument for sticking with a *broad* division, instead of a more detailed one, and putting up with the inconvenience of cases that do not fit well, whereas what Aristotle has just offered is a claim that we should not try for too general an account but should preserve the specialized subcategories.

Especially in view of the last sentence, I. 6 looks not very well fitted in to the text. Those inclined to speculate about Aristotle's development might wish to explain both 101ᵃ18–24 and the present passage as later additions intended to reconcile apparent differences between the *Topics* and other treatises (in particular the *Prior Analytics*): Aristotle, or some later editor, is saying 'these outline remarks will do for our present purposes, even if they conflict with what we say elsewhere.'

Contrast these reasons against looking for a 'single universal method' with Aristotle's claim, *An. Pr.* I. 30, to have discovered a universally applicable system for finding premisses from which conclusions may be deduced (46ᵃ3–4; the system is expounded in I. 27–8). This might imply that the *Prior Analytics* is a later work and that Aristotle has changed his views. However, what Aristotle says in I. 6 is that such a universal method would be both hard to find and inconvenient for the practical purposes of an art of dialectic. It seems to me that, from the standpoint of the practical concerns of the *Topics*, that description fits the theory of the *Prior Analytics* quite well.

102ᵇ38–103ᵃ1. Aristotle indulges in a bit of play with words here that it is hard to resist trying to reproduce: if we give a 'unique method' (*idia methodos*) for each genus (*genos*) that has been 'defined' (*dihoristheis*, from the verb *dihorizesthai*) ... Thus he manages to use the names of the first three of the predicables accidentally (or, as he might say, *kata sumbebēkos*) in this sentence.

CHAPTER 7

103ᵃ6–39. The opening 'first of all' is puzzling: first of *what*? Interpreters generally suppose the explanation is the remark at 102ᵃ6–9 that the best part of argument about definitions concerns whether things are the same or different (102ᵃ36–ᵇ3, which refers to the question whether things are in the same genus or not, may also be relevant). But Aristotle offers no argumentative strategies concerning whether things are the same or different (those appear instead in VII. 1) and instead only distinguishes types of sameness. This is reminiscent of the 'philosophical lexicon' preserved for us as *Metaphysics* Δ, and in fact what Aristotle says here about 'same' (*tauton*) overlaps the remarks he makes in *Metaphysics* Δ 6 about 'one' or 'single' (*hen*: note that in the present chapter he sometimes says 'one' rather than 'same').

103ᵃ7–14. Under 'same', Aristotle includes two different kinds of case. 'Same in number' amounts to 'identical'; thus, if two things are the same in number there is only one thing, not two. Sameness in species and in genus, however, are clearly relationships between different things. This leads to a certain awkwardness. On Aristotle's account, sameness in number looks like a relation between *expressions*, that is, two expressions that refer to the same individual. The clearest case of sameness in number would then appear to be an individual with two proper names, e.g. the one man known both as Mark Twain and as Samuel Clemens. Unfortunately, Aristotle's account is less clear-cut: see the discussion of 103ᵃ23–31 below.

103ᵃ11. 'indistinguishable with respect to species': the word 'species' means 'appearance' or 'look' in ordinary parlance, and so this phrase (*adiaphora kata to eidos*) might also be rendered 'indistinguishable with respect to their appearance'. (Compare *Met.* 1016ᵃ18–19, where Aristotle says that things are 'indistinguishable' if their form cannot be differentiated by perception.) Since Aristotle is almost certainly thinking of species in the technical sense here, it would be misleading to translate otherwise, but the association with appearance may still be present: cf. the remarks immediately following on water from the same spring.

103ᵃ14–23. The case of water from the same spring at first seems to raise no particular difficulty. Two buckets of water from the same spring are different in number (since they are separate things) but the same in species (since each is water); how then are they the same in a way that two arbitrary buckets of water are not? As the commentators interpret him, Aristotle's response is that things the *same in species* are so called because they share some likeness or other (cf. 103ᵃ10–11 and Commentary). Buckets of water all share a certain likeness, and so they are the same in species; buckets of water from the same spring simply share a *stronger* likeness. Alexander compares the likeness shared by all humans and that shared by a pair of twins. But this has discomfiting consequences if we suppose that definitions and what-it-is-to-be are correlated with species: each pair of twins would constitute the entire membership of a species, and—assuming that there is only one correct definition for a thing—water from different springs would be *different* in species.

Aristotle may instead have something else in mind. Water is a stuff or material: it is not naturally divided into units in the way that e.g. people and horses are. Putting the same point linguistically, 'water' is a *mass term*. In English, mass terms are marked by a resistance to pluralization, indefinite articles, and discrete quantifiers: we do not say 'two waters', or 'a water' as we do 'two horses' or 'a dog'. Nouns like 'horse' and 'dog' which do accept pluralization and indefinite articles in this way are *count terms*. Now Aristotle's paradigmatic examples of words for substances are count terms (e.g. 'man' and 'horse' in *Cat.* 5). The status of mass terms is more problematic, both for Aristotle and for modern philosophers.

From an Aristotelian perspective, individuals falling under count terms have relatively clear-cut criteria of unity and identity: marginal problem cases aside, knowing what a cow is involves knowing how to count cows and how to tell the difference between one cow and another. By contrast, water, sand, air, mud, and other stuffs do not come in natural units, and there are no natural demarcations separating 'one' from 'another'. Pour a bucket of water into three cups, and one bucket becomes three cups, but it is still the same thing. How are we to understand 'the same' here? Is it one thing that now exists in one place and now in three, or are the bucket and the cups instances of a single species?

Aristotle just may be responding to a specific way of viewing stuffs, namely, as *distributed individuals*: water, for instance, is a single entity consisting, at any moment, of all the water that there is. On such a view, different bits of water are like different parts of Socrates, and when I point to three buckets of water and say of each, 'this is water', it is like pointing to Socrates' various limbs and saying of each 'this is Socrates'. All water would then be the same *in number*. There is some intuitive plausibility to this in the case of water from the same source. At the same time, it is quite problematic to conceive of an individual the parts of which exist in separation from one another. Aristotle avoids this difficulty by assimilating 'same' applied to different pieces of *the same stuff* to sameness in species. However, he recognizes (as his commentators have generally not done) that this assimilation requires a defence, and therefore he gives one.

103ª15. 'has some differentia apart from those mentioned': the phrase *echein tina diaphoran para tous eirēmenous tropous* has vexed translators, since it seems a very clumsy way to say 'is different'. But *diaphora* is the technical term 'differentia', and Aristotle has just given the characteristics which differentiate three senses of 'same'. I take him to be saying 'you might think that this case exhibits a further differentia apart from those three'. Of course, since a species is characterized by its differentia, this amounts to 'you might think there is another species of sameness besides these'.

103ª23–31. 'indicated in several ways': the word *apodidotai* often means 'explain' or even 'define', but in the present case Aristotle most likely is thinking of different ways of indicating *something which is the same as X*:

I can do so by using a word with the same meaning as X, or X's definition, or X's unique property, or some expression which under the present circumstances just happens to designate the same thing as X. Of these possibilities, Aristotle thinks of the first two as the 'strictest' or 'most representative' cases. (Compare *Met.* Δ 6, 1016ᵇ35 ff., which discusses senses of 'one' that correspond very closely to these senses of 'same'.) But he has earlier explained 'same in number' as 'one thing with several names'; and if we take that explanation seriously, the *last* case seems best to illustrate it. After all, under the circumstances envisaged 'Socrates' and 'the one sitting' actually are two names for the same individual. By contrast, it is not at all clear what the 'one thing' is that has the two names 'cloak' and 'coat', since there are many *different* things called by either name. One might add that these different things are all cloaks and coats because they are the same *in species*.

A possible response is this: synonymous terms like 'coat' and 'cloak' *mean* the same thing. That is, they do not simply designate the same things but do so in virtue of having the same meaning. The same holds for a term and its definition. Unique properties (apart from accidental ones) do not have the same meaning but nevertheless are necessarily coextensive: thus, they necessarily designate the same things. By contrast, expressions which accidentally designate the same thing do so only because under the special features of a situation, one of them turns out to designate exactly what the other does. Thus, they do not have the same meanings, and it is only a coincidence that they designate the same things.

If this is what Aristotle has in mind, then he may be distinguishing between what an expression applies to and the way in which it applies to it. Comparable distinctions do occur in Aristotle: thus, he will sometimes say that two things 'are the same, though their being (*einai*) is different'— meaning that they coincide, even necessarily, but are distinct in nature or definition. There may be a hint of such a distinction in Aristotle's way of describing his cases. When he says that 'this is customarily indicated in several ways', we may take him to mean 'there are several ways in which I may *indicate something that is the same as X.*' One way to do so is to use an expression which *means* the same as X (a synonym or a definition): this can be thought of as the primary way to indicate 'what is the same' because the two expressions not only necessarily apply to the same thing but do so *in the same way*, that is, in virtue of the same meaning. A second, and less strict, way to do so is by giving a unique property of X, which necessarily applies to the same thing but in virtue of a different meaning. The least strict way is to find something which happens to apply to the same thing as X, but only coincidentally.

103ª32–9. This explanation applies only to the last case, things accidentally the same. Presumably, Aristotle regards this weakest case as so weak
that someone might object that it does not even count, and therefore he
gives an argument for it. Underlying it there may be a hint of the principle
that two expressions are the same if they can be substituted for one
another without change of meaning (thus, the command given is the same
when we replace a name by 'the one sitting').

<h3 style="text-align:center">CHAPTER 8</h3>

103ᵇ1–19. Aristotle now tries to establish the claim asserted in 101ᵇ13–18
that all dialectical arguments are 'made from' (*ek*) and 'about' (*pros*) the
predicables. Here, 'from' and 'through' correspond to 'from' in 101ᵇ13–18
(perhaps distinguishing premises from other parts of the reasoning), while
'about' corresponds to 'about' (*pros*) and 'concerning' (*peri*) in earlier
text. Since he has already recognized a sort of equivalence between the
problems arguments are about and the premises they are made from,
what he needs to do is establish that in every predication, the predicate
stands in one of the predicable relationships to the subject. 'Proof': pistis,
as at 100ᵇ19 (cf. Commentary on 100ª27–ᵇ3). Aristotle offers two proofs,
one through induction (*epagōgē*) and one through deduction (according to
I. 12 and passages in other works, induction and deduction comprise the
two species of argument). The proof through induction simply consists in
telling us what such a proof would rest on, viz. the examination of individual problems and premises to see that each one always falls under the
fourfold division.

The proof through deduction makes use of the scheme of division shown
in Fig. 1:

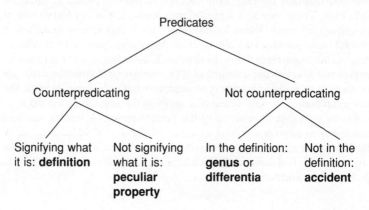

Since each division in the schema is a dichotomy, using a property and its negation, every predicate must fall into one and only one of the four lowest classifications. Therefore, Aristotle has a sound argument for the completeness of the classification presented here. However, it is not obvious that this schema corresponds to the divisions made in I. 5.

The problem is the definition of 'genus' (definitions and unique properties are defined as before, accidents in accordance with the first definition at 102ᵇ4–5). The division which captures genus and differentia yields the following definition:

A is genus or differentia of B = A is predicated of B and does not counterpredicate with B and is in the definition of B

We might see the first two components of this as equivalent to 'A is predicated of B and of other things besides', which in turn is close to the 'predicated of many things' in the definition of 'genus' at 102ᵃ31–2. Unfortunately, a case can be made that differentiae are usually, if not always, counterpredicated of their species. Furthermore, we now find 'stated in the definition' in place of 'predicated in the what-it-is'. This allows Aristotle to make explicit the conception of a definition as composed of genus and differentia, but he does not tell us what the difference between these two is nor explain why a definition must have this form (nor does he do so in I. 5). What his argument actually establishes is the unexciting result that if A is predicated of B, then A must be the definition of B, a unique property of B, one of the things in B's definition, or *something else*. This hardly shows that every predicate must be in one of the *four* predicable relations Aristotle has defined, since differentiae are now included; it does not explain how this division is related to the earlier definition of 'genus', nor how to distinguish genus and differentia; and, as in I. 5, it says nothing about the *second* definition of 'accident' at 102ᵇ6–7.

We can perhaps improve Aristotle's argument by calling on other texts, especially *Top.* IV. 2, IV. 5, and VI. 6 (the last is the closest thing in the *Topics* to an account of differentiae). First, the distinction between a genus and a differentia is that a genus 'signifies what its subject is' (*ti sēmainei*) whereas a differentia 'signifies what sort it is' (*poion ti sēmainei*: see e.g. VI. 6, 144ᵃ17–22). This can be put into rough correspondence with the requirement of 102ᵃ31–2 that the genus is 'predicated in the what-it-is': it is appropriate to give a thing's genus, not its differentia, in answer to the question 'what is it?' (Aristotle gives this distinction in IV. 6, 128ᵃ23–6). Thus, we could add a subdivision to the schema shown in Fig. 1 (see Fig. 2).

For this to work, then, there must be a difference between 'predicated in the what-it-is' and 'stated in the definition'. Unfortunately, Aristotle is not

73

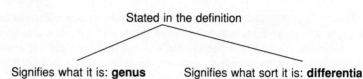

Stated in the definition

Signifies what it is: **genus**   Signifies what sort it is: **differentia**

very clear on this point: at VII. 3, 153ᵃ17–22, he says that both genus and
differentia are predicated in the what-it-is, and elsewhere (e.g. *An. Post.* I.
4) 'in the what-it-is' just seems to mean 'contained in the definition'.
Aristotle's views here may be unsettled: IV. 6, 128ᵃ20–9, the closest thing
in the *Topics* to an explicit account of the difference between genus and
differentia, begins 'Since some people think the differentia is also predicated of the species in the what-it-is'. See the Introduction for more on this
topic.

103ᵇ15–16. 'composed of a genus and differentiae': Aristotle usually insists that a definition is composed of a *proximate* genus and its specific
differentia, so the plural 'differentiae' is a bit surprising. However, he
sometimes recognizes another conception according to which a definition
consists of a higher genus and progressive differentiae of a species of this,
a subspecies of that species, etc., and he may have this in mind here.

CHAPTER 9

103ᵇ20. This section introduces one of the most famous of Aristotelian
doctrines, that of the *categories*. In fact, the word *katēgoria* simply means
'predication', and Aristotle says here that he is distinguishing 'kinds (or
genera) of predications' (*ta genē tōn katēgoriōn*). Almost immediately,
however, these become simply 'the predications'. We find him using this
sort of shorthand elsewhere, e.g. 'the problems' in the *Prior Analytics* for
'the kinds of problem' (i.e. the types of statement), 'the causes' for 'the
kinds of cause'. This is nicely reflected in the phrase 'the four predications
mentioned': the *kinds of* predication in which the aforementioned four
predications (the predicables, or expressions thereof) are found. Having
said that, I have retained the traditional 'category' for *katēgoria* (but note
that, as we should expect from the origins of the shorthand, the word is
always plural here).

The expression 'categories of predications' may seem to imply that the
categories are themselves classes of predicates. However, they may be
given two other interpretations. First, different types of predicate may be
related to the subjects of which they are predicated in different ways.
Second, different types of predicate may correspond to different types of

entity. In fact, all three interpretations may be involved in the uses to which Aristotle puts the categories elsewhere. We find the categories as types of predicate–subject relation in *An. Post.* I. 22 (and cf. below, 103ᵇ36–9); they are clearly types of entity, with corresponding senses of 'is', in the *Metaphysics* (B 3, Δ 7, E 2, Z 1), where each category is linked to a different sense of 'exists'.

I have for the most part retained the traditional names of the categories. Literally, they are 'what it is' (*ti esti*) 'how much' (*poson*), 'what sort' (*poion*), 'in relation to something' (*pros ti*), 'where' (*pou*), 'when' (*pote*), 'to be situated' (*keisthai*), 'to have' (*echein*), 'to do' (*poiein*), 'to undergo' (*paschein*). However, it is clear that these are already technical uses for Aristotle, since he uses them elsewhere in the *Topics* as, in effect, indeclinable nouns or adjectives. No gain in clarity would result from literalness.

The first category is an exception. Aristotle identifies this as 'what it is', but soon varies this with 'substance' (*ousia*), his preferred term for this category elsewhere. Interpreters also differ on the correct rendering of this term, which is derived from the verb 'be' (*on-* + *sia* = 'being-ness') and in everyday Greek can mean simply 'wealth' or 'possessions'. Something like 'entity' (Owens's rendering) is probably close to the mark: I choose 'substance' on the authority of tradition. The translation of *ti esti* is more problematic: 'essence' is favoured by tradition, but modern philosophical usage of this term is so variable that this is not likely to help. The unnatural look of my rendering, 'what-it-is' with hyphens, is intended to remind us that this is a technical locution for Aristotle.

Aristotle presents the categories as arising out of classifications of the answers to questions about something—evidently, about anything whatsoever. Ackrill (1963, 78–9) notes that we can imagine two different series of such questions. First, we may ask about something (e.g. Socrates), 'What is it?' When we get an answer (e.g. 'A man'), we repeat this question about that, getting another answer (e.g. 'An animal'). At each step, we obtain a higher genus; the process continues until we reach the highest genus possible, which will be a *category* (in the example, 'substance'). Alternatively, we may classify the different kinds of question we can ask about a single thing: 'What is it?' 'Of what sort is it'? 'Where is it?' Answers appropriate to one of these questions will generally make no sense in response to another. The categories will then emerge from these classifications of answers.

As Ackrill notes, the first series of questions leads to a classification of *subjects*, while the second leads to a classification of *predicates*. Although the results of the two series are (as Ackrill says) equivalent, they nevertheless reflect the ambiguity of interpretation of the categories noted above (the second series could also be seen as leading to a classification of predications as well as of predicates).

Aristotle gives lists of categories elsewhere, though only the *Categories* (4, 1ᵇ25–7) repeats the ten given here: elsewhere we find shorter lists of eight (*Phys.* V. 1, 115ᵇ5, *Met.* K 12, 1068ᵃ8, *An. Post.* I. 22, 83ᵃ21, ᵇ16), six (*Met.* E 4, 1029ᵇ4, *Phys.* I. 7, 190ᵃ34, *EN* I. 6, 1096ᵃ23, *EE* I. 8, 1217ᵇ28), five (*Met.* E 2, 1026ᵃ36, *Rhet.* II. 7, 1385ᵇ5), or even four (*GC* I. 3, 317ᵇ9, *Met.* Z 7, 1032ᵃ15). In general, the *Categories* most closely resembles the *Topics* in its account. One similarity is that neither treatise makes any kind of attempt to defend the list of ten categories (on this score, *Categories* 4 is even sparer than *Top.* I. 9).

103ᵇ29. 'the example under consideration': *to ekkeimenon*, literally 'what is set out'. Some translators take this rather vividly, so that Aristotle is imagining someone in the presence of a concrete individual (in the first case, some individual human being) 'set out' for some kind of consideration. The verbs *ekkeisthai* and *ektithenai* are sometimes associated in Aristotle with argumentative procedures in which an individual is singled out for consideration (see e.g. *An. Pr.* I. 41, 49ᵇ33–50ᵃ4), but this need not refer to actual contemplation of a concrete individual.

103ᵇ36–9. 'said about itself': Aristotle has previously given definitions and genera as the two types of predicates which 'say what it is' about their subjects. Since he explicitly mentions the genus as the second alternative, we would expect this first one to refer to predicating a thing's *definition* of it. However, it would be odd to call that 'saying it of itself', and the examples he gives do not seem to include definitions. If we take those examples to be predications with a concrete individual as subject, 'said of itself' is again odd, since a concrete individual cannot serve as a predicate. And predicating its *species* of a concrete individual, e.g. saying 'That is human' or 'That is white' of something indicated by ostension, also hardly qualifies as something 'said about itself'. (This is another reason for translating *to ekkeimenon* as I do above.)

It is better to see Aristotle as distinguishing between absolute and relative senses of 'what-it-is'. Substantial predicates like 'man' and 'horse' signify a what-it-is in the absolute sense. However, every predicate, whether substantial or not, can be defined, and the definition of a predicate says what it is in the relative sense. Generalizing, Aristotle says: predicating any species of itself, or any genus of one of its species, counts as 'saying what it is' in the relative sense, regardless of the category of the predicate. However, in predications that cross categorial lines, the category of the predicate also indicates the relation of predicate to subject. This distinction is important to Aristotle elsewhere, e.g. *An. Post.* I. 22.

103ᵇ39–104ª2. At 101ᵇ11–13 Aristotle said that it would be sufficient for his purposes to explain what arguments are about, what they are made of, and how we may be equipped to deal with them. As these lines note, I. 4–9 accomplish the first two of these tasks (by giving a system for classifying premisses and problems). It remains to say how we are to be 'equipped to deal' with these. Some interpreters suppose that the 'means by which' is the four 'instruments' Aristotle discusses in I. 13–18 (cf. 108ᵇ32, which refers retrospectively to 'the tools by means of which deductions come about'). In that case, we should expect I. 10–12 to explain 'how we are to obtain' something, but that is not what we find. Brunschwig nevertheless sees a reference to premisses in the verb 'obtain' and supposes that Aristotle is referring to the discussion of premisses in I. 10. A better solution, I think, is suggested by the end of Book VII: 'The locations, then, by means of which we shall be equipped to deal with each of the problems have been enumerated with reasonable adequacy.' It is therefore the contents of Books II–VII that give 'the means by which' we have an argumentative facility. But those contents are in turn useful only if we understand what premisses and problems are (I. 10–11), and Aristotle says that the four 'tools' are themselves to be used in connection with these locations (108ᵇ33). Aristotle is referring here, then, to everything that follows through the end of Book VII. 'The means by which we are to be equipped to deal with them' says what 'How we are to obtain them' means in concrete terms ('and' is explicative).

104ª3–8. This passage gives an especially clear picture of the real meanings of 'premiss' and 'problem': the words get their force from their cognate verbs *proteinein*, *proballein*, which designate types of argumentative procedures (cf. Note on 101ᵇ28–36). I have tried to bring this out with redundant translations of the verbs: *proteineie* as 'hold out as a premiss', *probaloi* as 'make a problem'. 'What nobody thinks' (*to mēdeni dokoun*) recalls the link between *endoxa* and what people think. 'Contains no puzzle' (*ouk echei aporian*) recalls Aristotle's emphasis on 'working through the puzzles' (*diaporein*) as the first stage of a scientific inquiry.

Premisses and problems are distinguished by their argumentative functions. When Aristotle says that not every premiss or problem is dialectical, we should ask what the non-dialectical ones look like. To judge by what he says here, non-dialectical premisses would at least include statements which have no support from any quarter, while non-dialectical problems at least include whatever has never been called into question by anyone. I. 1 implies that scientific principles are also non-dialectical, and the same would presumably hold for the conclusions of scientific demonstrations. However, many scientific principles might also appear to be the case to one of the relevant groups; many demonstrable propositions will also be denied by those lacking the relevant science. Elsewhere, Aristotle says that the many and the wise often have exactly opposed sentiments about what is obvious and what is puzzling (see e.g. *Met.* A 1–2). Hence controversial scientific principles and conclusions should qualify as dialectical.

104ᵃ8–12. 'the asking of something acceptable' (*erōtēsis endoxos*): that is, putting an acceptable proposition forward as a question. Note that this again emphasizes that a dialectical premiss is a kind of question asked: cf. *An. Pr.* I. 1, 24ᵃ24–6, 24ᵇ10–12.

104ᵃ9–10 exactly parallels 100ᵇ21–3 except that the word *endoxon* now replaces 'what seems so' (*ta dokounta*). This indicates that even in the earlier passage, Aristotle is not defining *endoxa* but instead specifying the different types of *endoxa*. The conclusion is that the term *endoxon* really is a relative term: to be acceptable is to be acceptable *to someone*. If we keep this in mind, a number of puzzles disappear.

'contrary to opinion' (*paradoxos*): 'paradoxical' is too narrow. What Aristotle says is only that one cannot use an opinion of 'the wise' as a dialectical premiss if it is *contrary* to what most people think: the view need not be 'paradoxical' in a stronger sense, e.g. supported by a paradoxical argument. This would imply that the opinions of the wise might be used as dialectical premisses under two circumstances: if they *agree* with the opinions of the many, or if there simply is nothing about the subject in question which counts as the opinion of the many. Note that this must only apply to the opinions of the wise, since it would be otiose to say that what all or most people think is 'not contrary to opinion'.

104ᵃ12–15. Aristotle follows his definition by listing three further classes of acceptable premiss. The first two classes depend on logical transformations which, when applied to acceptable premisses, yield other premisses that are (or at least 'appear to be') acceptable; the third class amounts to 'expert opinions'.

104ᵃ15–20. First transformation: if some term in an acceptable premiss is replaced by a similar term, the result is also acceptable. Aristotle's examples make the point clear enough. However, he does not explain just what use is to be made of such transformations. In fact, the *inference* from one such premiss to another here recalls a type of move often found in Plato's dialogues, that is, reasoning from one case to another similar one. Aristotle may therefore be proposing a general strategy for obtaining premisses: in order to obtain *p* from an opponent, try first to obtain some premiss derived from *p* by replacing some term with a similar one.

104ª20–30. To understand Aristotle's second group of transformations, we must look ahead to II. 7, which uses very similar examples in discussing another question. Suppose that we have a compound term containing two terms A and B, each of which has a contrary. As an example, consider the compound 'doing good to one's friends': its components 'doing good' and 'one's friends' have as contraries 'doing ill' and 'one's enemies'. We can form various other expressions by substituting the contrary of A, or the contrary of B, or both, in the original expression. Which of these are contrary to which? Aristotle's answer in II. 7 is that if we replace *one* term in a complex with its contrary, the new complex is contrary to the old, but that if we replace *both* terms the new complex is not contrary. For instance, 'doing good to one's enemies' and 'doing ill to one's friends' are both contrary to 'doing good to one's friends', but 'doing ill to one's enemies' is not.

Now the simplest way to describe the rule on which he is relying would be something like this: if a premiss is acceptable, then the premiss we get by replacing one term in it with its contrary and negating the result is also acceptable. This is in accordance with the results of II. 7: when *one* term in a complex is replaced with its contrary, the resulting complex is contrary to the original. The phrase 'put forward as a negation' recalls the dialectical context, in which premisses are questions: the transformed premiss will get an *affirmative* answer if we pose it in the manner of a negation.

(Two complications should be mentioned in passing. First, is Aristotle thinking of relations of contrariety between terms or between propositions? He is sensitive to this point elsewere, e.g. *De Int.* 7; however, it is difficult to find evidence of it in the present passage. Second, in Greek, as well as in English, 'must not' is not the negation of 'must': the negation of 'One must do good to one's friends' is 'One *need not* do good to one's friends'. Aristotle's translators and commentators have generally missed this point as much as Aristotle; I shall ignore it.)

104ª28–33. Now Aristotle turns to the other case considered in II. 7: replacing *two* terms in a complex with their contraries. II. 7 says that this transformation does not produce contraries. Therefore, the new premiss will not be contrary to the old premiss, and we cannot expect it to be acceptable when put forward as a negation. But Aristotle goes beyond this to say that the two-term transformation *itself* will be acceptable. He may be relying on a rule similar to that stated in II. 8, 113ᵇ27–34 (see Excerpt A): if A goes with B, then the contrary of A goes with the contrary of B.

The phrase 'in parallel' (*en parabolēi*) has vexed interpreters, but it seems most natural to take it as contrasted with 'as a negation': what distinguishes the present case from those before is just that the premiss obtained from the transformation is *not* negated and is thus 'parallel' to the original.

104ª30–3. 'What we say about contraries' probably refers to II. 7, where Aristotle argues at some length that A + B and Contrary(A) + Contrary(B) are not contraries, using the very terms found here (113ª1–8); this suggests that some of his contemporaries were inclined to think otherwise.

104ª33–7. Since doctors and geometers are 'the wise' when it comes to medicine and geometry respectively, it would seem that their opinions on their areas of expertise automatically qualify as *endoxa*. But if we suppose, as I have, that there are many lists of *endoxa* for different types of interlocutor, Aristotle may be making the different point that expert opinion can *always* be used as a source of dialectical premisses: *anyone* would concede what the relevant experts think.

CHAPTER 11

104ᵇ1–5. Aristotle has already explained what a problem is, to wit, some proposition considered as a subject for debate. He now explains which problems count as *dialectical*. An earlier remark in I. 10 (104ª6–7) implies that in order to be dialectical, a problem must be susceptible of real disagreement. The second part of Aristotle's definition reflects this: a dialectical problem is something about which people hold either conflicting opinions or no opinion. The term 'point of speculation' (*theōrēma*) is derived from the verb *theōrein*, Aristotle's usual designation for the activity of pure intellectual inquiry. However, in wider Greek usage a *theōrēma* could be anything intended to be beheld or looked at (such as a theatrical spectacle). Aristotle himself uses the term in application to the 'phantasm' or mental representation which he thinks is necessarily involved in sense perception.

A dialectical problem, then, is by definition a subject about which people can disagree. But Aristotle's definition also includes a specification of subject-matter: 'choice and avoidance' or 'truth and knowledge'. If we take this as a limitation, then any problem not concerned with either of these will fail to be dialectical. However, it is difficult to imagine an example of such a problem: it would need to be a subject about which genuine disagreement is possible but which is concerned neither with practical choices nor with theoretical understanding. The specification of subject-matter is better understood as a very general classification of problems, derived from observation of the subjects of actual dialectical exchanges (see the comments on the following lines and on 105ᵇ19–29).

104ᵇ5–12. The threefold division of problems is often taken to correspond to the division of premises and problems into 'ethical', 'scientific', and 'logical' at 105ᵇ19–29. This identification is given some support by the use of the example 'whether the universe is eternal' in both passages but it is hardly certain. In any event, Aristotle is not stipulating what counts as a subject of dialectical discussion but rather classifying the actual subjects encountered in dialectical exchanges. To use terminology common in his own later works, some of these problems are *practical*—concerned with deliberation and action—while others are *theoretical*, i.e. concerned with knowledge only. In fact, the way in which he makes the distinction later in the chapter is very much in accordance with the treatment of 'theoretical wisdom' (*sophia*) and 'practical wisdom' (*phronēsis*), the two principal intellectual virtues, in *EN* VI. However, the present distinction is not explicitly correlated with that pair (see the Commentary on 105ᵇ19–29 for further discussion.)

104ᵇ6. 'know the answers to some problems': literally, just 'know some problems' (*enia eidenai*). But the standard expression of a problem is with a 'whether' clause, and thus the problem itself fits exactly (in Greek as in English) as a direct object of 'know': 'to know whether *p*'. I have supplied 'answers' to make this sense clear.

104ᵇ12–17. The essential characteristic of a dialectical problem is that it is something which can be meaningfully debated. Although Aristotle initially defines a dialectical problem in 104ᵇ1–5 as something about which there is actual disagreement, he now observes that debate may be possible in two further cases even if divergence of opinion does not exist. In a sense, his two cases are opposite extremes. First, it may be the case that there are *arguments* for and against a given view (regardless of whether there is a real difference of opinion about it). In such a case, the arguments themselves make debate possible (as examples, we might think of almost any philosophical issue). Second, the question may be so 'vast' that we simply do not know what to say: we have *no* arguments. Either of these types of question, says Aristotle, might give rise to an inquiry, and thus both are dialectical.

The term 'puzzle' has a special significance in Aristotle's usage. He approaches philosophical questions with the assumption that human knowledge itself progresses in a manner similar to a dialectical discussion: understanding increases by first recognizing the 'puzzles' that exist concerning a subject and then discovering solutions to them. According to *Met.* A, philosophy—theoretical inquiry—always begins in 'wonder' (*thaumazein*), that is, the recognition that a certain state of affairs is in need of explanation. The goal of philosophy is then to find this explanation and thereby dispel the wonder or puzzlement. Aristotle normally begins his discussions of subjects by first laying out all the puzzles that have been raised concerning them, a procedure he designates with the verb *diaporein*.

A much-discussed passage in the *Nicomachean Ethics* (VII. 1, 1145^{b}1-7) says that any inquiry should begin with the 'appearances' (*phainomena*) and, by a process of working through the puzzles, try to 'solve' these puzzles while retaining the greatest number possible of the *endoxa* concerning the subject-matter. G. E. L. Owen (1961) proposed that the 'appearances' include not only observations of natural phenomena but also opinions held by the general public or by other philosophers—in other words, things that are *endoxa*, according to the *Topics*. We could take this to mean only that the fact of general acceptance is a prima facie reason for supposing that an opinion is true, so that we should at least take any such opinion seriously. However, the closing words of the *Nicomachean Ethics* passage hint at something stronger: 'for if the difficulties are solved and the *endoxa* remain, that would be proof enough'. On this basis, some have concluded that some kind of dialectical justification is *constitutive* of truth for the first principles (see Nussbaum 1986, Irwin 1988). I do not find such arguments persuasive (see Hamlyn 1990 for criticism of Nussbaum and Irwin); in any event, no such view need be read into the *Topics*.

104^{b}18-28. A 'thesis' or 'position' (*thesis*), as defined here, is a startling or incredible view that is taken seriously only because some famous person has maintained it, or because some argument can be advanced for it. Note that these will correspond to the views 'contrary to opinion' disqualified as dialectical premisses at 104^{a}10-12. The tone of the discussion again shows that Aristotle is not introducing a new term but instead fitting established terminology into his own framework. Evidently, 'problem' and 'thesis' were both current in dialectic, probably without being sharply distinguished from one another. Aristotle proposes a distinction according to which a thesis is a kind of problem; argues for it; and then tries to mollify any offence the argument might offer by saying that names do not really matter so long as we understand the underlying distinctions they are meant to capture.

Since *thesis* is connected with *tithenai*, the verb that indicates the acceptance of a premiss, it is a surprise to find 'thesis' defined here as quite the opposite of something 'acceptable'. However, what makes something a *thesis* in the sense of 104^{b}19ff. is principally its acceptance *by someone famous*. Thus, Aristotle's qualification at 104^{b}22-4 is intended to make it clear that not just anyone's acceptance of a proposition makes it a *thesis*.

Compare Alexander on 105^b10: 'he used the word "thesis" here because of agreeing, i.e. supposing [*tithesthai*]' (91. 12–13).

104^b26–7. 'the musician who is literate': the point Aristotle is making is easier to see than the example with which he makes it. His intent is merely to illustrate the second class of theses, those supported by argument. The conclusion of the argument is clear: 'not everything which is either has come to be or is eternal'. No one would be inclined to take such a thesis seriously but for the fact that an argument can be constructed in its support. Moreover, since Aristotle characterizes the propounders of the argument in question as sophists, he intends to include as theses of this sort any paradox in the usual sense of the term.

The argument he has in mind is almost certainly the one which appears in fuller form in *Met.* E 2, 1026^b18–20, and K 8, 1064^b23–6. One possible reconstruction is as follows: Suppose that X, who is literate but not musical, becomes musical. After this has happened, we can say 'X the musician is literate'. However, it does not appear that X the musician *became* literate: there was a time when there was no such thing as X the literate musician (i.e. the time at which X was not a musician), but there is never a time at which *X the musician* changed from being illiterate to being literate. Other reconstructions are possible. The word translated 'musical' may also mean 'cultured' or 'educated', so that it presupposes literacy (the ability to read and write). In that case, it would be impossible for anyone 'musical' to *become* literate, since 'musicality' in that sense presupposes literacy: 'X the cultured becomes literate' cannot ever be true. But as Brunschwig (1986) notes, the form of the argument in *Met.* K seems inconsistent with this interpretation. However it is to be interpreted, the argument is smoother in Greek, where nouns and adjectives are more parallel in syntax than in English: *ho musikos* and *ho grammatikos* ('the musical one', 'the literate one') behave like *ho anthrōpos* ('the man'). See Brunschwig (1986: 128–9), Kirwan (1973: 191–2) for further discussion.

104^b29–105^a2. This section also shows that 'thesis' is not Aristotle's coinage but had an accepted technical use in dialectic as he knew it. The sense seems to be that in dialectical exchanges (exercises?), the proposition under discussion is always referred to as a thesis, even if it is not a controversial opinion of a famous philosopher. As in other cases, Aristotle tries to provide a rational basis for an existing terminology.

105^a3–7. Perception and punishment can be associated respectively with theoretical science and ethics. Aristotle holds that a good upbringing is a necessary condition for understanding philosophical ethics: moral judgements rest ultimately on dispositions formed in childhood through habituation, and habituation results from rewards and punishments. Those who have the wrong dispositions are in need of punishment, not argument, to correct them. In the sphere of science, Aristotle holds that perception is ultimately the basis of knowledge: he is frequently distrustful of attempts (Platonic or otherwise) to construct scientific theories a priori, and he rejects Plato's view that learning is a kind of remembering.

These lines, then, imply that dialectical argument is pursued in an attempt to resolve questions: Aristotle's point is that it cannot make the wicked good nor the blind see. Does he then mean that certain questions, for instance the examples he gives here, cannot be the subjects of dialectical argument? I think he is instead concerned with the limits of what argument can accomplish. He has already allowed that dialectical theses may include paradoxical assertions supported either by famous authority or by argument, and we have plenty of examples of these from Aristotle's time that fly in the face of accepted morality and common sense. Aristotle is not claiming that these cannot be debated dialectically. However, there is a difference between debating them for the sake of argument and debating them 'for real'. Arguing with the depraved is a waste of time, if our goal is to change their behaviour; arguing about what can be decided through perception, if we need that decision for practical purposes, is silly.

105ᵃ7–9. The 'demonstrations' Aristotle refers to here are presumably arguments which establish one or the other side of a problem. Aristotle's contrast between 'near' and 'remote' demonstrations probably does not refer so much to the intrinsic difficulty of the problems (earlier, he included 'vast' questions as dialectical) as to the length of the arguments themselves. A very short argument is too obvious to engage anyone's attention; a lengthy argument in the style of a mathematical demonstration could hardly be developed or discovered in a verbal exchange. 'Too much for exercises' should not be taken to imply that *all* dialectical arguments are exercises (see I. 2 and Commentary). Aristotle never suggests that dialectical arguments are a means for discovering *demonstrations*, though they may have a role in developing the argumentative skills required for demonstration and also in discovering the *principles* of demonstrations. A truly difficult demonstration is likely to be discovered only by a solitary thinker; trying to come up with it during an argumentative exchange is bound to be a waste of time.

CHAPTER 12

105ᵃ10–19. *Induction* (*epagōgē*) is the ancestor of the modern philosophical notion (or notions) of inductive argument. As defined here, an induction is an argument from many instances to a universal generalization.

Broadly similar definitions are present or implicit in VIII. 1, 156^{a}4–6; *An. Post.* I. 1, 71^{a}8–9; *Rhet.* I. 2, 1356^{b}14–15 (see also below, I. 18, 108^{b}10–11 and Commentary).

Aristotle often repeats the claim that all arguments are either inductive or deductive (*An. Pr.* II. 23, 68^{b}13–14; *An. Post.* I. 1, 71^{a}5–11; *Rhet.* I. 2, 1356^{a}35–^{b}4, II. 20, 1393^{a}24–5; *EN* VI. 3, 1139^{b}27–9). Elsewhere he hints at the same point by giving inductive and deductive arguments for the same point (a good example is I. 8 above). Given the connections between dialectic and Socrates, it is noteworthy that in *Met.* M 4, 1078^{b}27–30, Aristotle credits Socrates with two advances in dialectic, one of which is inductive arguments. Aristotle often contrasts induction and deduction as moving in opposite directions: induction is from individuals to universals, deduction from universals. In the theory of demonstrative science, induction plays an epistemic role as the source of knowledge of the first premisses of sciences which (Aristotle argues) cannot be known by deduction from other principles. Thus, induction and deduction are the two sources of knowledge, as well as the two forms of argument.

In modern philosophical usage, an inductive argument is an argument from individual instances to a universal generalization:

X_1 is an A and an F
X_2 is an A and an F
. . . . .
X_n is an A and an F
Therefore, every A is an F

The inference from any number of premisses of the form 'X is an A and an F' to the universal conclusion 'Every A is an F' is, formally speaking, invalid: the truth of the conclusion is not a *necessary* consequence of the premisses. However, such inferences are indispensable for empirical knowledge. A critical issue for the modern philosophy of science has therefore been just the problem of induction: what is the nature of the inference from a finite number of instances to a universal generalization, and when are such inductive arguments good ones ('inductively valid')?

From this modern viewpoint, what Aristotle has to say about induction is disappointing. Though he distinguishes between induction and deduction, he does not really recognize a 'problem' of induction. Since he practically defines 'deduction' as 'argument in which the premisses necessitate the conclusion', and since he says that inductions are not deductions, it would seem to follow that the conclusions of inductions are not necessitated by their premisses. But this is an interpreter's conclusion, not one Aristotle draws. Moreover, some of his remarks about induction (notably the role he attributes to it in *An. Post.* II. 19) have sometimes been taken

85

to imply that it is *more* secure in some way than deduction. A complicating factor is that Aristotle does not distinguish clearly between the type of inductive argument given above and a second type:

> Every X is an F
> Every Y is an F
> Every Z is an F
> X, Y, and Z are species of A
> Therefore, every A is an F

In fact, the example in I. 12 is of this form. So understood, inductive arguments can easily be supplemented so as to make them deductively valid: we need only strengthen the last premiss to 'X, Y, and Z are the *only* species of A.' Aristotle proposes just this in *An. Pr.* II. 23.

A full discussion of Aristotle's views concerning induction would take us even farther from the *Topics*. But if we confine ourselves to induction as a device in argumentative exchanges, then we could ask: under what circumstances am I entitled to infer a general conclusion when my respondent has conceded a number of its instances? In Book VIII we get some indications of Aristotle's answer to this question; see below, I. 18, 108ᵇ10–11; VIII. 1, 156ª3–7; VIII. 2, 157ª18–ᵇ33; VIII. 8; and the associated Comments. For more of Aristotle's views on induction see *An. Pr.* II. 23–4; *An. Post.* I. 1, I. 18, II. 19; *Rhet.* I. 2, 1356ª25–ᵇ37; *EN* VI. 3, 1139ᵇ26–35.

105ª16–19. Aristotle thinks inductive arguments are less sophisticated or less artful than deductions. Induction starts with what is perceptible to the senses, which is more intelligible or familiar 'to us' (that is, to people in general), and proceeds to universals, which are remote from sensation and less intelligible to us but more intelligible 'by nature' (that is, give the true explanations of the phenomena we perceive). In the order of acquisition of knowledge, then, induction is prior to deduction, and it is therefore more comprehensible to ordinary people unskilled in reasoning. Furthermore, on Aristotle's account, all inductive arguments have essentially the same structure: instances followed by a generalization.

Deductions, by contrast, take many diverse forms, and it requires some skill not only to construct them but even to understand them. A complex deduction may be utterly lost on an unsophisticated audience, even though its conclusion is indeed necessitated by its premisses. Anyone who understands a deduction will understand the inescapability of its conclusion given its premisses; but in many cases only a few will understand. Not surprisingly, Aristotle has very much more to say about deductions than about inductions, both in the *Topics* and in the *Prior Analytics*.

Aristotle's characterization of deductions as 'more coercive' than inductions is perhaps an acknowledgement that a good inductive argument may be deductively invalid, so that its premisses do not necessitate its conclusion. However, he does not actually say this, nor does he do so clearly elsewhere. He may mean something like this instead. As instances are adduced, it quickly becomes clear where an inductive argument is headed. Such arguments therefore are easier to follow, but for the same reason they require a certain amount of co-operative spirit: a recalcitrant adversary will be unlikely to grant the needed instances. Deductions, by contrast, require fewer premisses and no goodwill on the part of the respondent in order to reach their conclusions, and thus they are more coercive. A good dialectician can deduce a conclusion from premisses conceded by an otherwise recalcitrant answerer. Refutations are coercive in just this way, forcing people to inconsistent admissions on the basis of their own concessions.

105ᵃ17. 'more intelligible in the way perception is': What we know through sense perception is more intelligible to us but less intelligible in itself; since induction is closely tied to sense perception, inductive arguments are also more intelligible to us, though they are incapable of providing the understanding of causes required for science. This harmonizes with the remainder of the passage, which emphasizes the ordinary and common-sense character of inductive argument.

CHAPTER 13

105ᵃ21–33. At I. 4, 101ᵇ11–13, Aristotle said that an adequate account of his dialectical 'procedure' would state 'the number and kinds of things that arguments are about, and what they are made of, and how we are to be supplied with these'. He now turns to the last component of this, enumerating four 'tools' (*organa*) by means of which we are to be equipped with deductions. Of course, this means 'equipped with deductions for any conclusion desired'. After enumerating these, Aristotle discusses each. The first, 'obtaining premisses' (*protaseis labein*), receives a detailed treatment in I. 14, and the second, 'distinguishing the number of ways a word applies', an even longer one in I. 15; the third and fourth, 'finding differences' and 'the examination of likeness', rate only cursory discussions (I. 16, I. 17).

One thing missing from this list, and indeed not mentioned at all until the very last sentence of Book I, is the 'locations' or 'places' (*topoi*) which have given the *Topics* its name. Since these occupy by far the largest part of the treatise, commentators have been much exercised to fill in the gap left by Aristotle's reticence and to answer the closely related question just what a *topos* is. My view is spelt out in the Introduction. Aristotle's dialectical art is to be a procedure for finding premisses that meet two requirements: (i) they will be conceded by our opponent and (ii) they will imply the conclusion we want to establish. To meet (i), we need to know what sorts of things our opponent will accept, whereas to meet (ii), we need to know what follows from what. A solution to the problem would result if we had a double system for classifying propositions: first as lists of opinions of different sorts of people, next as possible premisses for deriving a given conclusion. Aristotle's method, as I reconstruct it, rests on just such a system of classification. First, he tells us in I. 14 that we should compile lists of the opinions of various kinds of person. Next, in Books II–VI of the *Topics*, he gives us 'locations' (*topoi*) which consist of recipes for constructing arguments for various conclusions (Brunschwig characterizes a *topos* nicely as 'a machine for making premisses beginning from any given conclusion'). To use the method, we first determine our conclusion (which is simply the denial of the answerer's thesis). Then, using the collection of *topoi*, we find some premisses from which it would follow. Finally, we search for those premisses among the relevant collection of opinions. Once we have found them, all that remains is to present them to our opponent in an appropriate manner as questions (cf. VIII. 1, 155ᵇ4–7).

105ᵃ23-4. The second tool, being able to distinguish the different meanings of a word, includes two distinct abilities: being able to tell *whether* a word has different meanings and knowing *what* these meanings are. Aristotle devotes considerable attention to the second of these in other works: there are, for example, many alternative definitions for terms offered in the *Rhetoric*, and *Met.* Δ consists entirely of discussions of 'how many ways'. No such discussion is contained in the *Topics*, however. What we find instead is a lengthy series of tests (in I. 15) for addressing the complementary question whether a word has multiple senses. Aristotle discusses what this tool is useful for in I. 18, 108ᵃ18–37.

The phrase 'how many ways something is said' (*posachōs legetai*) is worth some attention in itself. One possible meaning of *legetai* ('is said') is the simple passive voice 'is called'. In this sense, different *things* to which the same word applies may sometimes be *called the same thing in different ways*. Just this use appears, for example, in 106ᵃ4–5: justice and courage are *called good in one way*, the healthful and what produces fitness called good in another way. (As I interpret it, the same construction is found in 105ᵃ27–38: see below.) Here, the subject of *legetai* is the thing to which the word applies, not the word. In Aristotle, however, another use of *legetai* is also common: if A is predicated of B, then A is 'said of' (*legetai kata*) B. Here the subject of *legetai* is the word itself. Finally, the verb *legein* can mean 'mean' (having either person or utterance as its subject). These senses are interrelated. If X and Y are both called A—that is, if A is 'said of' them— but in different ways, then X and Y are *called* (A) in many ways (*pollachōs legetai*); therefore, since A is *said of* (*legetai*) both X and Y but in different ways, the term A is *said of* (other things) in many ways (*pollachōs legetai*). The upshot is that *pollachōs legetai* is itself 'said in many ways', and in a way that it is difficult to capture in English translation. Most often in the *Topics* (for instance in I. 15), it is clearly a *word* that *pollachōs legetai*. I have therefore opted for the somewhat artificial 'said in many ways', with the intention of suggesting that Aristotle's expression may also be some- what artificial. In some places, however, syntax requires me to resort to 'is called'.

105ª24. 'finding differences': although I have generally translated *diaphora* as 'differentia', the less technical 'difference' fits better with what Aristotle says later in I. 16 and I. 18 (the point may be that finding differen- ces is important, among other reasons, because it can yield differentiae).

105ª25–31. Each of the tools is a procedure of some sort; Aristotle's point is that the *results* of using the last three can be expressed as propositions (cf. Alexander, 88. 25–30). There may be more than a trivial point at work here. In the terminology of modern logical theory, if B follows logically from A, then 'If A then B' is logically true; therefore, the premisses of an argument may include statements expressing the logical relationships of other premisses. This passage may indicate Aristotle's awareness that rules of inference which *apply to* a deductive system may also be *expressed within* the system. However, the question whether, and how, Aristotle distinguished logical truths from other truths is a most difficult one.

CHAPTER 14

105ª34–ᵇ3. This section, and what follows, closely parallels the discussion of dialectical premisses in I. 10. When Aristotle speaks of 'collecting' or 'selecting' premisses, I take him to mean 'drawing up separate collections of premisses for each of the groups indicated'. 'Making ready for use': *procheirizomenon* could mean just 'choosing', but its root sense is 'to make ready to hand' (*procheiros*). The whole point of the process of collecting premisses is to have collections of various classes of opinions prepared in advance in a form convenient for use. See the Note on 105ᵇ12–18 below.

'or the contraries': it may seem perverse to include the contraries of opinions, but these are to be used as premisses by 'putting them forward as negations', as Aristotle says immediately, with an allusion to his earlier remarks (104ᵃ13–14) that 'the contraries of things which appear to be acceptable, put forward by negation' are also acceptable.

105ᵇ3–10. Earlier (I.10, 104ᵃ15–20) Aristotle said that whatever is similar to an acceptable premiss is also acceptable. Now he says that while producing collections, we should also add to them other premisses similar to those collected. In other words: since what is similar to an acceptable premiss is likely to be accepted, it saves time to construct these in advance and add them to the list.

105ᵇ10–12. This remark makes it particularly evident that the collections are intended to be premisses a respondent will accept. People will think that they accept a universal claim if it is *usually* true, provided that they have not noticed any exceptions to it. Aristotle calls such a premiss an 'apparent concession' (*dokousan thesin*), that is, something which the answerer will *think* he agrees with.

105ᵇ12–18. 'Written works': as Brunschwig notes, *Rhet.* II. 22, 1396ᵇ3–8, which refers to this passage, makes it clear that these are the written works of others, not (as some have suggested) 'written collections of arguments'. 'Tables' (*diagraphai*): Aristotle uses this term at *EE* III. 1, 1228ᵃ28, of the tabular representation of moral virtues and their corresponding vices in *EE* II. 3. The point of drawing up tables is to make it easy to find these premisses. To that end, we should have an appropriate system of classification. Aristotle's system classifies by way of the subject of predication in the opinion. He assumes that, in accordance with what he has said earlier, any premiss will predicate something of something, and he then groups together opinions with the same subject. The phrase 'about each genus' could be a reference to the categories of I. 9 (the 'kinds—*genē*—of predications'), in which case Aristotle would be using the system of categories as a further principle of organization. The phrase 'and about every ⟨sense of⟩ good' is more problematic, but if Aristotle is thinking of the categories an interpretation suggests itself. Aristotle holds that 'good' has different senses which fall under the different categories (cf. 107ᵃ3–12). Therefore, if he intends the categories to serve as the highest divisions for his tables, these various senses will fall under different divisions. The 'marginal notes' giving attribution would be useful if our purpose were to appeal to the authority of an *endoxos*; they might also be important to someone undertaking to respond in accordance with the views of a well-known philosopher.

105ᵇ19–29. 'Ethical' and 'scientific' (*phusikai*: *phusikē* is 'natural science') premisses and problems correspond well with the two kinds of problems distinguished at 104ᵇ1–2, and perhaps also with Aristotle's dis-

tinction between practical and theoretical wisdom in *EN* VI and elsewhere. 'Logical' (*logikos*) is more difficult both to translate and to interpret. The example Aristotle gives of such a premiss is something he
elsewhere identifies as a 'common starting-point': one of a class of
premisses applicable to any subject-matter which, according to *On Sophistical Refutations*, have a special connection with dialectical argument (see
the Commentary on 101^a36–^b4 and on 162^b24–30). We might therefore
want to conclude that logical propositions are the special province of the
dialectician. If we make the further supposition that both theoretical and
practical sciences presuppose a more fundamental study of the nature of
argument and proof, and if we suppose that the contents of such a study are
'logical' propositions, we can arrive at an overarching picture of philosophy or science as having three components: theoretical wisdom (physics),
practical wisdom (ethics), and logic (here understood as the study of
argument and proof). The Stoics divided philosophy in exactly this way
and with exactly the names found here: logic, physics, ethics. Should we
understand Aristotle in the same way?

There are many obstacles in the way of doing so. To begin with, Aristotle's usual distinctions of kinds of wisdom or knowledge do not seem to
leave any place for a science of 'logic'. The contrast between practical
wisdom, which has as its goal knowing how to act, and theoretical wisdom,
which has as its goal the possession of understanding, is familiar in his
works. Often he adds the third category of 'productive' knowledge or arts
which have as their goal the production of artefacts; he generally views
productive arts as subservient in character. However, 'physics' is for him
only part of theoretical wisdom: he takes pains in the *Metaphysics* to argue
that 'first philosophy', the theoretical science which studies being as such,
is not identical with physics. Neither does he use 'ethics' as a synonym for
'practical wisdom'; and the beginning and the ending of the *Nicomachean
Ethics* may be taken to suggest that the study of conduct and character is
itself subordinate to the practical science of politics. And in none of these
divisions do we seem to find a place for a science called 'logic' or 'dialectic':
SE 11 even denies that dialectic constitutes a science of any sort. Finally,
Aristotle's use of the word *logikos* itself does not support the picture of a
'science of logic'. He uses it of arguments or propositions with a wide
generality of application, but often with the further implication 'merely
verbal': he describes 'logical' arguments as 'empty' and contrasts them
with genuinely scientific proofs 'according to the subject-matter': see *GA*
II. 8, 747^b27, 748^a7–13; *An. Post.* I. 22, 84^a7–8, 84^b1–2; I. 24, 86^a22; I. 32,
88^a19; II. 8, 93^a15. Sometimes it seems only to mean 'especially apt for
disputation': *Top.* V. 1 characterizes a 'logical' problem as one 'about
which there arise arguments both numerous and fine' (129^a29–31). See

also the Commentary on 162ᵇ24–30. (The term also has another sense, 'rational', that is not involved here.)

The ancient commentators interpret the passage against the background of a much later controversy about the place of logic in philosophy. Alexander and other later Peripatetics rejected the Stoic conception of logic as a division of philosophy on a par with theoretical and practical wisdom, maintaining instead that it is merely an 'instrument' of philosophy. They saw the origins of this view in Aristotle himself. Thus Alexander (74. 11–33) takes the threefold distinction in the present passage to be parallel to the classification of dialectical problems given at I. 11, 104ᵇ1–5: those useful for truth and knowledge, those useful for choice and avoidance, and those that work in conjunction with something else. Alexander supposes this to be a three-way partition and equates the last group with the 'logical' problems; the study of them will consequently be of no intrinsic value and important only in so far as it contributes to theoretical or practical issues. But the division in I. 11 can equally well be read as a double dichotomy: among both theoretical and practical problems, some are worth pursuing intrinsically while others are important because of their connection with other issues.

In view of all this, my translation of *logikos* as 'logical' should not be taken to carry modern technical associations. Non-philosophical uses of the term 'logic' are extremely broad and varying, but all have some connection or other to logic and reasoning, and that is all that I intend here.

105ᵇ25–9. 'the familiarity which comes through induction': this highly suggestive phrase may be linked with Aristotle's picture of scientific education, in which some form of familiarization is required to make the first principles 'more intelligible' to us.

105ᵇ30–1. Brunschwig says that this line has little special connection with what follows and accordingly makes it a paragraph by itself, rather than the beginning of a new paragraph. I have taken it instead as a final comment on the subject of 105ᵇ19–29, so that Aristotle is indicating that his threefold division holds for all propositions, not simply dialectical ones.

105ᵇ31–7. Compare the advice given at VIII. 14, 163ᵇ32–164ª2.

CHAPTER 15

This lengthy section (106ª1–107ᵇ37: almost a fourth of Book I) is almost entirely concerned with tests for detecting things 'said in many ways'. What Aristotle says is sensible and could still serve as a useful guide for detecting ambiguities and distinctions of type. Despite his initial remarks, Aristotle does not also try to give definitions for different senses, but that is hardly surprising: the tests are general tests, whereas definitions would necessarily concern specific cases.

106ᵃ1–8. There is an ambiguity in the term *legetai*, 'is said' or 'is called', which should be borne in mind here. Any case of things 'said in many ways' will involve two *things*, X and Y, and one *name* N which applies to both. In such a case, X and Y are 'called' (*legetai*) N, and the question whether this is 'in many ways' is the question whether they are so called in the same way. But as noted above (Comments on I. 13), Aristotle may also say that the name N is 'said of' (*legetai* again) the things X and Y. So construed, the question becomes whether N is said of X and Y in many ways or in one. Of these two ways of interpreting 'is said', the first (where the subject of 'is said' is the things the name applies to) is more fundamental. Aristotle's example in 106ᵃ4–8 can only be taken in this way ('justice', etc., are in the nominative case and thus must be the subjects of 'called'), and I have taken this to be true for the entire opening section 106ᵃ1–8. But as the discussion progresses, we often find that it is clearly the word which is 'said in many ways' of several subjects; sometimes the phrase 'said in many ways' (*pollachōs legetai*) can plausibly be read either way. I have tried to use an unambiguous construction when only one sense of 'is said' will fit, but in many instances my text is as ambiguous as Aristotle's.

Aristotle uses the brief phrase 'the how many' (*to posachōs*) to abbreviate the longer name of the second tool at 105ᵃ23–4. I translate with an equally compressed 'the number of ways'. The 'definitions' are not necessarily definitions of the different senses but perhaps only accounts of the *ways* in which they differ.

The rules which follow use a set of grammatical and syntactical categories prominent in several places in the *Topics*. For a fuller discussion of these categories and their functions, see the Introduction, and for fuller examples of Aristotle's use of it see II. 8–11, translated as Excerpt A. In the present chapter, we find first a discussion of 'opposites' (106ᵃ10–ᵇ28), subdivided into contraries (106ᵃ10–ᵇ12), negations (106ᵃ13–20), and privation/possession (106ᵃ21–8); next, inflections (106ᵃ29–107ᵃ2); and a brief mention of rules involving 'more and less' (107ᵇ13–18). These tests appear to be offered not as devices for convincing someone else in argument that a term has many senses, but as a means for determining this for oneself.

106ᵃ9–10. This sentence begins, word for word, 'Whether it is said in many ways or in one way in species'; I take 'said' to continue to mean 'called', as in the preceding passage. 'In species' is difficult. Sameness in species is one of the three types of sameness distinguished in I. 7, and the phrase 'in species' naturally recalls that distinction here. But then, Aristotle would be contrasting ways of application of a word which are *specifi-*

cally the same with those which are either *generically* or *numerically* the same; and it is obscure just what those alternatives might be. Alexander instead reads the phrase as equivalent to 'in definition' (97. 20–98. 3) and appeals to Aristotle's definition of 'equivocal' in *Cat.* 1ª1 ff. as 'with one name but different definitions' (see Comments below on 106ª20–2); *pollachōs tōi eidei legetai* would then mean something like 'called ⟨by the same name but⟩ in many ways with respect to definition'. This may be what Aristotle means, but it is hardly well expressed. One final possibility is that 'in species' here has some connection with its use in 106ª23–35, where it refers to the species of the *things* to which the term in question applies (see Comments below). None of these solutions is very convincing.

106ª10. 'To examine': Aristotle uses an infinitive (*skopein*) because he is giving a list of things one can do to test for ambiguity. See the Introduction, pp. xxix–xxx, on the comparable use of infinitives in expressing 'locations'.

106ª10–22. Suppose X and Y are both called N; what, in the case of X and Y respectively, is the contrary of N? If in application to X it is M, while in application to Y it is P, then X and Y are called N in different ways. Thus, Aristotle appeals to an underlying principle that to a term used in a single sense there can be only a single contrary.

The examples are naturally difficult to reproduce nicely in English, since they depend on ambiguities of Greek words. 'Sharp' (*oxu*) really means 'high' in application to a musical pitch; its opposite in this sense is *baru*, which means 'heavy' in application to bodies and is thus opposed to 'light' (*kouphon*); my 'flat' and 'rounded' are attempts at maintaining the parallel. And a knife that is not 'sharp' is 'blunt' (*amblu*).

In translating I. 15, I have been rather free with the use of inverted commas. It is possible to indicate, in Greek, that one is mentioning a word or phrase rather than using it by prefixing it with a neuter definite article. Sometimes, this construction is unequivocally recognizable: if, for instance, the phrase is not a neuter noun (*to aretē* could only mean 'the word "virtue"'). However, in many cases the same construction could equally well express abstraction: *to oxu*, for instance, could be either 'the word "sharp"' or 'the sharp' (i.e. that which is sharp, or sharpness). Aristotle's examples in I. 15 generally fall into this ambiguous category.

106ª20–2. ' "fine" is equivocal': The term 'equivocal' (*homōnumon*) can be understood in two ways, corresponding to the two readings given above for 'said in many ways' (see 105ª23–4 and comments). But in most instances, for Aristotle it is things not words that are *homōnuma*, 'like-named'. In *Cat.* 1ª1–15 Aristotle defines 'equivocal' to mean 'sharing *only* the name, not the definition'; thus, 'equivocal' things are things to which a single term applies but with different definitions. Such equivocals are 'called the same thing in different ways'. Things which share both a term and the associated difference are 'univocals' (*sunōnuma*: literally, 'named together'). This is not easy to align with English usage: we say that the *word* 'sharp' is equivocal because it applies to cheeses and to knives in different ways, whereas Aristotle says that *cheeses and knives* are equivocally called 'sharp' because the same word applies to them but in different ways. English 'homonym' and 'synonym' are still further removed in sense from their Greek cognates, Aristotle's *homōmunon/sunōnumon*.

If X and Y are both called A but different definitions of A apply to each, then X and Y are equivocally A. However, Aristotle also says in such a case that the term A is equivocal; similarly, if X and Y are univocally A, then A is univocal. As with the expression 'said in many ways', the latter senses of 'equivocal' and 'univocal' are the more common in I. 15.

Kalon (which I translate 'fine') means 'beautiful' (in application to anything), but in connection with persons can also mean 'noble' (in application to persons, especially in the phrase *kalos kai agathos*). The word I translate 'picture' (*zōion*) literally means 'animal', but the sense 'picture' seems to fit better with the passage.

106ª23–35. We should now expect Aristotle to turn to the case in which the contrary of N, in application to X as well as Y, is the same term M. He does give such an example: 'bright' and 'dark' are contraries of one another both in application to colours and in application to sounds, and so 'bright' is not detected as equivocal by the first test. We should then expect him to continue on these lines: even though the same *name* 'dark' applies to the contrary in each case, nevertheless these differ 'in species'; therefore, since 'dark' is equivocal, so is its contrary 'bright'. Instead, Aristotle gives an independent argument that sounds and colours are not the same in species. In other words, instead of arguing that M must be applied in different ways to X and Y because its contrary is different for each, he argues that M must be applied in different ways because *X and Y themselves* are different in species. On what principle does this argument rely? There is no reason to suppose that in general a term must take on different senses when it applies to things different in species: cows and horses are different in species, but 'black' applies to both in the same way. However, it is possible that 'species' here means 'category' (in the technical sense), so that the principle is: a term cannot be said in the same way of items in distinct categories. Such a principle is important elsewhere in the treatises. For instance, it underlies the argument in *EN* I. 6 that there cannot be a single Idea of good because the term 'good' can be applied to substances, qualities, and relations (1096ª19–23).

The example involving touch and taste repeats the terms I translate earlier as 'sharp' and 'flat'. Here, to get a better English example, I switch to 'rough'/'smooth'.

106ᵇ13–20. 'Contradictory' opposites are the third variety of opposite. It may be worth noting that the verb I translate 'see' (*blepein*) means both 'look at' and 'be able to see'; it is not cognate with the word I translate 'sight' (*opsis*). 'Multiple ways' (*pleonachōs*): though this seems equivalent to 'many ways' (*pollachōs*), it carries a suggestion of '*too* many ways'.

106ᵇ21–8. The third kind of opposite is the pair 'privation and state' (*sterēsis kai hexis*). As 106ᵇ25–8 indicates, a privation is the absence of something which it is natural for things of a particular kind to have, as for instance blindness is the absence of ability to see in an animal which naturally or normally is sighted. The term opposed to this, 'state' (*hexis*), is derived from the verb *echein* ('have'). Aristotle uses it in a wide range of meanings: 'condition', 'disposition' (thus both knowledge and virtue are *hexeis*), even 'characteristic'. In the present context, it means having that of which the privation is the lack. (On privation and state, see also *Cat.* 10, 12ᵃ26–ᵇ37; *Met.* Δ 20, Δ 22.)

What exactly are the two senses here in which something can be said to be 'insensible' (*anaisthēton*)? Alexander suggests that the point is the ambiguity of the verb *aisthanesthai*, which can apply either to sensory perception or to mental apprehension (similar ambiguities apply to many verbs of perception in English). Thus, perceiving 'with respect to the soul' would mean 'understanding', while perceiving 'with respect to the body' would refer to sense perception. The 'insensible' corresponding to the first of these would then be either 'unconscious' or 'lacking in understanding'; that corresponding to the second, some deprivation of a sensory modality. If this is correct, then the last sentence is problematic, since Aristotle does not believe that all species of animals naturally have both sense perception and the ability to understand: we would have to interpret it to mean something like 'animals naturally have each kind of perception that they do have'.

A different ambiguity may be involved instead. In Greek, 'perceive' (*aisthanesthai*) is a deponent verb, having passive endings but an active meaning. As a result, some of its forms can mean both 'perceive' and 'be perceived'. It is the soul of the perceiver which *aisthanetai* in the first sense, the object perceived which *aisthanetai* in the second. This ambiguity carries over to *anaisthētos*, which can mean either 'not such as to be perceived' or 'not such as to perceive' ('insensible' catches a little of the same ambiguity). Aristotle's last sentence will then amount to 'it is natural for animals both to perceive and to be perceived'.

106ᵇ29–107ᵃ2. The second major component of the *Topics* system, 'inflected forms' (*ptōseis*), makes a brief appearance here. Under this heading, Aristotle usually includes only the adverbial forms of adjectives ending in *-ōs* (rather like English adverbs in -ly), but occasionally other grammatical inflections of a noun or adjective are called *ptōseis* (conjugated forms of verbs are included at *Cat.* 3, 16ᵇ16–17).

The second example ('healthful') is difficult to translate. I have translated his adverbs *poiētikōs*, *phulaktikōs*, *sēmantikōs* with inelegant English adverbs 'productively', 'preservingly', 'indicatingly', because paraphrases like 'productive of health', etc., obscure the fact that Aristotle is appealing to the forms of the words themselves. (These are not common words in Greek and may have sounded just as inelegant to Aristotle's contemporaries.)

107ᵃ3–17. Suppose that N applies both to X and to Y. We may then ask: what *category* of thing is N in X and in Y respectively? If the answers are different, then X and Y are only equivocally N. Aristotle's examples illustrate this, but their structure is complex since he gives more than one example for each of the contrasted senses of application. Suppose that N is 'good', X is food, and Y is a soul. Then, X is called good in virtue of being productive of something, but Y is so called in virtue of being of a certain sort. This is a distinction of 'category' since the first falls under action, the second under quality. We get the same results if we let X be medicine, or if we let Y be a person. Again, to take Aristotle's last example, let N be 'sharp' and let X and Y be a sound and an angle. Then, N applies to X in virtue of X's being rapid (which may be seen as a quality) and to Y in virtue of Y's being in a certain relationship to something (i.e. less than a right angle). The middle example, 'bright' in sound and in colour, is less easy to characterize. Colours are paradigmatic Aristotelian examples of qualities; it is less certain what category 'easy to hear' falls under, but Aristotle may be thinking of it as a relative, which would give the middle example the same structure as the last.

The discussion of senses of 'good' closely resembles a position stated in *EN* I. 6, 1096ᵃ23–9: 'good', like 'is', has a different sense in application to each category, and thus there cannot be a single Platonic Idea of goodness. In the present text, Aristotle only advances the more modest claim that since 'good' is applicable to things in *several* categories, it must be equivocal.

The doctrine that 'good' and 'one' systematically vary their meanings in application to the different categories is of major importance to Aristotle's mature views, especially in the *Metaphysics*. It may therefore be significant that from this point until the end of I. 15, Aristotle switches from 'said in

97

many ways' to 'equivocal'. (The one exception, at 107ª34, is in a passage
that draws on a result from the earlier part of the chapter: see below.) This
may be slight evidence that the two halves of I. 15 were written at different
times, which in turn may have some bearing on the development of the
doctrines in the *Metaphysics*.

107ª12–17. Alexander assigns the bright in bodies to the category of
quality, that in sounds to action (i.e. having a certain effect on the hearer).
He interprets the three kinds of sharp as belonging to the categories of
action ('rapid motion'), relation (less *than a right one*), and quality (i.e. a
certain shape). 'Those who do numerical harmonics' are Pythagorean
music theorists.

107ª36–ᵇ5. A 'complex' is something denoted by a phrase, e.g. a pale
man. (Aristotle noted that definitions of phrases may be given in 101ᵇ38–
102ª2). This test rests on the general rule that equivocal things share only
a name, univocal things both a name and its definition (cf. *Cat.* 1). The
underlying rule bears a certain resemblance to one of Aristotle's favourite
examples of a 'common premiss' or 'common starting-point': 'if equals are
subtracted from equals, the remainders are equal'.

107ᵇ6–12. The test just given can be iterated: if the definitions as well as
the words are the same, we may nevertheless ask whether the definitions of
the terms in the definitions are the same. In order to show that X and Y are
univocally F, we must show that X and Y are both called F, that the same
definition of F applies to each, that the same definition of each term in the
definition of F applies to each, etc. Thus, it appears that (verbal) sameness
of definition is only a necessary, not a sufficient, condition for univocity.
The nature of Aristotle's example is difficult to see unless we remember
that he is still discussing the definitions of complexes. We need a case in
which two things have both the same name and the same definition, but a
definition containing something equivocal. Such a case can be provided if
we suppose, with Alexander, that the complexes are 'indicative of health'
(*sēmantikon hugieias*) and 'productive of health' (*poiētikon hugieias*).
These both contain the words 'of health'. Now, Aristotle considers definitions of these complexes which replace 'of health' in each case with
'commensurately related to health' (*summetrōs echon pros hugieian*):
'commensurately related to producing health' (*summetrōs echon pros to
hugieian poiein*) 'commensurately related to indicating health' (*summetrōs
echon pros to hugieian sēmainein*). (In Greek, the phrase 'commensurately
related to health' remains intact in both cases.) If we then delete what is
unique to each, we have left the same phrase, 'commensurately related to
health', so that this passes the test just stated. However, Aristotle notes
that 'commensurately related' has different meanings in the two cases.

Just what are these two meanings? Aristotle may have either, or both, of two things in mind. First, the two senses may involve different categories. What is productive of health is 'of such an amount' as to produce health (and thus a quantity), whereas what is indicative is 'of such a sort', i.e. a quality. Second, he appears to be saying that what is productive of health tends to produce *good health*, whereas what is indicative of health indicates *what state one's health is in*, whether good or bad. There may be more in this example than at first appears. Aristotle makes much in the *Metaphysics* of things which are neither strictly equivocal nor strictly univocal but rather designated 'with reference to a single thing', as all healthy things are called healthy neither in equivocal ways nor in the same way but in a way that always makes reference to health (see *Met.* Γ 2). G. E. L. Owen (1960) argued that the recognition of such '*pros hen*' equivocity in the *Metaphysics* represents a kind of partial recantation on Aristotle's part of an earlier position. Owen held that in the logical treatises, Aristotle is hostile to Plato's conception of a 'mistress-science' embracing all other sciences and taking all reality for its object; part of the argument against such a science, on Owen's view, is the claim that 'being' does not designate any single genus of things but instead has a different sense for each category. However, Owen argued, in the *Metaphysics* Aristotle retreated from this view and argued that *pros hen* homonymy could give a rational basis for a science of being as a science of substance. Many scholars today dispute Owen's claim that there is any real inconsistency between the *Metaphysics* and 'earlier' works on this point (see Code 1986). In any event, the present text does not seem to me likely to settle the issue. Even though Aristotle's examples are similar to those used in *Met.* Γ 2 to illustrate *pros hen* homonymy, there is no reason why he should mention this type of ambiguity here: *pros hen* homonymy is still a form of homonymy, whatever its metaphysical importance.

107^{b}13–18. The test proposed is straightforward: things to which an expression applies univocally can be meaningfully compared with respect to the degree to which it applies to them. Since, therefore, it makes no sense to ask whether this sharp taste is as sharp as this sharp sound, the taste and the sound are equivocally sharp.

Note here that this is a brief appearance of the third major element in the *Topics* system of classifying arguments: 'more and less and likewise' (see the Introduction).

CHAPTER 16

107^{b}38–108^{a}6. Aristotle's brief remarks about finding differences distinguish two cases: comparing things within the same genus and comparing things from different genera (he makes this same distinction again shortly below in discussing the study of similarities). Finding differences is not discovering *that* things differ but discovering *in virtue of what* they differ. Within a single genus, the difference in virtue of which one species differs from another is the differentia in a technical sense. Thus, as Aristotle says in VI. 6, 143ᵇ3–10, the differentia is 'the difference that makes a species' (*eidopoios diaphora*: 'specific difference').

When Aristotle says that 'the differences are completely obvious' in the case of very different things, he must mean, not that it is completely obvious *that* such things differ, but that it is completely obvious *how* they differ. This is not beyond question: questions like 'What is the difference between a frog and a bicycle?' or 'How is twelve different from being on the left?' can seem puzzling. Aristotle would presumably say, of very different things in different genera, that they fall in different genera. Thus in these cases the difference will not be a differentia, since differentiae only fall within a single genus.

CHAPTER 17

108ᵃ7–17. Studying similarities is a complementary process to finding differences, and Aristotle's remarks about it are comparably brief. As with finding difference, he distinguishes the two cases of things in different genera and things in the same genus. For things in different genera, Aristotle proposes looking for analogical relationships. This may reflect the fact that it will be harder to find a single predicate true of such cases, but this may also be a device Aristotle recommends for discovering wider and wider genera: cf. 108ᵇ23–31 and *An. Post.* I. 5, 74ᵃ4–25.

He may recommend concentrating our practice on widely different things either because the other cases are easy (cf. what he says about the analogous case for differentiae in 108ᵃ4–6) or because this will make us better able to deal with all cases. I have tried to retain this ambiguity in translation, though the following sentence makes the former interpretation more likely.

CHAPTER 18

The final chapter of Book I discusses the usefulness of three of the tools: studying the numbers of ways something is said, finding differences, and finding likenesses. There is no discussion of the usefulness of the first tool, obtaining premisses. This may be because, as Alexander suggests, its use-

fulness for constructing arguments is obvious. But Aristotle also said in I.
13 that the other three tools might in a way be reduced to finding
premisses.

108ª18–37. Aristotle lists three reasons why it is useful for dialecticians to
have studied the numbers of senses of terms. On clarity, compare VIII. 7:
in dialectical exchanges, the answerer had a right to refuse to answer
ambiguous questions and to demand, or offer, a clarification. 'Arguing
about a word' is the speciality of sophists and 'eristics'. What Aristotle says
here makes the most sense as a way of avoiding their arguments, i.e. taking
note of multiple senses and then assenting to a question only on one
construal (which would indeed make an opponent who persisted with the
other sense look ridiculous).

The second use is limited to the answerer in an exchange. The mention
of producing fallacies as well as resisting them might be taken to support a
more combative view of dialectical argument in which no holds are barred.
But Aristotle has already defined dialectical deductions as *valid* arguments, and here he adds at once the remark that producing fallacies is not
appropriate to dialectic. Even so, it is curious that he implies it might be
acceptable to resort to this kind of sophistry when all else fails. Perhaps he
means: 'If you have fallen in with sophists, you may be forced to resort to
sophistry'.

108ª38–ᵇ6. It is obvious enough that finding differences will yield arguments about what is different (and thus, negatively, about what is the
same). A short compendium of such arguments appears in VII. 1. The
phrase 'unique account of the being of anything' corresponds to the definition of 'definition' as 'account of what it is to be' (101ᵇ38), with 'being'
(*ousia*) in place of 'the what it is to be'. In I. 4 Aristotle distinguished
definitions from (other) unique properties on the grounds that definitions
signify what it is to be; here, he makes the complementary move of separating definitions from other predicates in the what-it-is on the basis of
their being unique to their subjects. The phrase 'we usually separate'
shows that Aristotle is reminding his audience of a practice of defining by
genus and differentia with which they are already familiar.

108ᵇ7–31. The three uses for the study of similarities give us glimpses of
other aspects of Aristotle's logical theory (one could wish that they were
more fully developed).

108ᵇ9–12. 'Inductive arguments': the general point here is that an inductive argument must rest on a collection of *similar* cases about each of which
the same thing is true. If these similar cases were (perceptible) individuals,

then the relevant criterion of similarity would be a perceived likeness, something not likely to be advanced by the kind of study Aristotle has in mind. Therefore, induction here must rather be the generalization from many similar *species* to a genus containing them all.

'Bringing in': *epagein* commonly means 'lead in', 'bring in', and can be used of introducing witnesses in a legal case. Although Aristotle often uses it to mean 'perform an induction', some indication of the root sense makes this passage clearer: thus, I translate *epagōgē* as 'bringing in'. 'Claim a right' (*axioun*) is used, especially in Book VIII, of moves we are entitled to make in a dialectical exchange. Aristotle says that if the answerer accepts the particular cases on which an induction rests, the questioner can expect him to concede the generalization; if this is refused, the questioner has a right to demand a contrary instance. See the Commentary on VIII. 2, 157ª34–ᵇ33, and VIII. 8.

108ᵇ12–19. 'Deductions from an assumption': the arguments considered here have a fairly precise structure. Aristotle says, first, that they rest on the general principle that it is 'accepted' that like is true of like, that is, that the *general* premiss 'like is true of like' is something we can always count on getting accepted. The ensuing argument then is, in effect, an argument from analogy: we obtain a case similar to the one we want to deal with, establish a result about it analogous to the conclusion we want, and then say that the same thing goes for our original case. Aristotle describes this as resting on an explicit agreement: we 'establish an agreement in advance' with our respondent that whatever holds of one case holds of the other.

He does not make it clear whether he regards these as the *only* kinds of 'arguments from an assumption'. Other sorts appear in other discussions (see *An. Pr.* I. 29, 45ᵇ15–20, I. 44). Both ancient and modern commentators have been much exercised to determine exactly how such arguments are related to other aspects of Aristotle's logical theory.

108ᵇ19–31. Aristotle's remarks about the usefulness of a study of similarity in connection with giving definitions recall the twofold division into cases involving things in the same genus and cases involving 'very different' things, as in I. 16 and I. 17. Concerning the first, he gives us a definition of 'genus'. Earlier, he said that a thing's genus was predicated in the manner of what it is of it and of other things as well; I take 'common' here to reflect this, so that a thing's genus must be a predicate common to it and other things. 'Most in the manner of what it is' presumably differentiates the closest (narrowest) genus from higher genera.

In the case of 'greatly differing' things, Aristotle again makes use of analogical similarities (cf. 108ª7–17 and Commentary).

108ᵇ32–3. This last sentence introduces the 'locations' (*topoi*) contained in Books II–VII. The 'aforementioned' are presumably the tools, which it would be natural to call 'useful'. See the Introduction for further discussion of what a *topos* is and how it would be employed to find premisses.

BOOK EIGHT

CHAPTER 1

155^b3–16. 'Arrangement' (*taxis*), the determination of just what questions to ask one's opponent, in what order, and in what way, is the subject of Book VIII. Aristotle begins with a striking comparison of dialectical and demonstrative ('philosophical') arguments which gives valuable clues about his understanding of several notions. To begin with, he describes both the philosopher and the dialectician as seeking for premisses from which to establish a given conclusion. Next, the 'locations' are useful to the philosopher as well as to the dialectician in their quests. Third, the critical difference between the two procedures lies in the epistemic qualities sought in the premisses. What the dialectician needs is premisses an opponent will accept; what the philosopher needs is true and intelligible premisses.

There is, of course, a difference in *form* between dialectical arguments, which consist of questions, and demonstrations, which consist of assertions. Underlying this, however, is a difference of purpose. The dialectical questioner aims at getting a conclusion *from an opponent*: and an opponent will usually have the opposite aim of not conceding that conclusion or anything which will lead to it. If we abstract from their form of presentation, then, premisses which would make for a totally perspicuous argument would yield a good demonstration and a bad dialectical argument for exactly the same reason, to wit, that it is obvious where it is leading. (Compare the remarks on concealment below, especially 156^a13–15.)

If we bear this in mind, then we shall be less tempted to think that dialectical argument has a deceptive character, as some have concluded. To begin with, a dialectical argument aims at drawing a conclusion which *actually does follow* from premisses an interlocutor accepts; if the conclusion only appears to follow, then the argument is not dialectical but contentious. At most, the procedures of concealment, etc., that we find here might keep an answerer from refusing to concede a premiss just in order to avoid an unwanted conclusion. But in that case, the answerer would probably have to fall back on answering on the basis of his actual opinions, and it is scarcely deceptive to show someone what consequences follow from his opinions.

155^b5. 'devising questions' (*erōtēmatizein*): this unusual word (from *erōtēma*, 'question', + verbal suffix-*izein*: 'questionize', 'devise questions') may be Aristotle's own coinage. It seems not to be a mere synonym for *erōtan*; it has a technical, perhaps slightly humorous ring. Aristotle uses it of the process of arranging (e.g. in thought) a series of questions to be asked in an exchange. As emerges from the discussion of this process (VIII. 1–3, 155ᵇ18–159ᵃ14), it is mostly a matter of keeping your opponent in the dark about what your argument actually is until it is too late.

There are two stages in determining the questions to put to an opponent. The first is the discovery of the premisses themselves, relying on the locations and the tables of accepted premisses. This is already 'directed at another', since the nature of the opponent must be taken into account in selecting the premisses. This would yield a bare-bones argument consisting of undecorated premisses and conclusion. The process of devising questions transforms this into a script for a dialectical exchange by setting the order in which the premisses will be presented and the verbal form in which they will be asked, and perhaps by adding other premisses for a variety of reasons. All this is then to be rehearsed mentally (presumably with allowances being made for various possible answers from the respondent).

Given the close association of Book VIII with an institutionalized form of dialectical exchange, all this can be seen as a very specific point in a round of gymnastic dialectic: we may imagine that after a pair of contestants has chosen or been assigned a thesis, the questioner is allowed some period of time in which to think through a strategy. However, it is equally plausible that Aristotle is offering relatively general advice on how to get ready for arguments with anyone.

155ᵇ10–16. 'close to the initial goal': since both dialectician and demonstrator start out with a conclusion and try to discover an argument for it, the conclusion to be proved is 'the initial thing' (*to ex archēs, to en archēi*): I supply 'goal' interpretatively. Aristotle makes frequent use of this phrase in the *Analytics* as well as the *Topics*, and it appears to have been an established technical term of dialectic. We find it in the phrase *to ex archēs aiteisthai*, 'asking for the initial thing', which is the ancestor of that somewhat bizarre English phrase 'begging the question' (see the Commentary on VIII. 13). In a dialectical exchange, the 'initial thing' sought is the contradictory of the answerer's position. In dialectical terminology, this may be called the 'problem' or 'thesis' (cf. 104ᵇ33–5), hence my translation (see below, 156ᵃ13, 156ᵇ5). 'Claims' (*axiōmata*): the word *axiōma* appears to take on a narrower technical sense (or senses) elsewhere (see *An. Post.* I. 2, 72ᵃ16–18, I. 7, 75ᵃ41–2, I. 10, 76ᵇ14–15; *Met.* B 2, 997ᵃ5–11, Γ 2, 1005ᵃ19–21, Γ 3, 1005ᵇ32–4), and there may in some cases be a justification for translating it as 'axiom'. However, Aristotle often uses it just to mean 'proposition' or 'premiss', as the Stoics later did (see e.g. 156ᵃ23). Its parent verb *axioun* often means 'claim' or 'have a right to' (cf. a premiss) in the rest of Book VIII (see the Commentary on 108ᵇ9–12), and it is reasonable to speak of the premisses of a demonstration as the demonstrator's 'claims'. Alternatively, the sense may be 'expectations', i.e. 'what the demonstration expects you already to know'.

155ᵇ17–28. 'Necessary' premisses: the phrase is verbally identical to that which Aristotle uses in the *Prior Analytics* to characterize modally necessary (as opposed to possible or assertoric) premisses. What is meant here, however, is 'premisses it is necessary to have in order to carry out the deduction'. 'Needful' might capture this better, but it is important to reproduce the verbal connection for historical reasons (for instance, it might be thought unlikely that Aristotle would have used 'necessary premiss' in the present sense after writing *An. Pr.* I).

The various sorts of 'non-necessary' premisses Aristotle lists do include some which have no effect on the deductive validity of the argument and only serve to make it fancy or harder for the respondent to comprehend (see 157ᵃ1–3, 6–13). However, the greater part of his attention under this head is given to the further premisses from which these 'necessary' premisses can be deduced or inductively inferred. Therefore 'necessary' is not contrasted with 'irrelevant' but rather with something like 'more than the minimum required for a deduction'. Alexander, calling on the theory of inference in *An. Pr.* I, takes this to mean 'the *two premisses* necessary for a deduction'. But all that Aristotle need mean is 'the premisses discovered by using an appropriate location'. (The plurals in 155ᵇ36–7, 'some by induction and others by deduction', suggest that Aristotle is not thinking of exactly two premisses.)

Aristotle lists four sorts of premiss it is legitimate to propose as questions, or rather four purposes which such a proposition may serve: it may be used as evidence for an induction, to add 'bulk' to the argument, to hide the conclusion, or to make the argument 'clearer'. As it appears, the first three of these really are concerned with 'concealment'. Of course, this will *not* be a matter of hiding the conclusion itself, since in a dialectical exchange both parties already know what it is that is being attacked or defended. Concealment is rather not letting your opponent see how you are trying to get to that conclusion. The fourth purpose, making the argument 'clearer', might seem to be opposed to this general aim, but as 157ᵃ14–17 show, Aristotle means 'making some *premiss* proposed clearer', i.e. making one's opponent more likely to accept it.

Although he makes no explicit mention of them in this list, he proceeds at once to distinguish a fifth class of 'unnecessary' premisses, namely, premisses from which the necessary premisses can be deduced. It might appear that these should be regarded as 'necessary' in the sense that they are not *deductively* superfluous to the argument (or to the argument that results from the substitution). In fact, we might think that such a replacement is analogous to the replacement of a premiss in a demonstration by further premisses from which it can be deduced. Since demonstrative science aims at just such a replacement, continued until the entire demonstration rests only on indemonstrable first principles, we might even think that in the present case there is a similar epistemic advantage. However, the epistemic situation in dialectic is different: the premisses must be something the respondent will accept. The procedure for finding premisses, as I have reconstructed it, will *already* have given us premisses our opponent is likely to concede. Replacing such a premiss with others from which it follows will not necessarily help us in a dialectical situation, and indeed may make things worse except in the lucky situation in which these other premisses are at least as acceptable to our opponent as the one they replace. Their real utility will lie, not in some superior epistemic status, but in the possibility that the answerer will not realize exactly why they are being put forward (i.e. to get further premisses from which the conclusion follows at once). Thus, their real value is for the purpose of concealment.

Aristotle's remarks about these four purposes are confusing. In keeping with his general position elsewhere that inductive generalization is how we establish universal propositions, he lists induction here as useful for obtaining 'necessary' premisses (155ᵇ34–7); later, however, it is classified (along with 'division') as an 'embellishment' (157ᵃ6–13). Induction itself is treated in only a few lines (156ᵃ4–7), which simply give a brief description of it. 'Bulk' is not clearly discussed anywhere, although that is probably the purpose of the section on 'embellishment'; 'clarity' gets a brief notice (157ᵃ14–17). Almost all of Aristotle's discussion (up to 157ᵃ5) is about 'concealment'.

155ᵇ24–5. 'should not obtain': most translators render this '*need* not try to get any other premisses', i.e. the types mentioned are all that is useful. But as the next sentence make clear, Aristotle's advice is that the four types mentioned are the only ones which *should* be introduced into an argument. Alexander gives it the even stronger sense 'it is *impossible* to take any further types of premisses' (522. 16–19), but this seems to me unwarranted.

155ᵇ26–8. Why is it *necessary* to use such devices? Presumably because there is no other way to bring the opponent we are faced with to the conclusion we are required to reach. But then, dialectic seems to blend insensibly into sophistical or combative argument, which reaches its conclusion by any means whatsoever. Such a result is probably unavoidable. It is really not possible to make sense of dialectic apart from the various uses to which it might be put, and these may include Socratic examination, argumentative persuasion, exercises for the improvement of dialectical skill, or philosophical inquiry. Greater or lesser degrees of trickery may be appropriate to these occasions: a Socratic refutation, for instance, must employ a little concealment if it is to be effective in revealing a subject's unrealized ignorance to him. Much the same thing could be said about our own uses of polemic, in philosophical writing and elsewhere.

155ᵇ29–156ᵃ26. This section outlines a general strategy for concealment making use of induction and a procedure called 'standing off'. We can best understand Aristotle's remarks if we remember that he is talking about the process of devising questions and that this process operates on an argument already discovered. Judging by the contents of the books of locations, this argument will probably be a simple one with only two or three premises from which the needed conclusion follows. However, a simple and obvious argument is hardly the way to proceed with an adversary who already knows the conclusion you are trying to establish and wants to avoid it: any reasonably perceptive respondent will see at once where you are going with your proposed premises and will try not to concede them. Therefore, you must find a way to conceal your *argument* even while getting your opponent to concede the premises you will need (the conclusion, of course, is already known to both parties and cannot be concealed).

Aristotle's general strategy for doing this is to add further layers of argument. Instead of actually putting forward the premises you want, offer other premises from which *those* premises can be derived. Failing that, put forward instances from which the needed premises can be got through induction; only ask for the actual premises you want as a last resort, or if they are highly obvious. The point of this process is not to strengthen the argument logically but to make its structure less apparent; the ideal is an argument in which all the premises can be stated without the answerer being able to see that the conclusion follows from them (156ᵃ13–15).

It is instructive to compare this notion with some Aristotle uses in *An. Pr.* I. He distinguishes there between 'complete' (*teleios*) and 'incomplete' (*atelēs*) deductions: the former are deductions in which it is manifest that the conclusion follows from the premises, the latter deductions in which this is not manifest. One of the products of the theory of the syllogism in *An. Pr.* I. 1–22 is a general account of how to transform any incomplete deduction into a complete one by adding additional steps between premises and conclusion. In the present case, Aristotle recommends what amounts to the use of deliberately incomplete deductions: we supply a set of premisses from which the conclusion we want follows through a variety of intermediate steps, but we do not supply the intermediate steps. (In 156ᵃ23–6 he recommends making it harder still by mixing up the order of the premisses.)

The strong contrast this implies between dialectical and scientific arguments seems to me a major difficulty for any interpretation that supposes dialectical argument can somehow establish scientific first principles. At the very least, such a view would have to regard this passage, and many others in Book VIII, as applying only to *some* dialectical arguments.

155ᵇ29–30. 'Standing off' is a matter of finding premisses from which the *premisses* of an argument follow, so that I 'stand off' from p by first discovering an argument for p and then discovering further arguments for the premisses of this argument (obviously, the process can be repeated for those further premisses, etc., each step leading to a greater degree of 'standing off'). It may be significant that essentially the same procedure plays a serious role in demonstrative science, where it is called 'packing full' or 'thickening' (*katapuknousthai*: see *An. Post.* I. 13). Parts of *An. Post.* I (especially I. 3, I. 19–22) are concerned with what we might call 'premiss regresses' in which a deduction is expanded in the same way by finding premisses from which its premisses follow, other premisses for those further premisses, etc.: Aristotle holds that in a demonstrative science, no such regress can go on indefinitely. From the standpoint of modern logic, the distinction between the premisses from which p follows and the premisses from which *those* premisses follow is imprecise at best: if a set S of premisses entails all the members of another set P, then S entails any statement p entailed by P. Even if we appeal to the order of steps in a deduction, there may be several deductive paths of different lengths from the same premisses to the same conclusion. In the relatively simple deductive theory of the *Prior Analytics*, however, it is easy to determine the shortest possible derivation of a given conclusion from given premisses.

155ᵇ34. 'If, however, he does not concede this': as Alexander points out, Aristotle's example shows that he thinks of induction and standing off as alternative means of obtaining a given 'necessary' premiss. The sense, then, is: if your opponent will not concede the more universal premiss needed for standing off, then try to get the *original* premiss you needed by induction.

155ᵇ35–156ᵃ3. The point of this somewhat tortuous passage seems to be this: standing off and induction have their value in concealment precisely because the answerer does not know what intermediate conclusion they are aimed at getting. However, this advantage would be lost if a questioner first tried to get a premiss outright and then, failing to get it, resorted to standing off or induction, for in that case the cat is out of the bag. There-fore, he advises, try standing off and induction *first*, and resort to putting forward the premiss itself only if these do not work.

156ᵃ3–10. The grammar of this passage is very difficult; as it seems to me, other translators have missed the point. It makes most sense if we see it as a complement to 155ᵇ35–156ᵃ3, which is about how to get *necessary* premisses. Here he explains how to get *additional* types of necessary premiss beyond those already mentioned at 155ᵇ19–24, explaining that they should be obtained for the sake of standing off or induction. And, since we have obtained them for that purpose, we then should use them in that way: some we shall use in inductions from particulars to universal; others, in preparatory deductions for the premisses from which the initial conclusion will follow.

156ᵃ5–7. 'from the familiar to the unfamiliar': Aristotle usually describes induction only as an inference from particular to general. He also holds that a scientific demonstration, which is a deduction, proceeds from more to less 'familiar' things. This clause must therefore be simply an explana-tory gloss, not part of the definition of induction. Elsewhere (e.g. *An. Post.* I. 2), Aristotle distinguishes between what is more familiar 'in itself' or 'by nature' and what is more familiar 'to us': the former include the first principles of sciences, the latter the objects of sensory perception. Alexan-der and others suppose the phrase 'either unconditionally or to most people' to be an allusion to this doctrine; but if it is, it is not a very easy one to catch.

156ᵃ7–9. 'when you are concealing': concealment here is a matter of making it hard to see where the argument is going by resting it on premisses at some logical distance from the conclusion (the degree of remoteness is a matter of the number of intervening steps of argument). As the remainder of the passage indicates, Aristotle recommends that we should obtain these premisses while trying not to divulge what we are going to do with them. Concealment of this sort may be deceptive, but it is not deceptive in the way that sophistical reasoning is deceptive (since all the arguments are supposed to be valid).

156ᵃ11–22. The 'conclusions' we are not supposed to state are the inter-mediate conclusions of preparatory arguments. Given the earlier sugges-tion to iterate the process of standing off, an ideal stealthy argument will consist of a set of premisses, from which the desired conclusion follows by many intermediate steps, but with none of those steps actually filled in. Thus, such an argument would contain neither actual inductions nor actual preparatory deductions, but only the materials from which to construct

them. Though Aristotle does not say so, presumably the questioner who
conceals in this way must be prepared, when challenged, to show that the
conclusion does indeed follow from the concessions made by the answerer.
Alexander supposes that this would require offering an 'analysis' that
supplied the intermediate steps. It is tempting to see here one possible
inspiration for the syllogistic theory itself.

156ᵃ11–12. 'deduce them all together later on': as Alexander observes,
Aristotle subsequently assumes that the intermediate conclusions are not
mentioned at all until the end of the argument. Therefore, he takes 'all
together' (*athroa*) to refer, not to these conclusions, but to the *premisses*:
get all the premisses at once, jumbled together in a heap, then state only
the desired conclusion. This does take care of one possible objection (if all
the other conclusions were actually drawn together, it would not be so
difficult to see why the main conclusion followed), but I do not see how to
get it out of the Greek. Aristotle may instead have in mind something like
this: get all the premisses you need without revealing your argumentative
strategy and then, once your answerer has made the necessary concessions,
work rapidly through all the steps of the argument to the ultimate conclusion in one continuous sweep.

156ᵃ13. 'the initial thesis': that is, the problem under discussion. According to I. 11, 104ᵇ34–6, 'thesis' and 'problem' were in practice interchange-
able terms. (See 156ᵇ5.)

156ᵃ19. 'spelt out' (*diarthrōthentōn*): literally, 'divided at the joints', 'articulated'. But even in anatomical contexts, Aristotle often uses this to
mean 'described in detail'. It is the opposite of 'described in outline': cf.
EN I. 7, 1098ᵃ20–4.

156ᵃ21. 'the premisses of that deduction' (*ta toutou lēmmata*): *lēmmata*
are 'things obtained'. If none of the premisses of a deduction is explicitly
stated and all are merely implicitly or potentially present as conclusions
from other premisses actually stated, then the deduction is at a kind of
maximum of incompleteness.

156ᵃ23–6. Continuing with his discussion of stealthy argumentation,
Aristotle recommends mixing up the premisses of different preparatory
deductions so as to confuse the answerer further. On 'claims' (*axiōmata*),
cf. 155ᵇ15, 159ᵃ4 and Commentary (the meaning is clearly 'premisses').
'Appropriate' premisses are those appropriate to a particular conclusion: 'if the premisses appropriate to each particular conclusion are
put together, it will be too obvious what those conclusions are going to
be'.

156ᵃ27–ᵇ3. In order to get a certain definition of a term, we should try first to get the corresponding definition of its *co-ordinate* (see the Introduction). It is a basic rule about *co-ordinates* that they have co-ordinate definitions: if F is a co-ordinate of G, then the definition of F will be an appropriate co-ordinate transformation of the definition of G (*Top.* VII. 3, 153ᵇ25–35). Therefore, if what we want to get is a definition of some term that has co-ordinates, we may instead try to get the co-ordinate definition of its co-ordinate. (Since we are asking for a premiss from which the premiss we want follows, this is an instance of standing off.)

This much is clear. What is less clear is the additional features of the case that Aristotle thinks make one coordinate easier to get than another. In the example, what we want is a definition of 'angry', and what we propose instead is the co-ordinate definition of its co-ordinate 'anger'. Aristotle says that an answerer might reject the proposed definition of 'angry' by offering a counter-example (the usual sense of 'objection': see 157ᵃ34–ᵇ33 and Commentary). He then says (i) this is probably not a valid objection; (ii) even so, it would be enough to permit an answerer to refuse the definition without seeming unreasonable; (iii) it would be harder to come up with the objection to the co-ordinate definition of 'anger'. But if the objection is not valid, then what is the advantage in making it harder to come up with? And if there were a valid objection, what would be the advantage in making *that* harder to find? In each case, the only advantage seems to be that the questioner makes a better showing (note that the advantage to the answerer in the case Aristotle imagines is that he does not *appear* to be rejecting the premiss without a reason).

Aristotle does not say why he thinks it is harder to find an objection to the definition of 'anger' than to the co-ordinate definition of 'angry', but the relevant point may be that the latter is more obviously a universal generalization: we look at once for an objection by asking 'Are there any angry people who do not want retribution because of an apparent slight?' It is less obvious what to look for in examining the definition of the abstract term 'anger'.

The word I translate 'fallaciously conclude' (*paralogizontai*) is usually associated with sophistical arguments, but here it means 'draw a conclusion that does not follow'. Evidently, Aristotle is calling attention to a common error in reasoning which a dialectician may exploit—presumably, failure to recognize the general rule that co-ordinate definitions of co-ordinates follow from one another. How could a questioner exploit this? Suppose that the answerer wrongly believes that *p* does not follow from *q* and consequently believes that one can accept *q* without accepting *p*. What good would it do to obtain *q* from *this* answerer as a means of obtaining *p*?

One possibility is that the questioner somehow appeals to judges, who overrule the answerer. A more satisfying possibility is that the questioner appeals to the general rule about co-ordinate definitions of co-ordinates, thus showing the answerer *why* he is mistaken.

156ᵇ4–9. These two sentences seem to offer independent advice, but in fact both involve concealment at a strategic level: keep your opponent in the dark about what premisses you are actually after and what you want to do with them. First, Aristotle proposes a strategy which exploits the procedure of concealment just discussed. An answerer skilled in dialectic will be aware that you may be engaged in 'standing off', advancing premisses useful for getting other premisses. If you can make it appear to such an answerer that that is what you are doing when, in fact, you are trying to obtain a premiss directly useful for the deduction of your conclusion, then you may have an easier time getting it accepted. (Presumably, sophisticated respondents will know that it is more work to argue from remote premisses, so they may be less reluctant to grant them.) As in fencing, so in dialectic: there are feints, and feinted feints.

Next, Aristotle advises against leading questions on the ground that the answerer will be inclined not to grant what you show yourself to want. His suggestion is to keep the answerer completely in the dark (rather than e.g. trying to make it look as if you want the opposite of what you want). Note that it is preferable to the questioner using Aristotle's method that the answerer respond as he really thinks.

156ᵇ10–17. The process described here is reminiscent of 'argument from example' as described in *An. Pr.* II. 24. Aristotle says that the 'universal gets by more readily' because in such an argument, the general premiss which comprehends all the examples is not actually used at all, as it is in induction (cf. again *An. Pr.* II. 23–4; this comparison is found in 69ª26–19). In effect, then, argument from example has the inferential power of argument from a generalization without the problems of first establishing the universal premiss.

We may wonder why Aristotle says the universal 'gets by' or 'escapes notice', since on his account it is not even used at all. Pacius' version of the text would give us 'it gets by more readily than the universal' (*mallon tou katholou*)—that is, the *argument* (or perhaps its conclusion) gets past an answerer better than an *argument* ('the universal') in which a universal premiss is required. Unfortunately, none of the manuscript sources appears to have had this reading. Another possibility is that the universal actually is present, but only implicitly: it is presupposed by the inference even if unstated (and if unstated it may escape the answerer's full attention).

The term I translate 'get answers' (*punthanesthai*) means 'find out through hearing', and Aristotle occasionally uses it of the questioner in a dialectical exchange (cf. *An. Pr.* I. 1, 24ᵇ10).

156ᵇ18–20. 'Playing fair in the attack' (*dikaiōs epicheirein*): in the *Topics*, *epicheirein* always means 'attack', not 'try'. What Aristotle recommends is clearly a matter of dissimulation: the point is to give an appearance, not of attacking *correctly*, but of being fair-minded.

156ᵇ25–7. An even more blatant species of dissimulation: make the premiss you need look like a mere illustration. Alexander offers a nice illustration: if the premiss you want is 'self-control is a virtue', then ask, 'Don't you think that, just as self-control is a virtue, so are courage and justice?' (531. 3–5).

156ᵇ27–30. This remark would be completely superseded by the preceding elaborate discussion of 'standing off'. Such passages probably result from the editorial process, whatever it was, through which our text of the *Topics* passed.

156ᵇ30–157ᵃ1. This is a purely tactical procedure, based (evidently) on observations of people's tendencies in arguments. On 'cantankerous' see VIII. 8 and Commentary. There is a certain malice in the remarks about people who 'think they are clever'.

157ᵃ1–5. Confuse your opponent by hiding the premiss you want among a heap of useless questions. 'Those who draw fake diagrams' (*pseudographountes*) appeared earlier in I. 1, 101ᵃ5–17 (see the Commentary on that passage and Excerpt C). The fake-prover's art rests on using diagrams that are not correctly drawn (e.g. certain lines shown to intersect cannot really do so, or lines claimed to be equal cannot be). This passage might be taken to suggest that outright deception forms part of the dialectician's arsenal, since fake proofs are clearly deceptive. But the point Aristotle is stressing is that these impossible diagrams typically include large numbers of *irrelevant* lines, making it harder to see how the trick works. Likewise, says Aristotle, it is often possible to get an adversary to accept premisses buried in a mass of irrelevancies which he would never accept if put forward all alone (presumably because in the latter case it would be obvious what conclusion would follow). 'The error': the diagram used in a fake proof must contain some impossibility, which is obscured by adding many irrelevant lines. I take this phrase to apply only to the case of the fake proof. The irrelevant premisses he is recommending that one add to a dialectical argument obscure how the argument *works*, not how it *deceives*: an argument that is invalid but appears valid is not dialectical but

contentious. 'Surreptitiously': the British idiom 'in a hole-and-corner manner' captures the sense of *en parabustōi* nicely, though it is meaningless to
most North Americans.

157ᵃ6–13. 'embellishment': this term seems to indicate that induction and
division are *merely* ornamental. But Aristotle regarded induction as an
important form of argument (cf. I. 12), and indeed he returns to it at length
in VIII. 2. Moreover, what he here calls division seems to be one of the
four instruments of I. 13. His present characterization of them as 'embel-
lishments' probably reflects the fact that his dialectical method is aimed
primarily at finding deductive arguments for a conclusion. Induction and
division will then be important, but only as subsidiary devices for establishing the premises used in a deduction.

There may also be a veiled criticism of Plato's concept of dialectic here.
As Alexander notes in his commentary (1. 16–19), Plato defined the dialectician's skill as consisting of the abilities to 'make one into many' (i.e.
divide a genus into its species) and 'make many into one' (i.e. collect
individuals into a species or species into a genus). Since the latter of these
may be identified with the purpose of induction, it appears that Aristotle
subordinates the two corner-stones of Platonic dialectic to the discovery of
deductions, the centrepiece of his own method (that would harmonize with
his harsh words about Platonic division in *An. Pr.* I. 31). But against this,
Aristotle himself encapsulates dialectical skill with almost the same words
at VIII. 14, 164ᵇ4–7 (see the Commentary on that passage).

157ᵃ14–17. The meaning of 'clarity' (*saphēneia*) is not entirely clear.
Aristotle's discussion suggests that examples and illustrations serve to
make the hearer better understand what we mean. Since the rules of
dialectic permit the answerer to say 'I don't understand' (see 160ᵃ18–19),
these may be intended to forestall such complaints, but they may simply
have the more general purpose of making the answerer understand (or at
least think he understands).

'from sources we know': any educated Athenian would know by heart
large portions of the Homeric poems, but the works of the epic poet
Choirilos would hardly be so well known (a rough parallel: '"as Shake-
speare says", not "as Albee says"'). Other translators (and Alexander)
suppose Aristotle is first making the point that illustrations should be
relevant and based on familiar things, then offering Homer's poetry as
exemplifying the right way, Choirilos' as exemplifying the wrong. I think
this is unlikely. The Choirilos referred to here is probably the fifth-century
epic poet from Samos whom Aristotle cites once or twice—with approba-
tion—in the *Rhetoric* (III. 14, 1415ᵃ3–4 and possibly 17–18). An Athenian
decree ordered that Choirilos' *Persica*, commemorating the Athenian

victory over Xerxes, be included in public recitations of Homer (*Rhet.* 1415ᵃ17–18 may be the *Persica*'s first lines), and this juxtaposition might explain Aristotle's choice of example. In any event, even if Choirilos did not enjoy Homer's unique status, there is no basis for Tricot's description of him as a 'bad poet'. Perhaps Tricot confused him with the notorious Choirilos of Iasos.

CHAPTER 2

157ᵃ18–21. Aristotle 'discussed this earlier' in I. 12 (induction is 'more persuasive' and 'common to the public', deduction is 'more compelling' and 'more effective' against *antilogikoi*); cf. also VIII. 14, 164ᵃ12–16. Nothing here suggests that induction is merely an ornament.

157ᵃ21–ᵇ33. To understand these remarks concerning induction, we must keep in mind that an inductive argument will begin within a series of questions about cases:

Is x_1 F? (Yes)
.   .   .
Is x_n F? (Yes)

After gaining these concessions, the questioner's next step would be to 'put the universal as a question', that is, ask for the universal generalization which these cases support. This will introduce some second general term, G, of which x_1, etc., are instances:

Is every G F?

A respondent who has assented to all the cases is under an obligation to assent to the universal or provide a counter-example, if asked (Aristotle discusses the details below and in VIII. 8).

157ᵃ21–33. The first problem Aristotle discusses points up an important difference between his conception of inductive arguments and most modern accounts. The latter suppose that the particular cases take the form '*x* is both G and F', so that each already contains both universal terms. What the inductive step introduces is simply a universal quantifier. However, this is clearly *not* what Aristotle has in mind, since otherwise an induction could not even be stated without having a general term for all its cases. His cases have instead the form '*x* is F', and the inductive step introduces the second universal as well as the generalization. This second universal must pick out what it is that all the cases have in common. If we cannot find such a term, we can still 'ask for the universal', but our question must take the much less satisfactory form 'Is every *such* thing F?'

Aristotle says that such anonymous generalizations should be avoided because they are too hard to deal with: lacking a universal which says what the various cases are cases of, questioner and answerer may fall into dispute about what counts as a similar case, and it will be possible for clever questioners (or answerers) to engage in cheating. Therefore, if no general term is available, we should coin one for the express purpose of covering the cases we want. This may seem to contradict his earlier discussion of 'argument from likeness' (156ᵇ10–17), which described the absence of an explicit universal generalization as the strong point of such arguments. However, he may be contrasting arguments in which a universal generalization is sought for its own sake with those in which it is sought only in order to infer from it one of its instances.

Compare Aristotle's note of the utility of a study of likenesses to inductive arguments at I. 18, 108ᵇ7–12. On coining names for unnamed universals, cf. *An. Post.* I. 5, 74ᵃ6–32; *An. Pr.* I. 35, I. 39. The assumed picture of induction is worth comparing with the notoriously problematic discussion in *An. Post.* II. 19, which also deals with the emergence of a universal from individual cases.

157ᵃ23. 'common name': since the names in question apply to 'similarities', not similar things, this most likely means 'commonly accepted name' rather than 'common name for all cases'.

157ᵃ27–9. 'hoodwink' (*parakrouontai*): this verb is often used, in Aristotle or elsewhere, of deception by means of fallacious arguments (thus it is a close synonym of *paralogizesthai*). AT *SE* 1, 165ᵃ13–17, Aristotle uses it of people skilled in numerical calculations who cheat the unskilled (see also *Pol.* IV. 12, 1297ᵃ10).

'some saying . . . others objecting': judging by what follows, these alternatives probably refer to questioners and answerers respectively.

157ᵃ30–3. 'similarly designated' (*homoiōs legetai*): this idiom recalls *monachōs legetai*, 'said in one way', and its contrasting 'said in many ways'. However, I do not see how the ambiguity of a term can be involved here. The problem is instead to determine whether the various cases of the induction fall under the same universal as the additional case we need to draw a conclusion about. Lacking a universal to characterize the similarity, this might be disputed, but once an appropriate term is coined those disputes are avoided. The point of the last sentence may be that cases which we at first think will fall under the same designation lose this similarity if we try actually to coin a single term to cover them all.

157ᵃ34–ᵇ33. An 'objection' (*enstasis*) is a counter-example to a generalization. As this section makes clear, the rules of dialectical exchanges permit a questioner to insist that an answerer who has conceded the cases of an induction either concede the generalization or provide a counter-example ('ask for an objection' is a technical term for the questioner's demand for such a counter-example).

157ᵃ34–7. It is the questioner's right to ask for counter-examples only in the specific case when the answerer has conceded the inductive steps but rejected the generalization. If the questioner simply asks 'Is every F G?' without a preceding objection, the answerer may say 'No' with no obligation to provide counter-examples. 'Your right': *dikaion* can simply mean 'legitimate', but the point here is to clarify the circumstances under which the questioner can require of the answerer something other than assent or dissent.

157ᵃ37–ᵇ2. The case presupposed by this further constraint on the answerer appears to be an induction followed by an inference to another instance: the answerer has conceded the cases and also conceded 'Every G is F' but now balks at the instance '*a* is F'. It is not clear just what the constraint is, but the most plausible solution is that when confronted with the unwanted case, the answerer decides to retract his earlier assent to the universal and uses that very case as the objection. The rule then appears to be: you can only do this if this case is the *unique* exception to the general rule. On a narrower interpretation, 'the very case proposed' would refer to the thesis under discussion. The implicit rule would then be that the answerer could appeal to this way out only if that thesis concerned a unique exception.

157ᵇ2–8. The advice here, which is obvious enough, would be a natural instance of applying the counsels of Book I about studying multiple senses of terms so as to be able to disarm such equivocations in advance.

157ᵇ8–33. Finally, Aristotle considers how to deal with a *sound* objection to a generalization. Overall, the tactic is straightforward: add a condition to the generalization that will avoid the objection. Thus, we replace 'Every G is F' with 'Every G which is H is F', and continue in this manner until (if we are successful) the answerer concedes a premiss we can use.

157ᵇ24–8. If we follow Aristotle's own claim that objections arise only in connection with inductions, then this passage must be recommending a means of forestalling objections. Evidently, the situation is this: the answerer has accepted the cases of an induction but refused the generalization. Before demanding an objection, the questioner then proposes instead a narrower generalization, subtracting a possible counter-example; this deprives the questioner of the example he was about to give, and he is therefore compelled to assent. Aristotle may have in mind deliberately choosing a generalization to which there is an obvious objection, then replacing it with a narrower generalization to throw the answerer off guard.

157ᵇ28–30. It seems not only obvious, but trivially so, that we cannot salvage a generalization by this kind of restriction unless it is indeed true in some cases and false in others. However, Aristotle may be supposing that these generalizations are stated (as are all his examples) without explicit quantification (thus making them all 'indefinite' in the terminology of the *An. Pr.* I. 1, 24ᵃ19–22 and *De Int.* 10). Statements of the forms 'A is B' or 'As are Bs' sometimes express universal generalizations ('Dogs are mammals'), sometimes things true for the most part ('Dogs make good pets'), and sometimes things true only sometimes ('Dogs bite'). Thus, Aristotle may be advising us to take note of which type of statement is actually being made.

157ᵇ31–3. In view of the discussion in I. 10, this can hardly be intended as a *definition* of 'dialectical premiss'. I suggest that Aristotle is thinking of what it is to *secure* or *obtain* a premiss in a dialectical argument: accepting a number of instances of a generalization and offering no objection just is to accept the generalization, in a dialectical context.

157ᵇ34–158ᵃ2. A number of difficulties arise concerning this brief passage. It will help to begin with a general picture of 'argument through the impossible' based on some of what Aristotle says elsewhere. He thinks of such an argument as consisting of two parts. One is the 'deduction *of* an impossible':

> Premiss₁
> . . .
> Premissₙ
> Assume that H
> (argumentative steps)
> Therefore, A (which is evidently impossible)

Given this deduction *of* an impossibility, we then conclude '*through* the impossible' that H is false (see *An. Pr.* I. 44, 50ᵃ29–38; *An. Post.* I. 26). This two-part conception forms the basis of Aristotle's present advice. A straightforward (*direct* in modern terms) deduction of a conclusion stands on its own: once the respondent has accepted the premisses, nothing more is needed to establish the conclusion. However, in a deduction through the impossible we must obtain the further admission that the 'impossible' result deduced really is impossible, and this leaves room for the respondent to protest.

This points up an important difference between Aristotle's way of understanding *reductio ad absurdum* argument and most modern conceptions. For Aristotle, the impossible result is simply an *obvious falsehood*: something which anyone would know to be false, or even something which the respondent has already agreed to be false. Thus, he says that arguments through the impossible resemble arguments from an assumption but differ in that no 'prior agreement' need be made since the falsehood of the impossibility deduced is obvious (*An. Pr.* I. 44, 50ᵃ32–8). By contrast, rules of *reductio ad absurdum* in modern formal systems typically specify that if from a set of premisses and an assumption H we can deduce a *self-contradictory* proposition (i.e. usually, a proposition of the form 'P and not P'), then we may infer the denial of H. Aristotle does not indicate that impossibilities are restricted to logical falsehoods.

So described, argument through the impossible may be distinguished from two other notions. The first is indirect proof, which has the following structure:

> Premiss$_1$
> .   .   .
> Premiss$_n$
> _____
> ~H (denial of the intended conclusion)
> .   .   .
> ~(Premiss$_k$)
> H

That is, if from a set of premisses and the denial of H we can deduce the denial *of one of the premisses*, then we may infer H. Examples of such arguments abound in Greek mathematics.

The second notion is something which Aristotle himself calls 'converting' (*antistrephein*) in VIII. 14 below. This is a process of transformation which derives one *deduction* from another. Suppose that the following is a valid argument:

> P$_1$
> .   .   .
> P$_n$
> _____
> C

Then if we replace *any* premiss P$_k$ by the denial of the conclusion ~C and the conclusion by the denial of that premiss ~P$_k$, the result is also a valid argument:

P₁
.   .   .
~C
.   .   .
Pₙ
_____
~Pₖ

This 'conversion' is a much more abstract process than argument through the impossible, since it allows the transformation of one *argument* into another. It can be used to show that an entire class of arguments of one form is valid by showing how to transform each such argument into another known to be valid: this is exactly what Aristotle himself does repeatedly in the proofs of the validity of syllogistic forms in *An. Pr.* I. 1–22. It is not clear how Aristotle understood the relationships among these various procedures. In *An. Pr.* II. 8–10 he discusses 'conversion', and following this (*An. Pr.* II. 11–13) he discusses deduction through impossibility; for one account of the difference between the two see 61ᵃ18–27.

'When it is possible to deduce': in the *Prior Analytics* Aristotle argues that *any* conclusion which can be reached by argument through the impossible can be reached without it, and *vice versa* (*An. Pr.* I. 29, 45ᵃ25–ᵇ11; II. 14, 62ᵇ38–63ᵇ21). Since these claims depend heavily on the theory of inference of *An. Pr.* I, which is generally not in evidence in the *Topics*, this might be taken as evidence that the *Topics* reflects an early stage in Aristotle's development as a logician. However, it might equally well indicate that he is trying to keep logical theory to a minimum.

'it makes no difference': Waitz notes that this seems to be inconsistent with *An. Post.* I. 29, which argues that proof through the impossible is inferior, and takes this as evidence that the *Topics* reflects a relatively undeveloped stage of Aristotle's thought. But it can also be argued that this *Posterior Analytics* text itself seems ignorant of the doctrines of the *Prior Analytics* (see Smith 1982, 1986); moreover, VIII. 14 shows Aristotle fully in command of the more abstract inferential procedure essential to the proofs of *An. Pr.* I. 1–22.

158ᵃ3–6. The first case seems identical with that mentioned above in 157ᵃ32–3. Therefore, it is the second case which is probably being emphasized: an objection that the answerer will be hard put to think of is as good as no objection at all.

158ᵃ7–13. To judge from this passage, the questioner was allowed (perhaps even expected) to state the ultimate conclusion in an exchange rather than putting it as a question. These lines raise an important issue about dialectical argument. Forcing an opponent to a conclusion requires not simply getting that opponent to concede premises which imply it but also getting the opponent to concede *that* they imply it: and what is to stop an adversary from simply denying that the conclusion follows? If only those opponents can be successfully refuted who agree that they have been refuted, then—paradoxically—slow-witted opponents will have a natural advantage; and what is to stop even clever ones from using this response? It may be that Aristotle supposes an audience to be present which can pass judgement on this point and award victory to the questioner. However, the phrase 'to those who do not understand . . .' might equally well mean that logically inexperienced audiences are sometimes taken in by this same device. We have, then, a sort of antithesis to the kind of contentious argument that appears to be valid but is not: an argument which actually is valid but does not appear to be so.

158ᵃ14–24. It is a basic rule of dialectical exchanges that the questioner must supply the premises for assent or dissent: all that the answerer is required to do, except under certain defined circumstances, is to say 'yes' or 'no'. Therefore, if the questioner needs something like a definition or a distinction of senses, he must formulate it for himself and try to get the answerer's assent (compare here the examples in I. 4, 101ᵇ29–33).

'At the same time': this suggests, if tentatively, yet another exception to the general restriction of answers to assent and dissent, namely, that an answerer who rejects a premiss stipulating the various senses of a term might be required to offer an alternative one.

158ᵃ25–30. 'a long time presenting a single argument': the verb I translate 'present' means 'ask', but dialectical arguments are always presented by asking questions; Aristotle is not only referring to asking the same *question* repeatedly but, generally, to spending excessive time on one argument. He outlines four possibilities. Either (i) the respondent is answering the questions, or (ii) he is not. If (i), then either (i*a*) the questioner is asking lots of different questions, or (i*b*) he is repeatedly asking the same question. But if (i*a*), he must have no argument, for no argument has a large number of premisses; and if (i*b*), he is rambling. In either case, it is clear that the questioner is doing a bad job. On the other hand, if (ii), then it is also clear that the questioner is doing a bad job because what he should do is either fault the answerer for not answering or abandon the argument.

The general principle that any very lengthy argument is bad (at least in dialectic) does not necessarily conflict with Aristotle's earlier counsels about 'stretching out' an argument (157ᵃ1–5): there is a difference between a long argument and a *very* long argument.

'Ramble' (*adoleschein*): sometimes, this term denotes a specific error in argument (also called 'saying the same thing twice') illustrated in the following example. Suppose that we define 'snub' as 'concave nose'; then, since we may always substitute a term's definition for it, 'snub nose' becomes 'concave nose nose', which—so goes the complaint—is nonsense. But nothing of the sort is involved here. Elsewhere Aristotle uses *adoleschein* to mean 'talk garrulously', 'chatter idly' (*Rhet.* 1390^a9, *EN* 1117^b35).

CHAPTER 3

158^a31–159^a2. Despite its opening sentence, the main purpose of this section is to explain what the questioner should do when confronted with a thesis that is 'hard to deal with', that is, when it is hard to find premisses that will yield the conclusion needed. The section as a whole is difficult, in part because of some terminological peculiarities; an interpretative summary will be useful. Aristotle's main point is that any thesis that is 'hard to deal with' has one of three properties: (i) what we need in order to establish the conclusion we want is a definition; (ii) some terms in the thesis may be equivocal and may be used metaphorically, without this being clear; (iii) the conclusion we need is close to 'the starting-points'.

The background Aristotle proposes is unusual for the *Topics*. He supposes that the questioner's role is much like that of a geometer searching for a proof of a proposition. The time-honoured way of doing this is to 'work backwards', i.e. ask what premisses would give us what we want, what further premisses would give us those, etc., until we reach something we have already established. Greek mathematicians called this 'analysis': evidently the term was already in use by Aristotle's time. We also know that his mathematical contemporaries were already producing systematic mathematical treatises in which propositions were proved in series, beginning with the most basic and proceeding to the more complex, and that in such treatments the proofs of later propositions depended on or incorporated the proofs of earlier ones. As I have interpreted it, the method of discovering premisses presupposed in the *Topics* also works backwards from conclusion to premisses, and therefore Aristotle may regard it as appropriate to compare the two.

A systematic development has the advantage that we can build on what we have already established. This works in both directions, provided we take up propositions in the right order: if we have established the things we need for a proof of a proposition, then it will be relatively easy to find its proof by working backwards to them. But there are two cases in which it may be particularly difficult to find a proof of a proposition in developing such a treatise. First, if the proposition is one that depends for its proof on a large number of others, then its proof, in full form, will include the proofs of those others; therefore, discovering it from scratch will be quite difficult. Such propositions are 'by nature last'. Second, if the proposition is a fundamental one which we shall require in the proofs of many others, we must find a proof for it before we have built up any body of proofs to call on. Such propositions are 'by nature first'; in establishing them, we shall have little to call on except the definitions of the fundamental notions used in the theory.

These are, I think, the cases Aristotle has in view in 158ª32–b4. The 'first things' are the propositions which should by nature come at the beginning of our treatment; they 'require definition' in that the *only* means of proving them is appealing to appropriate definitions. The 'last things' are not necessarily 'last' in any absolute sense, but we may think of them as the most advanced theorems our treatise aims at establishing. Strictly speaking, their proofs will rest on many subordinate propositions; anyone who wants to discover such an argument straight off will have to find all those intermediate steps. Thus, the lack of intermediate *results* to call on makes the first type hard to prove, whereas the large number of intermediate *steps* needed does so for the second.

This interpretation fits best with the geometrical example in 158b29–159ª1. Aristotle says that some geometrical theorems are virtually impossible to prove unless you have the right definition available, in which case the proof becomes obvious. These are 'the first of the elements'. He says that in mathematics, those propositions were called 'elements' the proofs of which were 'implicit in the proofs of others' (*Met.* B 3, 998ª25–7; Δ 3, 1014ª35–b2). This sense (which is the sense in which the propositions in Euclid's *Elements* are elements) fits exactly here: the 'first elements' are the first consequences of the definitions in a systematic treatise on mathematics, and these will use no other previously proved propositions in their proofs. The definitions required are the definitions of the 'principles' (*archai*), i.e. the basic constituents of the subject-matter of the proofs. In the case of geometry, these are points and lines.

What Aristotle says here is readily liable to misinterpretation because of what he has to say elsewhere, especially in the *Posterior Analytics*, about demonstrative sciences. It is a fundamental thesis of that work that every demonstration must proceed from 'starting-points' or 'first principles' which are themselves indemonstrable *propositions* (on some interpretations, they are in fact definitions). Here the 'principles' Aristotle mentions are not propositions but ingredients or constituent elements; and the 'first things' are not indemonstrable (since their proofs follow from definitions).

These terminological inconsistencies have made this passage an especially difficult one for commentators and translators.

A final problem of terminology is the word *epicheirein*. Throughout most of Book VIII this in effect means 'what the questioner does', in contrast to *hupechein* (which is what the answerer does). Since what the questioner does is try to refute the answerer's thesis, 'attack' is usually a good translation. (In wider Greek usage, it often means 'attempt'; its root sense is 'lay hands on'.) In the present case, it has another force. The questioner attacks by constructing a deduction of the denial of the answerer's thesis; therefore, *epicheirein* comes to mean 'construct a deduction'. Thus, the cognate noun *epicheirēmata* is used in 158ᵃ35 of attempted *proofs* (I translate 'argumentative attempts').

158ᵃ31–2. 'The same assumptions': 'assumptions' means 'premisses'. A different ranking in terms of ease of attack appears in *Topics* VII. 5, classifying in accordance with the four predicables. Definitions are harder to defend and easier to attack than any of the other predicables because there are more criteria which must be met in order to show that something is a definition; by the same token, accidents are the easiest predicable to defend, the hardest to attack. Another classification appears in *An. Pr.* I. 26, this time by categorical sentence type, with the criterion for 'ease of attack' the number of different argument forms (syllogistic moods, in traditional parlance) which can have a conclusion of the relevant type. The use of 'assumptions' here is similar to that of 'problems' at 158ᵇ16 or 'theses' at 158ᵃ24, 159ᵃ3.

158ᵃ36–7. 'beginning from the appropriate starting-points': Aristotle frequently claims that genuine demonstrations must be from the 'appropriate starting-points' that is, the basic principles of the relevant discipline. Sophistical demonstrations attempt to prove things from 'common' starting-points, and hence they fail actually to prove. In this respect, they have some resemblance to dialectical arguments (see Excerpt C). Here and at 158ᵇ2 it seems that 'starting-point' means 'basic premiss', not 'basic element'.

158ᵃ37–ᵇ1. 'answerers neither expect definitions': though Aristotle's attention is on demonstrations, his subject is really dialectical argument, and in such arguments a questioner cannot make use of a definition unless it is conceded by the answerer. The sense may be: 'answerers do not think themselves bound by definitions questioners want to use; therefore, if a definition is required to establish a conclusion, it will be hard to establish it'.

158ᵇ5–8. The first cause of being 'hard to deal with' was 'needing a definition', which applies primarily to naturally first propositions; the second cause, being 'too close to the beginning', applies to propositions which, though not naturally first and thus not requiring definitions, come early in the development of a system of deductions. It will be relatively hard to find proofs for these because at an early stage, few intermediate results will be available to use.

158ᵇ8–15. The third cause of being 'hard to deal with' has three ingredients: (i) some term in the thesis may have more than one sense; (ii) this term may also have been used metaphorically; (iii) it is not clear which of these things is going on. If the term in question is in fact equivocal, then distinguishing senses will lead to a means of attack. If, on the other hand, it is used metaphorically, then the answerer's thesis itself can be criticized for unclarity. Neither of these is especially difficult; the hard case with which Aristotle is concerned here is one which contains an equivocal term that may *also* be metaphorical. Since these require different courses of action, the questioner is faced with the problem of deciding whether to attack the thesis (as equivocal) or complain that it is unclear because metaphorical. (On 'criticism' see VIII. 11).

Aristotle says he is talking about the hardest *definitions* to deal with, but almost immediately he extends this to all kinds of problems (158ᵇ16–23). He may be giving special prominence to definitions here because the other causes of being hard to deal with cannot apply to definitions.

158ᵇ16–23. 'In general, you should assume': a problem is hard to deal with just so long as we do not yet know what makes it that way, for once we discover the cause we can remove it. Consequently, we should bear in mind that the cause is always one of these three, for then our only task will be to discover which one it is.

158ᵇ33–5. 'Reciprocal subtraction' (*antanhairesis*) is a process for finding the greatest common measure of two magnitudes parallel to Euclid's algorithm for finding the greatest common divisor of two numbers. Let A and B be lines, with A longer than B. Repeatedly subtract B from A until the remainder is less than B; subtract this remainder from B until a remainder less than it remains, and continue in the same manner, stopping only if an even fit is found. Two pairs of magnitudes A, B and A', B' have the same 'reciprocal subtraction' if the number of times each line is subtracted is the same for corresponding steps in the procedure as applied to each. Euclid's algorithm, the corresponding procedure applied to integers, always terminates; however, reciprocal subtraction for lines may go on indefinitely without reaching an exact fit (in which case the lines are shown to be

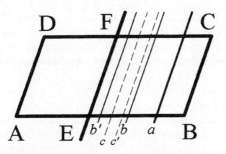

Note. Reciprocal subtraction of line segments AE, EB: (1) mark off on EB at *a* a segment equal to AE, leaving remainder *a*B less than AE; (2) from *a*, mark off at *b*, *b'* segments equal to *a*B, leaving remainder *b'*E; (3) from *b'*, mark off at *c*, *c'* segments equal to *b'*E, etc. The process continues until a remainder is reached which exactly divides the preceding segment.

incommensurable.) As Aristotle says, the application of this definition to the case of parallelograms and their sides is obvious if a figure is drawn (see above). The definition of proportionality in terms of reciprocal subtraction is older than the famous definition of Eudoxus (preserved in Euclid, *Elements*); this passage is important evidence concerning the early development of Greek mathematics (see Knorr 1975 for further discussion).

159ᵃ3–14. Aristotle switches briefly to the answerer's viewpoint. If the questioner proposes a premiss which you know to be harder to establish than the conclusion needed, what should you do? If you refuse it and thus require the questioner to argue for it, then you will be substituting a harder problem than the original one (in effect, the refusal makes the premiss into a problem). On the other hand, if you concede it, then you will be letting yourself be convinced from premisses less convincing than the conclusion (i.e., the argument will be a sham from an epistemic standpoint). Aristotle says: decide which of these is to be avoided and answer accordingly. In II. 5, 111ᵇ32–112ᵃ15, Aristotle discusses a 'sophistical' device that recalls this situation: try to get the answerer to concede a premiss (perhaps totally irrelevant to the thesis) which you already know how to refute. See also *An. Pr.* II. 25 on 'leading away' (*apagein*).

The closing remarks about teachers and learners are among the few in which Aristotle presents dialectical arguments in the role of instruction. It is tempting to suppose that an argument that teaches is a demonstration, or at least a demonstration transformed into a series of questions and answers. However, Aristotle says here that learners should only concede

what is more familiar. If this means 'what is more familiar *to them*', then
the resulting arguments cannot be demonstrations: Aristotle says many
times that what is more familiar to the uninstructed is generally less familiar in itself, and it is the latter standard that must apply to demonstrative
premises.

CHAPTER 4

159ᵃ15–32. Aristotle now turns his attention to the answerer's role, which
occupies him until the end of VIII. 10 (161ᵃ15). The general descriptions of
the tasks of questioner and answerer given here are refined immediately
below (159ᵃ26–36). Note that these goals are compatible and even complementary: it is quite possible for a questioner to succeed in deducing absurd
consequences from an answerer's thesis and for that answerer at the same
time to make it clear that these consequences follow as a result of the thesis
itself.

Somewhat different accounts of the roles of questioner and answerer
emerge in the section immediately following: see the Commentary on
159ᵃ38–160ᵃ16.

159ᵃ18–19. 'lead' (*epagagein*): the technical sense 'perform an induction'
would be out of place here.

159ᵃ25–37. The functions of questioner and answerer require further
definition in the case of answerers in 'arguments for the sake of exercise
and testing'. Aristotle discusses these additional details in 159ᵃ38 ff. But
first he digresses to distinguish three kinds of argument. In one, the questioner is a teacher and the answerer a learner; in the next, the questioner
and answerer are competitors, and the goal is victory; and the third kind is
'arguments for the sake of testing and inquiry'. To determine what these
three varieties are, we must look further afield for remarks on the different
sorts of argumentative practice and their goals. The most informative texts
are in the *Sophistical Refutations* (*SE* 2; *SE* 8, 169ᵇ23–9; *SE* 9, 170ᵇ8–11; *SE*
10–11, 171ᵃ28–ᵇ12, 172ᵃ21–36). What Aristotle says is not always clear and
may not be consistent; my interpretation tries to bring out the main lines of
his proposals.

Five types of situation involving argument make appearances in the
Topics: demonstration, rhetorical argument, contentious or sophistical argument, dialectical argument for the purpose of practice and inquiry, and
'testing' arguments (see the Introduction for further discussion). The first
two do not involve question and answer, although they may have an
audience. The demonstrator presents premises as statements, not questions, which the learner or hearer must simply accept, while the rhetori-

128

cian's audience simply listens. Each of the remaining three types of argument is dialectical in that it is put by a questioner to an answerer, and in each the questioner's ultimate goal is refutation. Though this takes different forms in the three cases, refutation is always a matter of starting with some initial thesis granted by the answerer and then getting further concessions, ultimately leading to an absurd or impossible result.

Contentious arguments are a form of combat, and the questioner's motive is to win at all costs. It makes no particular difference whether the absurd consequences deduced actually follow from the answerer's concessions or whether the answerer actually believes what he concedes; the questioner's goal is to *appear* to refute (to an audience or to an opponent).

'Testing' arguments are modelled on Socratic refutation and have as their goal bringing to light the answerer's unrecognized ignorance by exposing inconsistencies which follow from his opinions. Thus their purpose is educative, not combative. If they are to achieve this purpose, they must rest on the answerer's actual opinions: the answerer must therefore always say what he thinks.

Arguments for the sake of inquiry are most likely the formal dialectical exchanges presupposed by Book VIII. These seem to have two purposes. First, the participants improve their skill in argument. Second, these exercises are a means for exploring the consequences of different opinions as a part of philosophical inquiry. In either case, it is important to this variety of argument that the refutations produced are logically valid, i.e. that the contradictions deduced actually follow from the premises conceded. However, the opinions of the answerer are no longer at issue. Instead, the answerer undertakes to represent a particular point of view: perhaps the point of view of a specific philosopher, or a type of person, or perhaps the point of view of 'common opinion'.

On this interpretation, 'inquiry', 'testing', and 'exercise' are three different functions which can be served by dialectical argument in the broad sense. Exercise and inquiry are the goals of more formalized dialectical exchanges. Dialectic pursued for these goals would tend to presuppose participants who are more or less on an equal footing and understand the rules of the dialectical game. It is more difficult to say in what context testing might have taken place, but it might sometimes involve a more naïve answerer (especially if we take Plato's dialogues as portraits of testing dialectic). We may speculate that all three sorts of argument formed part of the philosophical education of the Early Academy: those newer to the subject would be put to the test more frequently, whereas those who had acquired some skill would pursue arguments for practice and inquiry. (For other views on the roles of questioner and answerer in this type of argument, see Ryle 1968, Brunschwig 1986, Bolton 1990.)

The syntax of 159ª25-37 is awkward. Aristotle says, 'Since it has not been defined just what these functions are in the case of dialectical arguments for testing and exercise and nothing has been said about this before, I shall try to say something myself.' However, in the midst of the sentence he launches into an explanatory digression (159ª26) and does not get back on track until 159ª36 (I have somewhat freely translated *oun* as 'to get back to the point').

CHAPTER 5

159ª25. 'But since': VIII. 5 begins here in the traditional chapter divisions, but a break would obscure the continuity of the argument.

159ª38-160ª16. The rules in this section apply to answerers in dialectical exchanges for the purposes of inquiry and practice: testing arguments presuppose answerers who answer according to their own opinions. Aristotle insists that this is his own original contribution. We might wish to see it as the counterpart, from the answerer's viewpoint, of another aspect of his method, namely, his emphasis on the importance of collecting and classifying accepted views. In order to follow the advice he gives here, an answerer would have to have a systematic compilation of *endoxa*.

Earlier, Aristotle said that the questioner's goal was to deduce the most unacceptable consequences possible from the answerer's thesis. Now he adopts a different perspective: the questioner's goal is to *deduce the denial of the answerer's thesis* from other premises conceded by the answerer. This is in accordance with the definition of 'refutation' in *SE* 1 as 'a deduction together with the denial of the conclusion' (165ª2-3; see also *SE* 2, 165ᵇ3-4, *SE* 9). This latter definition seems to be Aristotle's more considered opinion, since it treats refutations simply as a species of deduction (cf. *An. Pr.* II. 20). But these definitions are not equivalent. If my goal is to deduce absurd consequences from a given thesis, then I must use that thesis as a premiss; however, there is no specific absurdity which I must aim to deduce. If, on the other hand, my goal is to deduce the contradictory of a given thesis, then there is a specific conclusion at which I must aim and the initial thesis is not a premiss I can use. The remarks in VIII. 5-6 on answering make sense only in the latter context, since they require comparing the premises proposed with the desired conclusion.

159ª38-ᵇ35. In this section, Aristotle presupposes that propositions can be compared to one another with respect to acceptability. Given a scale of acceptability, the decision whether to accept or reject a premiss depends on two things: (i) its intrinsic level of acceptability, (ii) whether it is more or less acceptable than the conclusion. Briefly, his rules are these:

1. If the thesis itself is unacceptable (and thus the conclusion acceptable), concede only those premisses which are both acceptable and more acceptable than the conclusion.

2. If the thesis itself is acceptable (so that the conclusion is unacceptable), concede any premiss which is either acceptable or less unacceptable than the conclusion.

3. If the thesis itself is neither acceptable nor unacceptable (so that the conclusion is likewise), concede anything which is either acceptable or more acceptable than the conclusion.

These are just the obvious consequences of the general rule: the premisses must be more acceptable than the conclusion. Aristotle presents this here as, in effect, the dialectical counterpart of the requirement that in a demonstration, the premisses must be 'more intelligible' or 'more familiar' than the conclusion (159ᵇ8–9). This does not appear to be a general constraint on dialectical arguments, although the evidence is not conclusive. I would suggest that it is peculiar to dialectic for exercise and inquiry. Obviously, any serious attempt to apply these rules would presuppose an ability to make very fine distinctions of levels of acceptability. Aristotle does not tell us much about how that is done (see e.g. I. 10); compilations of *endoxa* might be ordered in such a way.

The standard of comparison itself may also be varied: acceptability may be measured either 'without qualification' (*haplōs*) or with reference to the opinions of some individual or some type of person. This at first recalls the varieties of *endoxa* listed in I. 10, although for present purposes we would also have to presuppose an ordering by degree of acceptability within each. However, the only cases of 'qualified' acceptables are those acceptable to the answerer and those acceptable to a specific person (see 159ᵇ23–35). (For an alternative view see Bolton 1990, which argues that the types of *endoxa* themselves are actually degrees of acceptability.)

159ᵇ8–9. 'Since whoever deduces well': we might take the requirement that the premisses be 'more familiar' than the conclusion to mean that the questioner must draw on premisses which the answerer more readily believes than the conclusion. However, Aristotle is here giving instructions to the answerer, not to the questioner. This shows that the standard for judging what is more familiar is not the answerer's own reactions, but instead an external criterion of acceptability. In exercises and inquiries, the answerer's job is to ensure that each deduction is a good one by allowing only premisses which meet the standard of greater acceptability (see 161ᵃ16–ᵇ10). Obviously, such a criterion is most at home in a gymnastic context.

159ᵇ19–20. 'for it would appear to have been sufficiently argued': that is, as before, the argument will conform to the rule that the premisses must be more familiar than the conclusion, even though the answerer has conceded some premisses which are in themselves not worthy of acceptance (in the case envisaged, the conclusion at which the questioner must aim is intrinsically unacceptable). Alexander paraphrases 'for he who answers in this way will not seem to transgress [the rules of] dialectical assembly'. But 'argue' refers to the questioner's activity, not the answerer's. The point is rather that in so far as the questioner follows these rules, the argument itself will be 'well argued'. Producing such an argument is the joint goal of both participants.

159ᵇ23–9. Taken literally, Aristotle's words imply that the answerer should choose which standard of acceptability to use based on whether the thesis is, as a matter of fact, absolutely or relatively acceptable or unacceptable. But this makes things sound too easy for the answerer: the same thesis could easily be acceptable to the answerer, unacceptable to another person, and neither acceptable nor unacceptable without qualification. It may be instead that the relevant standard for comparison was determined by the circumstances of the dialectical exchange, perhaps by advance agreement or by the rules of a particular engagement (Aristotle is silent on this).

Answering in accordance with one's own opinions sounds very much like 'testing', but if the two were identical we should expect Aristotle to have said so. The difference might have been a matter of who the participants are: testing might apply to beginning students (or with members of the lay public), whereas established members of a philosophical community answering in accordance with their own opinions might be part of philosophical inquiry. Answering for another could include impersonating a famous philosopher for the sake of exercise, or in order to examine that philosopher's position (thus, Aristotle gives the example of defending an opinion according to what Heraclitus would say). Unfortunately, Aristotle does not explain for us the tantalizing expression 'those who take over theses from each other'.

159ᵇ30–3. The illustration is something of an extreme case: if you have undertaken to defend a Heraclitean opinion in the style of Heraclitus, then you will have to accept and reject premisses as Heraclitus would, even though this may commit you to some strange views (e.g. that contraries can be true of the same thing at the same time). 'The opinions of others': this is the most likely meaning of *allotrias doxas* given Aristotle's usage, but it just might carry the suggestion 'outlandish opinions'.

CHAPTER 6

159ᵇ36–160ᵃ16. Another consideration for determining whether to concede a premiss: is it relevant to the argument (i.e. will it be of any use in
getting the desired conclusion)? Two general principles underlie Aristotle's rules: (i) let the questioner have any premiss that is irrelevant to the
conclusion; (ii) when you do have to concede something that will be useful
to the questioner, make it clear that you see what is coming (and if possible
claim that the questioner is begging the question). Both points nicely flesh
out the answerer's task, as defined at VIII. 4, 159ᵃ20–2, of making it clear
that any refutation deduced is a genuine consequence of the thesis and not
simply the result of the answerer's incompetence.

The premiss advanced, then, may be either relevant or irrelevant, and in
addition it may be acceptable, unacceptable, or neither. Aristotle's six
rules apply to the six cases we get by taking the product of these two
distinctions:

1. Concede anything acceptable but useless.
2. Concede anything unacceptable but useless, but add a note that you
   do not believe it.
3. Concede anything acceptable and useful, but say that it is 'too close'
   to the conclusion desired.
4. If a premiss is unacceptable but useful, say that it would yield the
   conclusion but that it is simple-minded to propose it.
5. Concede without comment anything useless but neither acceptable
   nor unacceptable.
6. If a premiss is useful but neither acceptable nor unacceptable, say
   that if it were conceded the thesis would be refuted (i.e. the desired
   conclusion established).

These rules are stated throughout in terms of absolute acceptability or
unacceptability rather than relative acceptability when compared to the
conclusion. However, the remarks in 160ᵃ11–16 suggest that the questioner's standard is really comparative: a good dialectical argument must not
rest on premisses less acceptable than its conclusion. Therefore, we should
probably take 'acceptable' throughout as 'at least as acceptable as the
conclusion'. So understood, Aristotle's rules tell the answerer to let the
questioner have anything useless, regardless of its degree of acceptability,
and anything more acceptable than the conclusion. He never says explicitly
that the answerer should reject premisses in any of these classes, but he
does not appear to recommend acceptance in cases (4) and (6). Most
likely, he means for the answerer to reject any premiss that is both less

acceptable than the conclusion and useful for reaching it. 'Neither acceptable nor unacceptable' presents a problem. Used absolutely, it would probably mean 'at the mid-point between the acceptable and the unacceptable'; comparatively speaking, it would then mean 'exactly as acceptable as the conclusion'. I do not understand what Aristotle wants the answerer to do in case (6). He says the answerer should 'add the comment' (*episēmanteon*) that granting the premiss gives away the conclusion, but he does not say clearly whether it is to be granted or rejected (or perhaps granted in some cases but not in others?).

160ᵃ1. 'accepted': for the rest of this section Aristotle substitutes *dokoun* ('apparent' or 'seeming') for 'acceptable'. Translating this 'it seems so' quickly becomes awkward and even ambiguous; I have preferred 'accepted', which preserves the connection with 'acceptable' (*endoxon*).

160ᵃ11–14. 'For in this way': this passage portrays dialectical exchanges as serious investigations of the logical consequences of a position. An answerer who makes concessions according to Aristotle's rules will have allowed the questioner any premiss that is at least as acceptable as the desired conclusion; thus, the questioner has the greatest possible leeway in finding premisses. Moreover, if we suppose that only premisses less acceptable than the conclusion are rejected by the answerer, then these are premisses the questioner should not really want to use anyway. With respect to what is actually conceded, then, the answerer's job is simply to keep the questioner from trying to use inappropriate premisses. However, in accordance with VIII. 4, 159ᵇ20–2, answerers should also make it clear that they see how the argument is going: in other words, it is no misstep to concede something your opponent could really use, just so long as you make it clear at the time that you realize this.

CHAPTER 7

160ᵃ17–34. This section concerns two exceptions to the general requirement that responses of answerers are limited to assent and dissent. First, the answerer need not give any response to an unclear question other than 'I don't understand' (presumably, the questioner is then obliged to offer a clarification). Second, when confronted with an ambiguous question, the answerer may offer distinctions of sense, assenting to some and dissenting from others. 'This is also how': as in VIII. 6, these are cases in which the answerer should not give merely a simple assent or dissent. The arsenal of the contentious reasoner included many tricks depending on unnoticed ambiguities or unclarities so designed that no matter which way one answers, one finds oneself presented with 'something vexatious'; hence, perhaps, Aristotle's caution about letting anything ambiguous or unclear go by.

Here again, answerers are expected to make it clear when they see where the argument is headed. Never being surprised is a large part of good performance as an answerer.

160ª33. 'dispute is easy': that is, the more ambiguous the term, the easier it is to make this sort of objection. As Aristotle has just noted, this is not as good a move on the answerer's part as catching the ambiguity in advance.

CHAPTER 8

160ª35–ᵇ13. This section discusses giving objections—in the narrow sense of counter-examples to universal premisses supported by inductions—from the answerer's viewpoint (for the questioner's side see 157ª34–ᵇ33). To paraphrase: 'You can tell that someone is trying to get a universal premiss through induction or similarity when he asks for a lot of similar premisses; let him have all the cases, so long as they are plausible, and worry instead about giving a counter-example.' (On argument by likeness see 156ᵇ10–17.)

160ᵇ4–5. 'cantankerousness': a verb in Greek (*duskolainein*). Its parent word *duskolos* means 'finicky', 'hard to please', 'quarrelsome' (the root sense is 'having a bad colon': cf. English 'dyspeptic'). *Duskolos* has slightly comic connotations and is often associated with bad tempered, unsociable old men who find fault with everything and agree with nothing—in a word, curmudgeons (the title character in Menander's *Duskolos* is a good illustration). Evidently, the cognate verb *duskolainein* was a technical term in dialectic for a certain kind of misconduct on the part of the answerer. Aristotle explains it later (161ª21–ᵇ10) as hindering the common work of questioner and answerer in producing a good argument. The *duskolos* carps at questions, refusing to concede premisses for pettifogging reasons or for no reasons at all, and generally does not enter into the co-operative spirit of a dialectical exchange.

160ᵇ5–6. 'counter-attack': since *epicheirein* denotes what the questioner does in attacking the answerer's thesis, *antepicheirein* would denote the answerer doing what the questioner does but to the questioner's own premiss. On the evidence of this passage, answerers must have been allowed to go on the attack and ask questions themselves, though Aristotle does not give us any further details.

160ᵇ6–10. In a corrective aside, Aristotle suggests a third form of cantankerousness: refusing to grant an obvious premiss just because an exotic argument exists against it. The case bears a certain resemblance to the error of 'giving what is not the cause as the cause' discussed in *SE* 5, 167ᵇ21–36, and *An. Pr.* II. 17, 65ᵇ13–40. In this error, which is peculiar to arguments through impossibility, we deduce an impossible result from some premisses and then take this as a disproof of one of the premisses, even though the same result could be obtained without that premiss. For instance, take any set of premisses whatever and add the (obvious) premisses necessary to get one of Zeno's arguments against motion; then, having deduced an impossibility, infer the denial of any one of the original premisses.

What exactly is wrong with such an argument? The natural response is that the premiss rejected is not relevant to the contradiction deduced. But how do we determine when a premiss is or is not relevant to a conclusion? Aristotle attempts to answer this in *An. Pr.* II. 17, but he does not seem happy with his solution (see 66ᵃ1–15). In hindsight, this is hardly surprising: the work of modern relevance logicians show it is more difficult to characterize relevance than at first appears.

160ᵇ10–13. This definition of cantankerousness says, in effect, that answerers are only allowed to impede the argument (by refusing premisses) under certain defined circumstances. It is not entirely clear what 'the ways mentioned' is to include: does this apply only to the rejection of universal premisses supported by inductions, or does it also include premisses proposed on their own? If the latter, then the relevant restraints are presumably those in VIII. 5–6.

CHAPTER 9

160ᵇ14–16. An obvious bit of advice: to be a good answerer, put yourself in the position of questioner and see what you would do. This may indicate that questioner and answerer were given time to plan their strategies before the beginning of a match, though Aristotle pretty clearly supposes that an ability to think quickly is necessary in dialectic.

160ᵇ17–22. This passage has generally been misunderstood. In ordinary usage, the term *adoxos* (which, as the opposite of *endoxos*, I have been translating 'unacceptable') usually means 'disgraceful'. If we take the first and last clauses together, the point is quite clear: be careful about defending a disgraceful thesis, for people will think you really mean it and hate you. However, Aristotle has previously been using *adoxos* in a technical sense, as the opposite of *endoxos*. Therefore, he (or some later editor) has added an explanatory note. (Aristotle offers no caution about taking on an *adoxos* thesis in VIII. 5–6.)

CHAPTER 10

160ᵇ23–39. 'Arguments that deduce a falsehood' are best understood, not as arguments through impossibility, but as paradoxical arguments, that is, arguments which seem to have true premisses and seem to deduce a false conclusion from those premisses through correct reasoning. Thus, they bind us in an intolerable position. To 'loose' or 'solve' such an argument is to find a way to escape from its absurd conclusion (we can also speak generally of 'solving' any argument which compels us to accept an unwanted conclusion). Aristotle's point here is that such a solution, if it is truly to dissolve the paradox, must rest on an understanding of the logical error that drives the argument. The example he considers is the following:

> He who is seated is writing.
> Socrates is seated.
> Therefore, Socrates is writing.

Suppose now that Socrates is seated and not writing; nearby, Plato is the only one among a group of others who is seated, and he is writing. A sophistical reasoner, adverting to Plato, says 'He who is seated is writing'; turning to Socrates, he utters the second premiss. The conclusion seems to follow because (as Aristotle notes) its first premiss may mean 'Everyone seated is writing', though as used it meant 'The seated one over there is writing' (this ambiguity works even more smoothly in Greek). The sophist has thus bound us to a false conclusion from premisses we believe to be true. To solve this paradox, we must realize that its first premiss is ambiguous in the way indicated.

Now, Aristotle's concern here is to show that another 'solution' is inadequate. Suppose that Socrates happens to stand up. Someone might then say, in response to the argument, 'But Socrates is not seated' (perhaps he stood up while our sophist was looking away). Aristotle's response is very much in the spirit of contemporary model theory: what counts is not the actual situation but whether there is an *imaginable* situation in which the fallacy would still work. We cannot always count on Socrates standing up; a true solution to the fallacy discovers 'that because of which the falsehood comes about'.

Although Aristotle's subject here is fallacies in general, the notion of 'that because of which the falsehood comes about' plays an important role in his understanding of arguments through impossibility (see VIII. 8, 160ᵇ6–10 and Commentary).

160ᵇ29. 'And yet the claim is false': that is, 'and yet—let us suppose—Socrates is not in fact seated'. Aristotle uses vivid language to describe the case he is imagining.

160ᵇ35–6. 'as in the case of fake diagrams': see the Commentary on 101ᵃ5–17. Fake diagrams will typically include various incorrectly drawn lines. Aristotle probably has in mind objecting to a mistake in such a figure which happens not to be the one on which the trick rests.

161ᵃ1–12. To 'hinder' an argument is to impede the questioner from reaching the desired conclusion. Sometimes the questioner is able to work around the impediment, but sometimes not. The four cases Aristotle distinguishes are best seen as criteria for third parties to use in evaluating arguments (thus they go with the section immediately following).

In each case, Aristotle supposes the answerer has refused to grant some premiss (here we must take 'objection' in this broader sense rather than in the more specific sense of a counter-example to an induction). If this premiss is 'that because of which the falsehood comes about', i.e. the crucial premiss in the argument, then the answerer has 'solved' the argument, and there is nothing the questioner can do: this is the first and best way to hinder an argument. In the second case, there is a way to counter the objection, but the questioner fails to see it and cannot go on. The answerer therefore succeeds in halting the argument, but only because of the questioner's incompetence: this objection is thus 'against the questioner'. In the third case, the questioner does see how to respond. Aristotle says that this is an objection 'against the questions asked'. This sort of objection, of course, does not really stop the argument from reaching its conclusion, although it may slow it down. However, Aristotle does imply that it was an error on the questioner's part to leave the way open even for such an objection. Finally, an answerer may give some objection, knowing that it can be answered but that the answer will take more time than there is available. This 'poorest' of hindrances verges on cantankerousness on the part of the answerer. Since there is no way to tell the difference between objections 'against the questioner' and objections 'against the questions asked' until the argument is finished, these criteria would be most appropriate for finished arguments.

The reference to the time allowed may indicate that some dialectical contests were timed (water-clocks were used in Athenian lawcourts).

161ᵃ16–ᵇ10. This section sheds important light on the nature of dialectical exchanges as co-operative enterprises. A 'criticism' (*epitimēsis*) is an ascription of fault to a completed argument; as above, Aristotle probably has in mind evaluations by judges or an audience (see below, 161ᵇ19–33: the verb *epitimān* is commonly used of the assessment of legal penalties), though the faults he discusses are not simply the violations of arbitrary rules of a game. The point of this section is that a good dialectical argument depends on both answerer and questioner. If the answerer is uncooperative and refuses to grant anything just so as to make trouble, then the questioner will be forced to use whatever arguments will work or even to resort to contentious tactics. When this happens, it is the answerer's fault, not the questioner's; a bad argument may be the best argument possible against a cantankerous adversary.

161ᵃ21–4. First case: if the questioner is ready to reject anything the questioner says, you have no choice but to respond in kind and attack the person rather than the thesis. It is therefore the fault of such an answerer if the questioner resorts to sophistry. 'The speaker' (*ton legonta*) is the answerer.

161ᵃ25–9. Second case: gymnastic arguments will sometimes be directed against a true thesis, in which case the conclusion that the questioner must deduce is false. Since dialectical arguments must be valid, this can be done only if the questioner is allowed at least some false premises. In a cooperative exchange, the answerer will recognize this and answer accordingly (e.g. using the kinds of consideration given in VIII. 5–6); an answerer who, in such a case, refuses premises simply on the grounds that they are false is being cantankerous.

161ᵃ29–37. Third case: an argument which refutes a false conclusion from false premises might actually be better than one which does so from true premises. The circumstance is one in which the answerer is more confident of certain false premises from which a refutation is possible than of the relevant truths. Most likely, Aristotle has in mind a testing argument (since the previous case concerned exercise, 'exercise and testing' at 161ᵃ25 refers to two different types of arguments). Such arguments proceed from the opinions of the answerer, who might fit the above characterization.

161ᵃ32–3. 'more likely be convinced or benefited' (*mallon estai pepeismenos ē ōphelēmenos*): other translators take *ē* as 'than' ('more convinced than benefited', 'persuaded rather than helped'). So interpreted, however, Aristotle would be suggesting that there is something mistaken about relying on the answerer's opinions in this case, which if anything seems to be the opposite of his view: if we suppose that the argument is a testing argument, then it cannot possibly work unless the opinions are genuinely the answerer's. Aristotle may mean to distinguish two cases: one in which we wish to persuade someone of a given conclusion and rely on beliefs of his which happen to be false but will serve (thus, he is persuaded), and another in which the answerer is subjected to a Socratic refutation and abandons a previously unrecognized bit of ignorance (thus, he is benefited). Alexander interprets the passage in this way, but he does not appear to have read 'or benefited'.

161ª33–7. 'change minds' (*metabibazein*): at I. 2, 101ª33, we are told that Aristotle's dialectical method is useful for arguing with the public because in arguing from what others think, we will be able to 'change their minds' about unclear opinions. A contentious argument can trick me into an apparent refutation, but it will not make me abandon my opinions. Dialectical argument, however, can be genuinely persuasive and educative precisely because it shows me that my opinions are in need of correction by deducing inconsistencies from them. A valuable passage to compare is *EE* I. 6: 'It would be best if everyone should turn out to agree with what we are going to say; if not, that they should all agree in a way, and that they *will* agree after a change of mind (*metabibazomenoi*)' (1216ᵇ28–30). See also Plato, *Phaedrus* 262a–c.

The comparison with geometry is more difficult to explain. I suggest the following: Aristotle often says that arguing 'in accordance with an art' is arguing from the premisses appropriate to that art. In the case of a science such as geometry, this means deducing from the first principles of that science. Now Aristotle has explained previously that 'dialectical' means 'from accepted premisses', which in the present case means 'from premisses believed by the answerer'. The comparison is strained but intelligible.

161ª37–9. The 'common work' is seeing to it that a good argument comes about. This is more evidently the goal in VIII. 5 than elsewhere (compare the definitions of the functions of questioner and answerer in VIII. 4, VIII. 5).

161ᵇ3–5. We have met with the answerer who 'will not grant what is evident' several times before. A cantankerous answerer might also refuse to understand any questions in the way the questioner obviously intends them.

161ᵇ11–18. This passage makes most sense if we take it—as other interpreters do not—to be a continuation of the remarks about cantankerous answerers. With such people, Aristotle says, it is hard even to know when you have won an argument. The questioner's aim is to force the answerer to admit something absurd or inconsistent with his earlier admissions. But 'these people' (*hoi anthrōpoi*—the phrase is slightly contemptuous) are the belligerent sort who often contradict themselves or change their minds even in the course of their own arguments (*kath' hautous legontes*, 'making statements on their own'). Therefore, it is hardly surprising that they will

140

change their position when answering and deny, not just *what* they formerly assented to, but even that they formerly assented to it (especially
when a questioner has just derived a contradiction from it). No questioner
can force an answerer to concede that he has been refuted unless the
answerer has at least the minimum goodwill to confess that he did agree
to what he did agree to and that an obvious contradiction is indeed a
contradiction.

I take the 'original conclusion' (*to en archēi*) to be the conclusion at
which the questioner aims, which is the contradictory of the answerer's
thesis. 'Contraries' are inconsistent statements. In VIII. 13 Aristotle discusses the related subject of 'asking for' such things, which is a fault that
may be committed by the questioner.

161ᵇ17–18. 'It is evident': this sentence marks the close of the entire
section which began at 161ᵃ16, not simply the brief section beginning at
161ᵇ11.

161ᵇ19–33. These criticisms of an argument 'in itself' concern only the
premisses and conclusion, not the manner in which they are asked or the
responses of the answerer. They give levels of argumentative vice, beginning with an argument that has every possible fault and proceeding
through types with progressively fewer. A list of the faults themselves will
help clarify Aristotle's remarks. Six vices appear, corresponding to the
following virtues of a good argument:

1. There must be a deduction, i.e. the premisses must imply some
   conclusion.
2. The premisses must imply the intended conclusion.
3. No premiss must be left out.
4. There must be no superfluous premiss.
5. The premisses must be more acceptable than the conclusion.
6. The premisses must not be more difficult to establish than the
   conclusion.

The first four of these are needed if the argument is to be a good deduction
of the conclusion; we might characterize them as logical. The last two,
which correspond to the requirement that a demonstration be from
premisses 'more intelligible' than the conclusion, are epistemic. Note also
that 2 implies 1, that 3 and 4 each imply 2, and that 3 and 4 are independent. With these relationships in mind, we can distinguish the following
levels of deficiency in an argument:

   I. No deduction at all (fails 1)
  II. A deduction, but of the wrong conclusion (fails 2 but not 1)
IIIa. A deduction of the right conclusion but with a premiss left out
     (fails 3 but not 1 or 2)

   IIIb. A deduction of the right conclusion but with a superfluous premiss (fails 4 but not 1 or 2)

    IV. A good deduction with premisses less acceptable than the conclusion (fails 5 but not 1, 2, 3, or 4)

     V. A good deduction with premisses not less acceptable than the conclusion but harder to establish than it (fails only 6)

This reconstruction (found in the commentator Herminus) gives us five levels by treating superfluous and missing premisses as subdivisions of the same vice. Alexander instead treats IIIa and IIIb as separate and groups IV and V together.

What precisely does it mean to say that 'no conclusion at all' follows from certain premisses? Nothing, from a modern viewpoint: logical truths follow from any premisses, and any premiss follows from itself. But Aristotle's own definition of 'deduction' implies that he is interested only in arguments in which something other than the premisses follows, and he shows no particular awareness of arguments in which logical truths are deduced from arbitrary premisses (if he ever did think about them, he might have regarded them as flawed, perhaps as using irrelevant premisses).

161ᵇ21–2. 'the premisses used': Aristotle ranks failure to be a good deduction as a worse fault than failure to have more acceptable premisses than the conclusion. Presumably, he includes this requirement here because the first level of criticism amounts to 'has no virtues at all'. But then there is no mention of an argument with totally inconclusive premisses that are nevertheless more acceptable than the conclusion.

It is mildly surprising that Aristotle says 'false or unacceptable' rather than 'less acceptable than the conclusion' (as he does for some of the lesser degrees of fault). As he has already observed, premisses can be unacceptable but still more acceptable than the conclusion, or again acceptable but less acceptable than the conclusion. In view of the next section (161ᵇ34–162ᵃ11), Aristotle may regard any argument with false or unacceptable premisses as bad, absolutely speaking, even though such an argument may be good 'with respect to the problem' if the conclusion proved is false or unacceptable.

161ᵇ26–8. The notion of an argument which becomes conclusive only when certain premisses are supplied is more problematic than at first appears. Informally, we can readily enough imagine cases in which there is enough present in an argument to indicate how it is supposed to work, though some premiss has obviously been left out. However, such cases blend by degrees into cases in which *most* of the needed premisses are missing (and *any* argument can be made conclusive by adding enough premisses). Aristotle's attention may be on the more limited type of case in which the omitted premisses were omitted because they are obviously true. The phrase 'inferior to the ones asked for and less acceptable than the conclusion' is difficult. I suggest this: if the premiss omitted is less acceptable than the conclusion then the answerer ought not to grant it, whereas if it is more acceptable then the answerer should concede it. An argument with an omission of the latter sort could therefore be in itself a good argument, even though the questioner failed to ask all the right questions; by contrast, one of the former sort would not be a good argument in its own terms. (Cf. below, 162ᵃ4–8.) Thus, 'inferior to the ones asked' may simply amount to 'less acceptable than the conclusion'.

161ᵇ28–30. This recalls the definition of 'deduction' in 100ᵃ25–7, but the phrase 'in virtue of their being so' is the form actually found in the corresponding definition in *An. Pr.* I. 1, 24ᵇ18–20 (the *Topics* version says 'through' the premisses). Here Aristotle takes this strictly: if there are superfluous premisses, then the conclusion does not result in virtue of *all* the premisses being so, only in virtue of *some* of them being so.

161ᵇ34–162ᵃ11. Just as an argument may merit a different evaluation on its own and with respect to how it is presented in questions, so its evaluation in itself may differ from its evaluation in view of the problem, i.e. the conclusion to be proved. A good dialectical argument is one that does the best job of getting the conclusion from the most acceptable premisses possible.

162ᵃ4–8. 'Sometimes, an argument': Aristotle says only that under certain quite specific circumstances an inconclusive argument *might* be better than a conclusive one. This is still a substantial concession, since the five levels of censure for arguments just stated treat inconclusiveness as the worst of vices. The case he offers is very detailed indeed: the conclusive argument has 'simple-minded' or 'silly' premisses, though its conclusion is serious, whereas the inconclusive one would be conclusive if we added one or two true and perhaps obvious premisses. He probably means this only as one example, not as the defining case. 'The argument does not lie in these additional premisses' means 'the *entire* argument does not consist of unstated premisses.'

162ᵃ8–11. 'from the *Analytics*': a very detailed study of the number of ways (with respect to syllogistic arguments) a deduction can have a true conclusion and one or more false premisses is found in *An. Pr.* II. 2–4, and some commentators see a reference to that here. But in fact, nothing more is required to establish *that* this is possible than the definition of 'deduction' itself. The reference could be to the bare statement that a deduction may have false premises and a true conclusion in *An. Post.* I. 12, 78ᵃ6–13.

162ᵃ12–15. 'When the argument stated': This probably concerns a view we find several times in the logical treatises (e.g. *SE* 11; *An. Post.* I. 7, 75ᵃ38–20, I. 9, 76ᵃ4–15) that every demonstration must be a demonstration proper to some definite science with its own definite genus, so that no demonstration from one field can be applied to the subject of another. The only exception Aristotle allows to the latter is applying a demonstration from one science to the subject-matter of one of its subordinate sciences, e.g. taking a demonstration from geometry and applying it to optics, or applying an arithmetical proof to harmonics. In such cases, the subject-matter of one science is in a specific relation to the other (superordinate to subordinate). Thus, no demonstration can be applied to a subject which has no relation whatever to its own subject genus. In 'not related in any way to the conclusion', the term 'conclusion' means 'subject-matter', a use found in the *Posterior Analytics*.

162ᵃ15–18. These lines (which Alexander does not seem to have read) are almost certainly spurious. The definition of 'philosopheme' corresponds to nothing else in Aristotle's works (in *De Caelo*, the word is used twice to mean 'philosophical treatise'); 'aporeme' elsewhere means 'puzzle' or 'component of a *diaporia*' (e.g. *An. Post.* I. 1, 71ᵃ29, 31; Met. Γ 6, 1011ᵃ6, M 2, 1077ᵃ1). Apart from that, these lines are quite irrelevant to what Aristotle is saying. They are probably a later editor's marginal note—prompted by the term 'sophism' in the preceding line—which has crept into the text.

162ᵃ19–23. The text here is extremely compressed and perhaps corrupt. Aristotle seems to be spelling out rules for the transmission of degree of likelihood or plausibility from premises to conclusion. But the rules he gives suppose that the conclusion can inherit not only plausibility but also *implausibility* from the premises: indeed, he appears to say that anyone who disbelieves the premises of an argument will *for that reason* disbelieve the conclusion. This would be a serious error, and one he would be unlikely to make. He understands clearly that a valid deduction may have false premises and a true conclusion—in fact, he just adverted to this above at 162ᵃ9–11. But to hold that disbelief in the premises of a valid deduction *is a reason for* not believing its conclusion is to make virtually the same error. The constraint imposed on belief by deduction is a constraint on *rational* belief: it is irrational to believe premises which imply a conclusion but disbelieve that conclusion for the simple reason that such a set of beliefs is inconsistent. But there is no comparable irrationality in disbelieving premisses which imply a conclusion and believing that conclusion. We might conjecture that Aristotle is really talking about the way people tend to reason, not the way they should, but nothing in the text hints that he is describing a species of error.

The phrase 'more than either' raises another problem, since it implies that a deduction can somehow bring about a degree of conviction or evidence in its conclusion that surpasses that of *any* of its premisses. This is hardly the view we find in the *Posterior Analytics* (cf. I. 2–3), where Aristotle generally treats justification as always flowing downhill, so that the conclusion of an argument could never receive a higher epistemic status as a result of that argument than that of its best-established premiss. On the evidence of the present passage, Aristotle would instead be a kind of coherence theorist. It may be that we should adopt the reading 'more than one', found in a few manuscripts.

162ᵃ24–34. This error is straightforward: giving a lengthy argument when a shorter one could have been constructed from a subset of the same premisses. Aristotle's example takes this to an extreme. 'Each thing itself' (*autohekaston*) was an Academic term for a Platonic Idea (cf. *EN* I. 6, 1096ᵃ34–ᵇ2). The Idea of F itself is supposed to be F to the highest degree, and thus more F than each of the particular F things (*ta tina*). Now the proposition to be proved in his example is 'one opinion is more so than another'—more expansively, perhaps 'one opinion is more properly so called than another.' Both the long and the short arguments take Platonic metaphysics for granted. I reconstruct the prolix argument as follows (the starred premisses are not stated in Aristotle's text):

[Premiss]	(1)	For any F, the F itself is F to the highest degree.
[Premiss]	(2)	There is a truly opinable itself.
[From 1, 2]	(3)	Therefore, the truly opinable itself is more truly opinable than the other truly opinable things.
[Premiss]	(4)	If *x* is called G in relation to *y*, *x'* is called G in relation to *y'*, and *y* is more F than y', then *x* is more G than *x'*.
[Premiss]	(5)	There is a true opinion itself.
[Premiss]	(*6)	True opinion is called true opinion with respect to the truly opinable.
[Premiss]	(*7)	True opinion itself is called true opinion itself with respect to the truly opinable itself.
[From 3, 6, 7]	(8)	Therefore, true opinion itself is more true opinion than the other true opinions.

(4) spells out the stenographic 'that which is so called in relation to the more so is more so'. (*6) and (*7) are not stated by Aristotle but easily

supplied; (5) and (8) are actually combined in one sentence: the future tense 'will be' indicates that the clause at the end is the conclusion. I take 'truly opinable' (*alēthōs doxaston*) and 'true opinion' (*doxa alēthēs*) as the correlative terms. Some translators instead take 'truly' and 'true' as adverbial ('there truly exists an object of opinion in itself'), but this seems to me less natural. As Aristotle points out, the same result can be reached at once from (1) and (5), in the same way that (3) follows from (1) and (2).

162ᵃ27–30.   Aristotle presents the imagined questioner's argument in indirect discourse with infinitive phrases; direct quotation is more natural in English and closer to the vividness of the Greek.

162ᵃ31–2.   'But he asked': Aristotle switches from stating the example to discussing it.

162ᵃ32–4.   'What is the fault?' Earlier (161ᵇ19–33) Aristotle listed—with an air of comprehensiveness—five (or perhaps six) points on which an argument in itself may be criticized. Under which should the fault just discussed be classified? We might put it under 'superfluous premisses', but there is an important distinction. An argument with superfluous premisses would, in the typical case, have premisses that are not actually connected to the conclusion by any line of reasoning. In the example just considered, however, there are two distinct arguments, and the longer argument makes non-trivial use of the full set of premisses. Therefore, if we consider the chain of reasoning in the prolix argument, none of its premisses is superfluous. The particular vice of prolix arguments cannot then be linked to the definition of 'deduction' (cf. 161ᵇ28–30 and comments). Aristotle diagnoses—somewhat tentatively—a different fault. The longer argument's detour through an unnecessarily complex path of reasoning obscures the 'cause' as a result of which the conclusion follows. This could be interpreted as a kind of opposite to the virtue Aristotle sees in a 'complete' deduction, which makes evident that its conclusion follows from its premisses: the arguments he is criticizing here have complex structures that not only fail to make evident how their conclusions follow but also positively obscure it.

CHAPTER 12

162ᵃ35–ᵇ2.   Aristotle offers three meanings for 'obvious' in application to arguments, though he makes no use of these elsewhere in the *Topics*. The first two senses suggest different contexts of application. Premisses of dialectical arguments are obtained by asking, and therefore an argument in which nothing further need be asked is an argument in which all the premisses have been made explicit. There may, however, be an allusion to another point. In *Rhet.* III. 18, 1419ᵃ20–ᵇ2, Aristotle discusses arguments (usually forensic) in which a questioner concludes with a final and accusing question rather than a direct statement. This leaves it open to the answerer to respond, not just with a 'yes' or 'no', but with a good retort: therefore, says Aristotle, stay away from this sort of thing unless you are very sure that your answerer has no way to reply. A connection between the two passages is further suggested by the use in both of the relatively uncommon verb *eperōtān* ('ask further').

The second sense of 'obvious' comes instead from the context of demonstrative arguments and may be equivalent to 'complete deduction'. The 'necessary' premisses are those needed to obtain the conclusion in question; the phrase 'concluded through conclusions' may mean something like 'all the intermediate steps between the premisses and the conclusion are filled in.'

In contrasting these two senses as, respectively, 'most popular' and 'most correctly so called', Aristotle follows the pattern of *Met.* Δ, which often begins with more popular or ordinary senses of a term and proceeds later to the more 'correct' and philosophically interesting.

162ᵇ2. Aristotle appends a third sense of 'obvious': if there are unstated premisses but these are obvious.

162ᵇ3–30. Aristotle, like modern logicians, generally resists applying the words 'true' and 'false' to arguments, but more popular usage (then as well as now) often speaks of false and true arguments, usually with an eye to the conclusion. There is a natural tendency to think that what is important is only the outcome, so that an argument with a false conclusion is false, one with a true conclusion true. In response, a logician could respond that the truth or falsehood of the conclusion alone tells us little about the logical character of an argument: both valid and invalid arguments may have either false or true conclusions. Instead, we must at the very least separate the question whether the conclusion follows from the premisses from the question whether the premisses are true. (Anyone who has taught elementary logic knows that this is often a difficult lesson.)

In this section, Aristotle considers a variety of senses in which the term 'false' might be applied to arguments. Since these are not generally matters of some proposition being false, it might seem better to translate with another word ('incorrect' or 'erroneous'). But the English word 'false' also has broader senses: false steps, false notes, false friends; and there is an important reason for keeping 'false' in the translation. Aristotle's goal here is precisely to convince us that we should *abandon* the characterization of

147

arguments as true or false, since the questions we should ask in evaluating them are more complex (see 162ᵇ24–30 below).

162ᵇ3–5. 'One way': Roughly, 'fallacious', invalid but apparently valid. Such arguments are one of the two types he counts among 'contentious' or 'sophistical' arguments in I. 1, 100ᵇ23–5 (cf. *SE* 2, 165ᵇ7–8). The other variety mentioned in that earlier passage, arguments from merely apparently accepted premisses, perhaps falls under the third type of 'false argument' below.

162ᵇ5–7. The second sense is more distinctively Aristotelian: valid but with the wrong conclusion. This is particularly associated with arguments through impossibility because such an argument may be used to refute a premiss not relevant to deducing the absurd conclusion (see the Commentary on 160ᵇ6–10).

162ᵇ7–11. The third sense is also peculiarly Aristotelian: an argument which tries to draw a conclusion about a given subject without using the premisses appropriate to that subject (this is the meaning of 'in accordance with the appropriate study'). What Aristotle says elsewhere is that it is a mistake (and a form of sophistry) to try to *demonstrate* conclusions about one subject without using the appropriate premisses: this implies that Aristotle is talking about arguments in general, not only dialectical ones.

'or dialectical, when not dialectical': it is quite surprising to find 'geometrical' and 'dialectical' arguments spoken of in parallel. Aristotle argues at some length in *SE* 11 (Excerpt C) that dialectic has no subject-matter, so that there cannot really be any premisses peculiar to dialectic: dialectic applies in a way to everything but cannot prove anything. But he also says that some sophistical arguments depend on premisses which seem to be *acceptable* but are not (I. 1, 100ᵇ26–101ᵃ1), and he sometimes uses 'dialectical' of arguments or premisses to mean 'accepted' (see 161ᵃ33–7 and comments).

162ᵇ11–15. This fourth sense amounts to the modern 'valid but unsound' (i.e. having at least one false premiss): it is only true of *valid* arguments that 'a falsehood is always concluded through false premisses'.

162ᵇ16–24. Alexander takes this section to be about arguments which are false in the fourth sense and have false conclusions. It is clear enough that Aristotle is concerned here with such arguments, but the connection with the preceding passage is less clear. I speculate that in fact he wants to consider yet another sense of 'false' when applied to arguments—namely, 'having a false conclusion'. His point is that this is not a particularly useful criterion for evaluation: whether an argument is a good one or not really cannot be judged simply on the basis of whether its conclusion is true or false, and thus arguments with false conclusions do not form a logically interesting category. (Note that he points out, for some of the four varieties of 'false' argument he has just defined, that they may have true as well as false conclusions.)

Aristotle contrasts two cases. In one, premisses with a strong degree of plausibility are shown to entail a known falsehood: this then yields a proof through impossibility that some widely held view is false, and thus it is a praiseworthy argument. In the second case, we have an argument which might be described as 'true' since its conclusion is true, but it has little merit because of its foolish premisses. His concluding remark then makes the general point: the truth-value of the conclusion alone does not really tell us much about whether the argument is a good one.

162^{b}16–17. 'fault of the speaker': this is not a return to the earlier business of distinguishing between the faults in the argument itself and the faults in the argument as presented (the term here is *hamartēma*, not *epitimēsis*). Instead, Aristotle is saying that the *only* case in which a conclusive argument with a false conclusion counts as faulty is when the person presenting it does not realize this.

162^{b}18. 'many true ones': I take this to mean 'true *arguments*'. Aristotle is considering (and ultimately rejecting as not useful) the characterization of any argument with a false conclusion as false. The corresponding sense of 'true' would be 'having a true conclusion'. Aristotle's point then is that an argument 'false' in this sense might be far more valuable than many 'true' ones (e.g. arguments with false and silly premisses but true conclusions).

162^{b}24–30. The three 'points of examination' differ from the argumentative faults which underlie the five levels of criticism of 161^{b}19–33 (see the Commentary on that section). Earlier, Aristotle did not include the truth or falsehood of the conclusion as a consideration at all. The arguments Aristotle characterizes here as 'logical' (*logikos*) seem to be at least a subdivision of dialectical arguments, since a dialectical argument might (but need not) have false but acceptable premisses (Alexander takes 'logical' as equivalent to 'dialectical'; on this term see 105^{b}23 and Commentary.) It is more difficult to say what an argument from true but unacceptable premisses might be. Aristotle often says that the first principles of demonstrative sciences appear implausible or even impossible to the uneducated, and thus demonstrations might fit this description. But why would Aristotle characterize such an argument as 'poor'? Perhaps in the sense that it would be a poor tool of persuasion, or poor as a dialectical argument.

CHAPTER 13

162^{b}31–3. Aristotle now turns to two additional faults which can be charged to a questioner: asking for 'the initial thing' and asking for contrary (i.e. inconsistent) premises. Before he begins discussing them, however, he makes a remark that raises serious questions. The issue is the following. 'Asking for the initial thing' is also discussed in *An. Pr.* II. 16; deductions from 'opposite premises' are the subject of *An. Pr.* II. 15, which also contains an explicit reference to the present section of the *Topics* at 64^{a}36–7 (see below for more on this). When we compare those discussions with the present passage, there are a number of discrepancies. There are other places where the *Topics* and the *Analytics* give different treatments of the same subject. *An. Pr.* I. 30 and *Top.* I. 14 both discuss 'selecting premises', and the former contains a reconciling passage similar to our present one (46^{a}28–30). *An. Post.* II. 13 and *Top.* VII. 3 are both about establishing definitions (VII. 3 alludes briefly to another 'more precise' treatment elsewhere at 153^{a}24–5). Finally, we should also note *An. Pr.* II. 17 and *SE* 5, 167^{b}21–36 on 'false cause' in arguments through impossibility (the first of these refers to the second: 65^{b}13–16).

Now alternative discussions of the same point are common enough in Aristotle; what is unusual about these sections is the presence of explicit acknowledgements that the treatments are different. It is not at all certain just how we should understand the distinction between an account 'according to truth' and one 'according to opinion'. The traditional position, represented by Alexander, is that since dialectical argument is only concerned with plausibility, its standards in general are only the standards of appearance. Therefore, in the present case, VIII. 13 is not about *actually* asking for 'the initial thing' or for contrary premises, only about *appearing* to do so. But that is a solution that brings with it problems.

One such problem is that it imputes a kind of validity-relativism to Aristotle: there may be different standards of argumentative correctness in different fields, and the differences between the *Topics* and the *Analytics* are just the natural outcome of these different standards. Such a view is, depending on one's perspective, either philosophically *au courant* or philosophically disastrous; in either event, the question whether Aristotle held such a view is important.

A quite different possibility is that the inconsistencies result, not from any theoretical distinction in Aristotle's mind between dialectical and scientific argument, but from his philosophical development. On this view, the *Topics* and *Sophistical Refutations* stem from an earlier period in his thought than the *Analytics*, and therefore the earlier works contain positions refined or corrected in the later. On this view, the reconciling remarks will be attempts—whether Aristotle's own or a later editor's—at papering over genuine inconsistencies.

My inclination is to treat different cases differently. VIII. 13 does seem genuinely inconsistent with the *Prior Analytics*, and there are enough other indications of the greater logical sophistication of the latter work to conclude that our present section is just not as well worked out. But even here, the difference of context of the two treatises explains a great deal of the difference in interest. In other cases (most prominently *An. Pr.* I. 30 and *Top.* I. 14), the differences may be completely explained by the difference in subject-matter.

162ᵇ34–163ª13. Aristotle distinguishes five varieties of asking for the conclusion:

(1) Doing it outright.
(2) With a conclusion which is particular, asking for a universal generalization of which it is an instance.
(3) With a universal conclusion, asking for a particular instance which falls under it.
(4) With a conjunctive conclusion, asking for its conjuncts.
(5) Asking for a premiss equivalent to the conclusion.

The first and last of these are relatively unproblematic, and Aristotle's remarks on the first case are straightforward enough. It is less certain just what case (4) is, but, judging by the example, Aristotle seems to have in mind establishing a conjunction by taking its conjuncts as premisses. (This does not imply a criticism of establishing a conjunction by *establishing* each of its premisses.) Cases (2) and (3) are more surprising: (2) seems counter to the counsels of 155ᵇ29–33 (which even uses the same example), and (3) would rule out all inductions. But it may be that Aristotle distinguishes between using either of these sorts of premisses directly in establishing the final conclusion of the argument and using them to get another premiss (either by induction or deduction).

The parallel discussion of 'asking for the initial thing in *An. Pr.* II. 16 explicitly recognizes only cases (1) and (5). Alexander therefore explains (2), (3), and (4) as *merely* apparent, not true, cases. But this is reading a lot into Aristotle's brief comments about (2) and (3). We should have to take 'apparent' to mean something like 'most people think this is a case of this error, but actually it is not'. If that is what Aristotle means, he has not said so very well.

163ª3. 'claims' (*axiōseie*): throughout VIII. 13 Aristotle uses this as a variant for 'ask'. Elsewhere, it often means 'expect': perhaps we should think of it as 'expect to get (sc. a premiss)'.

163ᵃ14–24. 'Same number of ways': though Aristotle says that the varieties of asking for inconsistent or conflicting premisses are equal in number to the varieties of asking for the initial thing, six different cases of the latter may be distinguished in his text:

(1) Asking for a premiss and for its denial.
(2) Asking for a premiss and its contrary.
(3) Asking for a universal and for the denial of one of its cases.
(4) Asking for a particular proposition and the denial of a corresponding universal generalization.
(5) Asking for the contrary of a consequence of the premisses.
(6) Not asking for the contraries themselves but for two (sets of) premisses from which they follow.

Aristotle explicitly numbers (1)–(3); therefore, if we take him at his word, one of (4)–(6) must be assimilated to another case. The anonymous commentator aligns (4) with the previous (4); Alexander, however, matches up (6) with the earlier (5). Evidently, Alexander treats (3)–(4) as one case, perhaps because of their proximity in exposition. But it is quite plausible to treat (6) as a subcase of (5), or even as an additional note beyond the five cases that appeals to the process of 'standing off'.

163ᵃ23. 'two sets of premisses': the text might, as Alexander thought, mean 'two premisses such that from them . . .', but Aristotle makes little use elsewhere of the *Analytics*' claim that every deduction has exactly two premisses. It is awkward but possible to take 'two' to mean 'two sets of premisses' (in this case, we should probably also take 'contradiction' to mean 'pair consisting of a proposition and its denial', as it often does in Aristotle).

163ᵃ24–9. 'Getting contraries differs': the error in asking for the conclusion as a premiss is, in effect, external to the argument, since it depends on what conclusion is being sought; by contrast, the error involved in asking for inconsistent premisses is internal to the argument.

CHAPTER 14

163ᵃ29–164ᵇ19. The closing chapter of the *Topics* turns to various techniques of practice with which we may prepare ourselves for dialectical exchanges. Since 'exercise' has been used earlier to designate a particular type of exchange, the phrase 'exercise and practice' probably serves to explain that it is such preparatory exercises Aristotle is talking about, not gymnastic arguments. In the course of discussing these exercises, Aristotle gives us a great deal of information about the workings of his dialectical method and the nature and function of *topoi*, 'locations'.

163ª29–36. 'Converting' as defined here is a process which transforms one argument into another: if

$P_1, \ldots, P_n$; therefore C

is a valid argument, then

$P_1, \ldots, P_{i-1}$, Not C, $P_{i+1}, \ldots, P_n$; therefore, not P_i

is a valid argument. This is a relatively abstract notion, and it is purely logical in character in the sense that it concerns only the relations of entailment among propositions, not their actual truth and falsehood. The contrast between the clarity of this section and the obscurity of many of Aristotle's remarks about arguments through impossibility probably results from the fact that the latter usually concern proof and thus must take account of the epistemic status of individual propositions. However, the process defined here is exactly the procedure Aristotle uses in *An. Pr.* I to show that certain deductive forms are valid.

163ª31–2. 'in learning a few arguments we will learn many': that is, each argument we learn can be transformed into many through this process. 'Learn': *exepistasthai* means both 'learn by heart' and 'repeat from memory'.

163ª36–ᵇ16. A more general form of solitary exercise: take some thesis and try to find a 'line of attack' to show that it is so and another to show that it is not so (a *thesis* is a *problēma*, and thus it is intrinsically two-sided). Then take on the answerer's viewpoint and try to find a 'solution' (i.e. an objection: cf. 160ᵇ23–9 and Commentary) for each. We have encountered examples of this before, e.g. answerers should prepare themselves by thinking through what a questioner might ask (160ᵇ14–16). Note that, like I. 2, this passage suggests an importance for dialectical skill far beyond its use in argumentative exchanges. In fact, the process of thinking through the arguments for and against a thesis, then trying to find answers to these, recalls the procedure of 'working though the puzzles' with which Aristotle typically begins his scientific treatises.

163ᵇ8–9. '⟨one's opponent⟩ must be on guard': though most interpreters take this phrase to mean something like 'you will be able to defend yourself against arguments from contrary directions', it is almost identical to *SE* 15, 174ª25–6, where Aristotle is clearly talking about ways to refute someone else. The point is roughly: 'if you are ready with arguments for and

against, your opponent will have to work twice as hard since attack can
come from either side'.

163ᵇ9–16. I take this section to rest on a comparison between scientific
knowledge and moral virtue. Aristotle holds that moral and scientific
educations are similar in that each requires a reordering of sensibilities
(see Kosman 1973, Burnyeat 1980). To become virtuous is not simply to
know the right thing to do, nor even to act in accordance with that knowledge: one must also have one's dispositions to feel pleasure and pain so
ordered that right action is pleasant and wrong action painful. Those who
act in accordance with the right reason but against their inclinations are
'continent' (*enkrateis*), not virtuous. Virtue and vice can be compared to
health and illness. The healthy are disposed to enjoy food and drink which
are actually wholesome, whereas those who are ill have perverted sensibilities. As a result, though different things may appear pleasant to those in
different conditions, only that which appears pleasant to the healthy is
pleasant by nature. Likewise, only that which the virtuous enjoy is naturally enjoyable. Extending the comparison to theoretical knowledge (as
suggested by *Met.* Z, 1029ᵇ3–12), those who achieve theoretical wisdom
must acquire the proper epistemic sensibilities and come to see that which
is in reality—by nature—a first principle as prior to and more convincing
than the consequences which follow from it.

Now, in the case of moral virtue, these two components—the intellectual
understanding of what is right and the emotional inclination to do it—are
to some extent separable. Some people grow up with the right inclinations
but without any real understanding why they are right: they have a kind of
inferior moral virtue which Aristotle calls 'natural virtue' (*phusikē aretē*)
in *EN* VI. 13. I take the last sentence of the present section to be a
reference to these naturally virtuous people: they have the right basic
dispositions to hate and love, and therefore they choose rightly in most
cases (though not always when real deliberation is required). The term I
have translated 'naturally gifted' (*euphuēs*) means, by its etymology, 'well-
grown': its senses include 'of good natural disposition', 'naturally suited'
(to something), or 'naturally clever'. It could be applied to the naturally
virtuous, and it could also apply to those with a natural talent or genius for
understanding things.

The argument of the passage, then, is this. Aristotle wishes to show that
the technique of becoming familiar with the arguments for and against any
thesis is an important instrument for theoretical inquiry. Now the purpose
of theoretical inquiry is to discover the truth; and this requires choosing the
right alternative with respect to any problem. A natural talent for doing
this will be a natural disposition to choose the true and flee from the false,

analogous to the natural dispositions to hate and love possessed by those with natural virtue. Such a natural disposition would be a kind of epistemic health: a person so disposed would be inclined to regard that which is true and primary by nature as most convincing.

Aristotle is then saying: 'Studying both sides of a question is valuable in the search for truth because, once we have before us all the arguments, we are in the best position to apply whatever natural ability we have to recognize the first principles.'

163ᵇ15–16. In some sources, this sentence reads: 'This is just what the naturally good are able to do well, for those who love and hate in the right way whatever is presented to them judge what is best.'

163ᵇ17–33. This is one of the few passages in the *Topics* to give us information about how Aristotle conceives of the *topoi*—'locations'— which give the treatise its name. I take Aristotle's main subject to be memorization: just what the dialectician should commit to memory and how it should be recalled (there are references to ancient mnemonic techniques: see the Commentary on 163ᵇ28–9). Aristotle tells us in *SE* 34 (Excerpt D) that his predecessors in teaching dialectic simply offered various arguments to be memorized—presumably, fully specific arguments for or against specific conclusions. But this, he says, is not teaching an *art* at all, any more than providing a collection of various sizes of shoes would be teaching the art of podiatry. A true dialectical art must instead teach how to construct arguments concerning any problem that may present itself (see the first sentence of the *Topics*).

Of course, an art for constructing arguments must construct them out of some materials, and the dialectician must have available in memory a stock of those materials. The present passage gives us a picture of just what practitioners of Aristotle's art are to memorize and how they are to recall it when and as needed. In general content, it resembles the picture of dialectic's sister art, rhetoric, in *Rhet.* I–II. There, Aristotle says that there are two sorts of inferences: those concerned with a particular subject-matter ('specific') and those applicable to any subject-matter ('common'). This is best construed as a distinction of two sorts of *premiss*. The 'common' premisses on which dialectical locations rest (see the Introduction) have no particular connection with any subject-matter. Rhetorical arguments, however, always try to persuade an audience to adopt an opinion about some specific subject, and therefore they must employ premisses concerning that subject.

In *Rhet.* I. 3–14 Aristotle gives us listings of such 'specific' premisses. He identifies three broadest species (*eidē*) of rhetorical argument—deliberative, forensic, epideictic—and then considers the premisses proper to each, in considerable detail. These discussions include both definitions (sometimes multiple) of important terms and listings of generally accepted opinions. Aristotle notes more than once that these treatments encroach on the territory of scientific accounts: in fact, they are not really within the competence of the rhetorician as rhetorician, and to the extent that one makes any of them genuinely accurate it ceases to be part of the rhetorical art and becomes a specialized science. An example will help. *Rhet.* I. 5 tells us that since deliberation is ultimately directed at the attainment of happiness, anyone engaging in deliberative oratory must have available premises and definitions concerning happiness and its constituents. Aristotle then enumerates a collection of such definitions, without any supporting argument. Obviously, this is not intended as a philosophical theory of happiness: we can see that by comparing *EN* I, in which Aristotle elaborates and defends his own definition. But neither would it be correct to call it a *rhetorical* account of happiness, for it is not the business of rhetoric (or dialectic) to give a theory of anything. It is simply a collection of propositions about happiness each of which might be useful in constructing rhetorical arguments and each of which might be acceptable to some type of audience.

The situation is different with the common premises, which Aristotle says are a proper subject for study by the dialectician and the rhetorician. The account of these in *Rhet.* II. 23 recapitulates (often in condensed form) many argumentative strategies found in Top. II–VII. Aristotle thinks of each as revolving around some central premiss, which may be embedded into an argument in a number of ways. This premiss is common in the sense that it may figure in arguments about any subject-matter.

To understand the relationships of these two types of premiss to actual arguments, we should bear in mind that the collections of specific premises Aristotle gives are also of general utility within their specific subject areas. Deliberative arguments aimed at many different conclusions may make use of the same definition of happiness, for instance. An actual argument may make use of common premises, specific premises, and premises expressing truths limited to a particular situation ('particular' premises).

One final point must be noted. Aristotle is aware that an argument usually consists of more than simply premises and a conclusion: it must have some articulate structure showing how the conclusion follows from the premises. Except in very obvious cases, this will require additional steps of reasoning. Consequently, the dialectical art requires more than simply having an inventory of common and specific premises available: one must also know how to construct arguments resting on them. A modern logician might suggest here that Aristotle needs to include some account of *rules of inference* stipulating that various types of conclusion follow from various combinations of types of premiss. Aristotle does not mention rules of inference as a separate component in arguments, but his discussions of common premisses include indications of how those premisses are to be used as starting-points for arguments. In effect, he treats knowledge of a common premiss as including knowledge of the consequences which follow from it in conjunction with other premisses. Each common premiss itself thus amounts to an index location—hence the term *topos*—under which are filed not simply the premiss but also a set of recipes for its use. Many different arguments will then fall under this heading. Dialectical skill, for Aristotle, requires memorizing the recipes, not actual arguments, and being able to recall and use them when they are appropriate.

This is the crucial difference Aristotle sees between his method and the teaching of his predecessors: what is to be committed to memory is not a set of arguments but a set of materials from which arguments can be constructed. As a practical matter, such a method will obviously be more flexible and efficient than trying to learn a separate argument for each possible occasion—the latter, indeed, would be an impossible task if we suppose that there is no limit on the number of problems that might be attacked or defended. (And of course any such 'method' would be totally dependent on the ingenuity of a teacher in coming up with those arguments—and obviously it could not have been the teacher's method for finding them.) From a philosophical viewpoint, the most important fact about Aristotle's method is that it contains, at least in germ, the notion of logical form.

I think we can find this picture in 163ᵇ17–33. It is perhaps clearest if we begin with the comparisons he offers in 23–8 between his method and two other procedures: learning the 'elements' in geometry and learning the multiplication table. The elements of geometry are basic propositions which can be used in the proofs of many others; committing them and their proofs to memory is a great aid to the construction of other proofs. Like-wise, memorizing outright the products of all pairs of one-digit numbers greatly facilitates figuring out the products of larger ones. What is signifi-cant about these cases is the interrelation between what is memorized and processes of calculation or deduction.

Now consider two different ways of learning to multiply. Imagine first someone who commits to memory only the basic definition of multiplica-tion and computes every product from scratch. Such a calculator could, of course, reckon up the product of any two numbers, but each calculation takes considerable time. At another extreme, imagine a reckoner who simply memorizes a vast number of products. This calculator responds instantly with those products he knows but is helpless when faced with any new pair of factors. A practical compromise is the sort of method we use ourselves. We memorize a table of some hundred products (all those for two one-digit factors) and then make this memorized table part of a generalized method for discovering any product. This gives us a much greater—in principle, infinitely greater—return on our effort of memorization, since each product that we memorize is now useful not only on its own but also as an element in indefinitely many other calculations. (This point is familiar to computer programmers. Values for a function may be calculated by using an algorithm and computing each value afresh when needed, or they may be entered in a table and simply looked up. The former procedure usually takes up less computer memory but may be slower; table look-up is usually faster but requires more memory space and can deal only with a fixed set of values. Practical programs usually combine both approaches to find an appropriate compromise between speed of execution and memory use.)

A similar point holds about the elements of geometry. One way to learn geometry (or any other axiomatic system) is to memorize only the minimal components of the system, i.e. its axioms and rules of inference, and to construct a proof for each proposition afresh. As anyone familiar with axiomatic systems will realize, this is a very slow way to proceed. At another extreme, we can imagine a student who learns geometry simply by memorizing separate proofs for various geometrical theorems, without ever learning how to construct a new proof. In between is the procedure typical of actual mathematical systems in which proofs of basic theorems are memorized and used as components of larger proofs. (See also the Commentary above on 158^a31–159^a2.)

In 163^b17–33 Aristotle recommends just such an intermediate procedure having three components: (1) memorize arguments about certain problems of particular importance; (2) memorize various definitions, accepted propositions, and common premisses, all of which can serve as starting-points for deductions; (3) master the common premisses that arguments most frequently fall under and have their use in constructing arguments at your fingertips.

Though I think this is the overall sense of the passage, a number of problems arise concerning the details; the text itself is also uncertain. I address these issues in the following comments.

163^b17–20. 'those problems which arise most often to deal with': one narrow interpretation of these lines is 'memorize *verbatim* arguments to handle the most frequent subjects of debate', but in that case there would be relatively little distance between Aristotle's method and the earlier style of teaching he condemns in *SE* 34. Instead, we should look ahead to the remarks about the 'elements' in 163ᵇ23–4: the problems in question are propositions which play a role in many different deductions. 'First theses': I take these to be 'starting-points', i.e. premisses with which arguments about many different subjects may begin. It would make sense to memorize arguments for these since they would be useful in many contexts; moreover, if the arguments themselves are sufficiently well known, answerers who try to avoid conceding these premisses would likely 'give up in despair' and grant the premiss as soon as they saw a familiar argument being deployed.

An alternative interpretation would link this section to the earlier remark in VIII. 3 concerning 'naturally first' propositions (158ᵃ31–ᵇ4). Aristotle would then be recommending that questioners commit arguments about these to memory because they are hard to discover. But it is *answerers* who he says 'give up in despair', and answerers do not present arguments.

163ᵇ20–2. 'Next, you should be ready': I take this sentence to be about three things: definitions, acceptable premisses, and 'first things'. The 'first things' are then the common premisses which serve as starting-points: 'a dialectician must have ready to hand definitions, acceptable premisses, and common premisses to use as starting-points, since these are what arguments are made from'.

Other translators suppose the entire passage is about definitions: the second clause then could be rendered either 'and have *the definitions of* acceptable and first things at your fingertips' or 'have acceptable definitions and first definitions at your fingertips'. But this implies a distinction between being 'ready with' (*euporein*) definitions generally and 'having at one's fingertips' (*echein procheirous*) certain definitions in particular, a distinction which seems out of place. Moreover, Aristotle would then be saying that deductions are made from definitions, a view not supported by the *Topics*.

163ᵇ22–33. What we are to 'master' and have 'at our fingertips' is the common premisses, which function as 'locations' or headings under which many different arguments fall. This mastery consists not simply in remembering them but in being able to recall them when needed and to use them in constructing arguments; since many arguments 'fall under' them, they will be of constant use to us. Compare VII. 4, 154ᵃ12–15: 'The handiest locations are those just stated and those from co-ordinates and cases. This is why you should master these above all and have them at your fingertips, for they are the most useful for the greatest number of cases.'

Note that *topoi*, in the system as I interpret it, can be regarded as locations for attacks in two senses: locations in a filing-system under which

they are stored, and locations (points) at which an opponent's position
may prove vulnerable to attack.

163ᵇ28–9. 'in the art of remembering' (*en tōi mnēmonikōi*): the phrase
might also be translated 'in someone with a trained memory' (Forster),
which comes to much the same thing. Aristotle almost certainly has in
mind some kind of mnemonic system based on 'locations' of the type
widely used in the ancient world. Though we have no direct evidence from
Aristotle's time about the details, an account of such a system is preserved
in the *Rhetorica ad Herennium* formerly attributed to Cicero. (For a thor-
ough discussion see Sorabji 1972, esp. ch. 2, and Solmsen 1929, 170–9.) This
system first required the user to commit permanently to memory a series of
detailed and vivid images of a sequence of actual locations—typically, the
buildings along a city street—and to associate each firmly with its number
in the series. Users were to become so practised with these imaginary
locations that they could quickly run through them in order, call to mind
any particular member (e.g. the tenth or the fiftieth location), or even run
through them backwards. Once the system was established, the user then
could memorize a series of items for recall by superimposing an image of
each item at its corresponding location. Then, all that would be required to
recall the seventh item in the list would be to think of the seventh location
and then recall the associated image. In effect, the user of such a system
remembers things by mentally locating them at various addresses, then
recalls them by inspecting the contents of those addresses. This system was
in wide practical use, and according to ancient testimony its most accomplished practitioners were capable of astounding feats.

References in Aristotle show clearly that mnemonic systems involving
places were in use in his time (cf. the examples in *De An.* 427ᵇ19, *De Mem.
et Rem.* 452ᵃ12–16, *De Insom.* 458ᵇ20–4). Though we cannot determine
how closely these resembled the later system, what is important for present
purposes is the general strategy of memorizing and recalling information in
an orderly fashion by associating items with 'locations' fixed in order.
Aristotle's methodical dialectician will also need to memorize a large
number of common premisses, along with instructions for their use, and an
inventory of acceptable propositions for use as premisses. However, it will
not be sufficient merely to be able to recall all this material in fixed order:
there will also have to be some device for locating material that will be
useful to the problem at hand.

I think there is evidence in the locations presented in Books II–VI that
Aristotle's method employed a variant of the place-memory system designed to achieve these goals. He often follows a fixed order in stating
topoi, beginning with those that concern opposites, then those involving

'cases and co-ordinates', then 'more and less and likewise'. Most *topoi* begin with 'next' or some other indication of sequence. A dialectician who had committed the *topoi* to memory in a fixed order could use that order as the basis of a methodical search; the search continues until some location is found under which the desired conclusion falls, at which point an argument can be constructed. Alternatively, a dialectician might simply identify an appropriate *topos* at once from the nature of the conclusion (roughly as a user of the place-memory system could go at once to a given position in the series). That is, the terms used for classification of arguments and premisses could serve as indices pointing into the memorized structure, just as numbers do for the place-memory system. This could work both with logical terms classifying argument forms ('contrary', 'negation', etc.) and with content terms classifying acceptable premisses ('good,' 'justice', etc.). All these devices could form part of Aristotle's system.

163ᵇ31-2. 'looking to these defined premisses in order of enumeration': the common premisses are 'defined' or 'limited' because they are relatively few in number. Compare the remarks in *SE* 34, 183ᵇ36-184ª2, about the earlier teachers of argument: they taught their students to memorize arguments which they thought most situations would come under. The superiority of Aristotle's method is its efficient use of the effort of memorization. Rather than having to commit to memory an enormous list of particular arguments and then review the whole list on every occasion to find (if possible) an appropriate one, Aristotle's dialectician memorizes a limited list under which many more arguments can be classified and which can be searched much more quickly.

Aristotle often uses enumerations in the presentation of his own views, making a point of specifying the number of cases before presenting them (cf. *Rhet.* III. 9, 1409ᵇ4-8 on enumeration as an aid to memory). Examples in the *Topics* include I. 4, 101ᵇ11-25; I. 9, 103ᵇ20-3; I. 13; II. 7; VIII. 1, 155ᵇ20-8.

163ᵇ32-3. 'is a matter of manageable difficulty' (*metriōs chalepon*): *metriōs* means 'in a measured way'; in Aristotle, it is usually contrasted with what is uncontrolled or excessive. There is an implied comparison: coming up with a starting-point for an argument is not unmanageably difficult, whereas memorizing a separate argument for every possible situation would be.

163ᵇ34-164ª2. This section makes most sense if we attach it closely to what precedes. 'Standing off' is a technique of concealing the conclusion one wants by starting with highly general premisses far removed from it (cf. VIII. 1, 155ᵇ29-156ª22). Those who are most successful at this technique will use premises so general that it is as obscure as possible what consequences they are aiming at. But if they are to succeed in drawing their intended conclusions, they will have to be skilled in making the right inferences from these general premises, breaking them up into their subordinate cases in the right way (cf. I. 14, 105ᵇ31–7). Here Aristotle compares this to the skill dialecticians must have in using the generalized arguments they are to commit to memory: these will be of no use to us unless we also know how to 'make them into many' by taking the subordinate cases we need. These arguments are 'powerful' (*dunatoi*) in the sense that they contain many others in themselves implicitly.

164ᵃ3–11.   As Alexander says, this is complementary advice for the answerer (for an analogous case see *An. Pr.* II. 19). Aristotle has just been recommending the use of the most general premises and arguments possible. This is advice for the questioner, who seeks to deduce; the answerer, who seeks to block a deduction, should therefore watch out for attempts to introduce more and more universal premises. (If we suppose instead that the entire passage concerns how to advance arguments, then it is hard to see it as consistent.)

The 'memorized accounts' must be the various materials to be committed to memory which Aristotle has been discussing since 163ᵇ17. Translators generally suppose these are written records or summaries of actual arguments, but written summaries would be useful in dialectical practice only if also committed to memory.

'common things': some interpreters see a reference to the admonition of *An. Pr.* II. 19, 66ᵃ25–32, that since every syllogistic deduction must contain a middle term which occurs in more than one premiss, we can prevent people from producing deductions if we never allow them two premisses with a term in common. Such an allusion to technical details of the syllogistic would be out of character with the *Topics* (but there may be another immediately following: see below). A sense more in character with the method of the treatise would be 'watch out for common terms' (that is, completely general such as 'contrary').

'it is not possible to deduce anything without universals': most likely, 'every argument must contain universal premises'. In *An. Pr.* I Aristotle gives a rigorous demonstration that every *syllogistic* argument must contain at least one universal premiss. But here again Aristotle may only have in mind a relatively imprecise claim, in this case that all deductions contain universal premises. From the viewpoint of modern logic, even this is false: apart from the fact that we can always infer 'Something is F' from '*a* is F', there are examples like the following:

Socrates was executed.
Socrates was the teacher of Plato.
Therefore the teacher of Plato was executed.

164ª12-13. Aristotle generally regards inductive arguments as more convincing and intelligible to the uninitiated than deductions; hence beginners should start with what is easy. The distinction between those skilled at induction and those skilled at deduction parallels the distinction in the *Rhetoric* between orators who are good at giving examples and orators who are good at reasoning (1356ᵇ21-3).

164ᵇ2-7. The questioner's skill consists in knowing just how to put forward premisses, while the answerer's consists in knowing just how and when to object; dialectical skill as a whole is the combination of the two. The aphoristic characterization of this as being able to make one thing many and many one is almost certainly intended to recall Plato's characterization of the dialectician (in his sense of the term) as making many one and one many (e.g. *Sophist* 253d-e). When Aristotle mentions Platonic dialectic elsewhere it is usually to deprecate it (see *An. Pr.* I. 31); the relatively forced nature of the present remarks may carry a touch of the same attitude, but he may also be trying to show that his method really meets Plato's expectations for dialectic.

164ᵇ8-15. 'You should not argue': Aristotle noted in I. 2 that his dialectical method was useful, among other things, for arguments with the public. This present advice is probably intended as a caution against using all one's dialectical skill against naïve opponents, especially contentious ones (the reasons why are quite familiar to any modern academic philosopher).

'This is why': this brief comment gives important insight into the nature and purpose of dialectical exercises. Aristotle presents dialectical exchanges as co-operative enterprises in which questioner and answerer both contribute to the common goal of producing a good argument. But arguments are also by their very nature contests, with winners and losers, and the desire to win can easily tempt participants to use devices more appropriate to the sophist (Aristotle must be speaking from experience here). The problem with engaging in this kind of argument is that it encourages bad habits of argumentation. And if trained dialecticians arguing with one another sometimes find sophistries too tempting to resist things are bound to be much worse when a dialectician takes on someone untrained: it will be all too easy, and too tempting, to hoodwink such a vulnerable opponent with shoddy argumentative tricks. In brief: don't practise your skill on untrained opponents, because it will just give you bad habits.

163

164ᵇ16–19. This section repeats part of what was said in 163ᵇ17–164ᵃ2, though the language is obscure and difficult to construe. Since it comes at the end of the work, it may be an isolated fragment of text placed here by a later editor.

Though the grammar is convoluted, the meaning is reasonably clear: 'For the sake of economy, you should try to work out in advance and memorize highly general [i.e. 'common'] arguments. In that way, your memorized arguments will be of maximum utility: the ability to remember each one will make you able to deal with the widest range of problems.' The arguments it is 'too difficult to come up with out of what is available on the spot' could be arguments about starting-points (cf. VIII. 3), but Aristotle may also have in mind any arguments that take more time to discover than is available in an extemporaneous debate.

EXCERPTS

EXCERPT A: *TOPICS* II. 8–11, 113ᵇ15–115ᵇ35

CHAPTER 8

And since there are the four oppositions: ⟨one location is⟩ inquiring **113ᵇ15**
from the negations, from a reversed consequence, both when rejecting and when establishing, and get them from induction. For
instance, 'if a man is an animal, then what is not an animal is not a
man'. (And similarly in other cases.) For in these, the consequence
is reversed: 'animal' follows 'man', whereas 'not an animal' does 20
not follow 'not a man', but, in reverse order, 'not a man' follows
'not an animal'. This may be claimed for anything, e.g. if the beautiful is pleasant, then what is not pleasant is not beautiful; and if not
the latter, then not the former. Likewise, if what is not pleasant is
not beautiful, then what is beautiful is pleasant. It is clear, then, that 25
the consequence we get by negation converts both ways when it is
reversed.

And in the case of contraries, there is inquiring whether the
contrary follows the contrary, either in the same direction or reversed, both for rejecting and for establishing (and also getting
these from induction, insofar as that is useful). Now there is a 30
consequence in the same direction, e.g. for courage and cowardice:
for virtue follows the one, vice the other, and it follows the one to
be worthy of choice, the other to be deserving of avoidance. Thus,
the consequence for these is in the same direction: for 'worthy of
choice' is contrary to 'deserving of avoidance'. And likewise for the
other cases, but the consequence is reversed: e.g. health follows 35
good bodily condition, but illness does not follow poor condition:
instead, poor condition follows illness. It is clear, then, that the
consequence is reversed for these. However, reversed consequence **114ᵃ**
rarely occurs with contraries, and for most of them the consequence is in the same direction. So, if contrary does not follow
contrary either in the same direction or reversed, it is clear that
neither in the case of the terms stated does one follow the other; 5
but if, on the other hand, it does happen in the case of their
contraries, then also in the case of the terms stated one necessarily
follows the other.

The same kind of inquiry can also be used for a state and a
privation, except that in the case of privations reversed conse-

quence does not occur and instead the consequence is necessarily
10 always in the same direction, as sensation follows sight and insensibility blindness (for sensation is opposed to insensibility as
state and privation, since one of them is a state and the other a
privation).

This may be used in the case of relatives in the same way as with
state and privation: for their consequence is also in the same direc-
15 tion. As an example, if a triple is a multiple, then a third is a
fraction: for the triple is so called in relation to the third, and the
multiple in relation to the fraction. Next, if knowledge is belief,
then what is knowable is believable; and if vision is sensation, then
20 the visible is sensible.

(Objection: 'it is not necessary for there to be a consequence as
stated in the case of relatives, for the sensible is knowable, but
sensation is not knowledge'. But in fact, this objection does not
actually seem to be true, for many people deny that there is knowledge of what is sensible. And moreover, what was said would be no
25 less useful against the contrary position, e.g. 'the sensible is not
knowable: for neither is sensation knowledge'.)

CHAPTER 9

Next is ⟨inquiring⟩ about co-ordinates and about cases, both when
rejecting and when establishing. Things of this sort are called co-
ordinates: just things and the just (with justice), courageous things
and the courageous (with courage). Likewise, what produces or
defends something is co-ordinate with that of which it is productive
30 or defensive, as e.g. the wholesome with health, or what makes fit
with fitness (and likewise with the rest). Now, these are what is
usually called *co-ordinates*, while justly, courageously, healthily, and
anything expressed in that way are usually called *cases*. But it seems
35 that whatever is expressed as a case is also a co-ordinate, e.g.
'justly' is co-ordinate with justice, or 'courageously' with courage,
and all those in accordance with the same co-ordination are called
co-ordinates ⟨with one another⟩, e.g. justice, just man, just thing,
justly. It is clear, then, that if any one whatever within the same co-
ordination has been shown to be good or praiseworthy, then the
114ᵇ remainder are also shown to be so. For example, if justice is something praiseworthy, then just people, just acts, and justly are also
praiseworthy. And 'justly' will also be called 'praiseworthily' since
5 it is the same case derived from 'praiseworthy' as 'justly' is from
'justice'.

166

And ⟨there is⟩ inquiring not only about the very term mentioned, but also about its contrary, e.g. 'the good is not of necessity pleasant: for neither is the bad painful' (or if the latter, then the former). And 'if justice is knowledge, then vice is ignorance'. And 'if justly is knowledgeably and skilfully, then unjustly is ignorantly and un- 10 skilfully'. But if not the latter, then not the former either (as in the case just stated: for unjustly would more likely seem to be skilfully rather than unskilfully). This location was given earlier among those about the consequences of contraries: for all that we are claiming here is that contrary follows contrary. 15

Next, about generations and perishings and productions and destructions, both for rejecting and for establishing. For those things of which the generations are goods are themselves goods; if they are themselves goods, then so are their generations; and if their generations are evils, then they are themselves evils. But with perishings it is reversed: that is, if their perishings are goods, then 20 they are themselves evils, and if their perishings are evils, they are themselves goods. The same relation holds for what is productive or destructive ⟨of something⟩: if whatever is productive of something is a good, then it is itself a good, and if whatever is destructive of something is a good, then it is itself an evil.

CHAPTER 10

Next, about similar things, if they are similarly related, e.g. if there 25 is a single knowledge of many things, then so for opinion; and if to possess sight is to see, then to possess hearing is to hear. Likewise in other cases, where things either are or seem to be similar. The location is useful in both directions: if it holds for one of a group of like things, then so also for the others, and if it does not hold for one of them, then not for the rest either. Also, inquiring if it is the 30 same way for one thing as for many (for sometimes these disagree). For example, if to know is to think, then to know many things is to think many things. (But this is not true: for it is possible to know many things but not think them. So if not the latter, then not the former—that, in application to one thing, to know is to think.) 35

Next, from more and less. The locations from more are four in number. One is if the more follows the more, e.g. 'if pleasure is a good, then the greater pleasure is a greater good', and 'if to do **115**[a] wrong is an evil, then to do greater wrong is a greater evil'. The location is useful in both directions. For if the qualification of the accident follows the qualification of the subject, then clearly it is an

5 accident ⟨of the subject⟩; but if the qualification does not follow, it
is not an accident. (This can be obtained by induction.)

Another location is from one thing said about two: if it does not
belong to what it is more likely to belong to, then neither does it
belong to what it is less likely to; and, if it belongs to what it is less
likely to belong to, then also to what it is more likely to belong to.
Next from two things said about one: if what would more seem to
10 belong does not belong, then neither does what would less seem to;
and if what would less seem to belong does belong, then so does
what would more. Next, from two things said of two: if one thing
that would more seem to belong to another does not belong to it,
then neither does another thing that would less seem to belong to
some other belong to it; and if the thing that would less seem to
belong to another does belong to it, then likewise with the remaining things.

15 Next, there are three locations from what belongs (or seems
to belong) alike, just as there are from 'more', as was said above in
the three locations mentioned last. For if one thing belongs or
seems to belong alike to two, then if it does not belong to the one,
then it does not belong to the other, and if it belongs to the one,
20 then to the other. Or, if two things belong alike to one, then if
the one does not belong, neither does the other, and if the one
belongs, then so does the other. And in the same way, if two things
alike belong to two others, then if the one does not belong to the
other, then neither does the remaining one belong to the remaining
one, but if the one belongs to the other, then the remaining one to
the other.

CHAPTER 11

25 So then, this is the number of ways in which it is possible to attack
from more and less and likewise.

Next, from addition: if one thing added to another makes it good
or white (when it was not good or white before), then what is added
will be good, or white, just as it makes the whole. Next, if something
30 added to what already is of a certain sort makes it more of that sort
which it already was, then it is also of that sort itself. Likewise in the
remaining cases. This location cannot be used in all cases, but only
in those in which there happens to be a surplus of that which is
'more'. And this location does not convert for rejecting. For if what
35 is added does not make something good, it is not yet clear whether
115ᵇ it is not itself good: for a good added to an evil does not necessarily

168

make the whole good, nor does white added to black necessarily **115^b**
make it white.

Next, if something is called more or less, then it belongs without
qualification: for what is not good, or white, will not be called more
or less good or white either (for what is evil will not be called more 5
or less good than anything, but instead more evil, or less evil). But
this location does not convert for establishing. For many things that
are not said to be more or less belong without qualification: a man
is not said to be more or less 〈man〉, but not for this reason is he not
a man.   10

Inquire in the same way about 'in some respect', 'when', and
'where'. For if something is possible in some respect, then it
is possible without qualification. Similarly for 'when' and 'where':
for what is without qualification impossible is not possible in
some respect, or somewhere, or sometime. (Objection: 'some 15
people are by nature good in some respect, e.g. the liberal or the
temperate, but no one is good without qualification by nature'.
Similarly, 'it is possible for some perishable thing not to perish at
some time, but it is not possible without qualification for it not
to perish'. In the same way, 'it is in one's interest to follow such-
and-such a diet somewhere, e.g. in unhealthy regions, but it is 20
not without qualification in one's interest'. Next, 'it is possible for
there to be only one person somewhere, but it is not possible for
there to be without qualification only one person'. And in the same
way, 'somewhere, it is a fine thing to sacrifice one's father—e.g.
among the Triballoi—but without qualification it is not a fine
thing'. But this last example does not signify 'where' but 'for
whom', for it makes no difference where they might be: every- 25
where, this will be a fine thing to them, since they are Triballoi.
Next, 'it is sometimes in one's interest to take drugs, e.g. when one
is ill, but without qualification it is not'. But here again, this does
not signify 'when' but 'to one in such-and-such a condition': for it
makes no difference whatever time it is, if only one is in such a
condition.) 'Without qualification' is this: what you will say is a fine 30
thing (or the contrary) without adding anything else. For instance,
of sacrificing your father, you would not say 'it is a fine thing', but
rather 'it is a fine thing to some people': so, it is not a fine thing
without qualification. But honouring the gods you will call a fine
thing, adding nothing, for it is a fine thing without qualification.
Consequently, that which, without the addition of anything else,
appears to be fine, or base, or anything else of the sort, will be 〈so 35
called〉 without qualification.

EXCERPT B: *TOPICS* III. 5–6, 119^{a}11–120^{b}8

CHAPTER 5

119^{a}12 The locations about more and most should be taken as universally as possible: for if they are taken in this way, they will be useful for more cases. It is possible to make some of the ones we have actually
15 mentioned more universal by a small modification in the expression, e.g. 'what is by nature such-and-such is more such-and-such than what is not by nature such-and-such'. Or: 'If one thing makes what possesses it, or what it belongs to, so-and-so, but another does not, then the one that does this is more so-and-so than the one that does not do it' (and if both do, then the one that makes more so-
20 and-so ⟨is more so-and-so⟩). Next, if one thing is more, and another less, so-and-so than some same thing. And if one thing is more so-and-so than something so-and-so but another ⟨is more so-and-so⟩ than something not so-and-so, it is clear that the first thing is more so-and-so. Next, from addition: if when added to the same thing it makes the whole more so-and-so, or if, when added to what is less
25 so-and-so, it makes the whole more so-and-so. Likewise also from subtractions: for that which, when subtracted, leaves the remainder less so-and-so is itself more so-and-so. And those which are more unmixed with the contraries are more so-and-so, e.g. what is more unmixed with black is whiter. Next, apart from what was mentioned earlier, that which is more receptive of the definition be-
30 longing to the term in question. For instance, if the definition of 'white' is 'colour that divides vision', then that is whiter which is more a colour that divides vision.

CHAPTER 6

If the problem is posed as partial and not universally, then to begin with, the universal locations mentioned for establishing or rejecting
35 are all useful. For when we reject or establish universally, we also show this of a part: if it belongs to all, then to some, and if it belongs to none, then not to some. (The handiest and most commonly applicable of these are the locations from opposites, co-ordinates, and cases.) For it will be equally acceptable to claim that if every pleasure is a good, then every pain is an evil as to claim that if some
119^b pleasure is a good, then some pain is an evil. Next, if some sense is not a capacity, then some lack of sense is not an incapacity; and
4–5 if something believed is known, then some belief is knowledge.

Again, if something done unjustly is a good, then something unjust is a good, and if something done pleasantly is to be avoided, then some pleasure is to be avoided (and on the same basis, if something pleasant is beneficial, then some pleasure is beneficial). Likewise for things destructive, and generations and perishings. For if something which is destructive of pleasure or knowledge is a good, then 10 some pleasure or knowledge is an evil. Likewise, if some perishing of knowledge is a good, or some coming to be of knowledge is an evil, then some knowledge is an evil (for example, if forgetting the disgraceful things someone has done is a good, or recalling them is an evil, then knowing the disgraceful things someone has done 15 would be an evil). Likewise also for the rest: in all of them, the acceptable is similar.

Next, from more and less and similarly. For if it is more likely that something from another genus is so-and-so, but none of them is, then neither is the thing in question so-and-so (e.g. if it is more 20 likely that some knowledge is a good than that pleasure is, but no knowledge is a good, then neither will pleasure be. Likewise from similarly and from less: for it will be possible both to reject and to establish, except that both are possible from similarly, whereas from less only establishing is possible and rejecting is not. For if it is equally likely that some capacity is a good and that knowledge is, and some capacity *is* a good, then so is knowledge; but if no capac- 25 ity is, then neither is knowledge. And if it is less likely that some capacity is a good than that knowledge is and some capacity *is* a good, then so is knowledge. But if no capacity is a good, it is not also necessary that no knowledge be a good. It is clear, then, that only establishing is possible from 'less'. 30

It is possible to reject not only by arguing from another genus but also from the same one, taking what is most so-and-so. For example, if what is supposed is that some knowledge is a good, and if it were proved that prudence is not a good, then neither will any other knowledge be a good, since the one that most seems so is not.

Next is arguing from an assumption, having claimed that if it 35 belongs or does not belong to one, then so likewise with all, e.g. if the human soul is immortal, then other souls are, and if this soul is not immortal, then neither are others. So then, if what is supposed is that it belongs to some, it must be proved that it does not belong to some (for it will follow by means of the assumption that it belongs to none). And if what is supposed is that it does not belong 120^a to some, it must be proved that it belongs to some (for thus again

it will follow that it belongs to all). Clearly, then, whoever makes an assumption makes the problem universal though it was put forward as particular: for he claims that whoever agrees about the part is
5 agreeing universally, since he claims that if it belongs to one, then likewise to all.

Now, if the problem is indefinite, then it will only be possible to refute it in one way, e.g. if ⟨your opponent⟩ were to say that pleasure is a good, or not a good, and made no further distinction. For if he said that *some* pleasure is a good, then you would have to prove
10 universally that *none* is, if what was put forward is going to be rejected. Likewise, if he said that *some* pleasure is not a good, then it would have to be shown universally that *every* pleasure is. It is not possible to reject in another way. For if we do show that some pleasure is not (or is) a good, what is proposed is not yet rejected. It is clear, then, that it is possible to reject in one way alone. But it
15 is possible to establish in two ways. For if we show universally that every pleasure is a good, or also if we show that some pleasure is a good, what was proposed will have been proved. Likewise, if what has to be argued is that some pleasure is not a good, if we show either that none is a good or that some is not a good, we will in both
20 ways—universally as well as partially—have argued that some pleasure is not a good.

If a determination has been added to the thesis, it will be possible to attack it in two ways, e.g. if it was supposed that being a good belongs to some pleasure and does not belong to another: for if either every pleasure or none is shown to be a good, what was proposed will have been rejected. And if our opponent supposed a
25 single pleasure alone to be a good, then it is possible to reject in three ways: for by showing that every pleasure, or no pleasure, or more than one, is a good, we will have rejected his proposal. With a thesis still further determined, e.g. 'Prudence alone among virtues is knowledge', it is possible to reject in four ways: for if it is shown that every virtue is knowledge, or that none is, or that another is as
30 well (e.g. justice), or that prudence itself is not knowledge, then what was put forward will have been rejected.

It is also useful to survey the particular ⟨species⟩ of that which something is said to belong or not belong to, just as with universal problems. Moreover, the survey of the genera should proceed by
35 dividing them up into species as far as the indivisibles, as was said earlier. For if it obviously belongs to them all, or to none, then when you have brought forward many cases ⟨your opponent⟩ is expected either to agree to the universal or to bring as objection a

case in which it does not hold. Next, in those cases in which the accident can be determined either by species or by number, see if none of these belongs, e.g. ⟨show⟩ that time does not move and is **120ᵇ** not a motion by enumerating how many species of motion there are: for if none of these belongs to time, then it is clear that it does not move and is not a motion. Likewise, ⟨show⟩ that the soul is not a number by determining that every number is either even or odd: for if the soul is neither even nor odd, then it is clear that it is not a number.

When it comes to accidents, then, you should attack through these means and in this way.

EXCERPT C: *SOPHISTICAL REFUTATIONS* 10–11, 171ᵇ3–172ᵇ4

... expecting someone to affirm or deny something is not for the **171ᵇ3** one giving proofs to do, but for the one making trial. For the art of making trial is a kind of dialectic and studies, not the one who knows, but the one who is ignorant and pretends to know.   5

Now, whoever studies the common things as they apply to a subject is dialectical, whereas the person who merely appears to do this is sophistical; and one kind of contentious or sophistical deduction is an apparent deduction about things about which dialectic makes trial (even if its conclusion should be true: for it is deceptive 10 about the reason why), while another kind includes those fallacies which, though not actually in accordance with the relevant treatment of the subject, seem to be according to the art. For fake diagrams are not contentious, since the fallacies apply to things that fall under the art—even if there is such a thing as a fake diagram about a truth. (Take for example Hippocrates' argument or the 15 way of squaring the circle that uses lunes.) But as for the way Bryson squared the circle, even if the circle is actually squared by it, still, because it is not in accordance with the subject, it is for that reason sophistical. Thus, an apparent deduction that applies to such-and-such is a contentious argument; and a deduction that apparently applies to its subject—even if it should be a deduction— 20 is also a contentious argument (for it only appears to apply to its subject, so that is deceptive and unfair).

For just as unfairness in a wrestling match takes a certain form— that is, it is a kind of 'dirty fighting'—so the contentious art is 'dirty fighting' in disputations. For in the former case, those who choose

25 to win at all costs use every kind of hold, and so in the latter case do the contentious. Now, those who behave like this for the sake of winning itself—these seem to be the contentious fellows and the lovers of strife; but those who do it for the sake of a reputation that gets them money are sophistical (for sophistry is, as we said, a way of making money from apparent wisdom). This is why they aim at

30 *apparent* refutation. Lovers of strife and sophists are men of the same arguments, but not for the same purposes, and the same argument will be both sophistical and contentious, but not in the same respect: insofar as it is for the sake of apparent victory it is contentious, but insofar as it is for the sake of apparent wisdom it is sophistical (for sophistry too is a kind of apparent but not real wisdom).

35   In a way, a contentious argument bears the same relationship to a dialectical one as a fake-diagrammer to a geometer: for it leads people into fallacies from the same premisses as dialectic, just as the fake-diagrammer leads the geometer into fallacies. However, he is not contentious, because he draws conclusions from these

172ᵃ starting-points that *do* fall under that art. But as for an argument falling under dialectic—now this clearly *will* be contentious applied to other subjects. For example, the squaring of the circle by means of lunes is not contentious, while Bryson's squaring is contentious; and the former cannot be transferred to another genus but applies

5 only to geometry, because it is from geometry's peculiar starting-points, while the latter can be ⟨transferred⟩—with the mass of people, who do not know what is possible and impossible in any individual case—for it will adapt. Or: the way Antiphon squared the circle. Or again: if someone denied that it is better to take a walk after dinner by means of Zeno's argument, it is no medical argument, for it is common.

10   Now if the relation of a contentious argument to a dialectical one were completely like that of the fake-diagrammer to the geometer, then it would not be contentious about the former subjects. But as matters actually stand, dialectical argument is not about some definite genus, nor does it constitute a proof about anything, nor is it a kind of universal argument. For all things are not in some single

15 genus; and even if they were, all beings could not fall under the same starting-points. Thus, none of the arts that gives proofs about some nature is interrogative: for it is not possible for it to grant either one of the parts ⟨of a contradiction⟩ indifferently (for a deduction does not arise out of both). Dialectic, however, *is* interrogative. And if it did give proofs, then it would refrain from

asking—if not everything—at least its first things and appropriate
starting-points. For if someone did not grant these, it would no 20
longer have anything from which to argue against his objection.

And dialectic itself is the art that makes trial. For an art of
making trial is not an art like geometry, but rather the kind of art
someone could possess even without having knowledge. For it is
possible even for someone without knowledge of a subject to detect
by trial another who does not know—if, that is, he answers questions—not on the basis of what he knows or the premisses peculiar 25
⟨to the subject⟩, but on the basis of consequences ⟨of what he says⟩
which are such that, though nothing prevents someone who knows
them from not knowing the art, one who does not know them must
necessarily be ignorant of it. So, it is obvious that the art of making
trial is not the science of any definite genus.

That is just why it applies to them all. For all the arts also make
use of certain common things (which is why everyone, especially 30
lay people, makes use in a certain way of dialectic and the art of
making trial: everyone tries to cross-examine people who advertise
their wares, up to a point), and these are what is common. For
people know *them* not a bit the less, even if they themselves should
seem to make utterly irrelevant statements. Therefore, they all
conduct refutations—that is to say, they participate without art in 35
that activity in which artful participation is dialectic—and he who
uses the art of deducing to make trial is a dialectician.

Since there are many of these ⟨premisses⟩ that apply to all things
but not in such a way that ⟨what they apply to⟩ is a certain nature or
genus—they ⟨apply⟩ instead rather as negations do—while others
are not like this but instead peculiar ⟨to some genus⟩, it is possible
for making trial about all subjects on the basis of these both to be
a certain art and not to be the same kind of art as those that give **172**^b
proofs. This is just why the contentious person is not entirely in the
same position as the fake-diagrammer: for it will not be from the
starting-points of some definite genus that he constructs fallacies,
but instead the contentious reasoner will deal with every genus.

EXCERPT D: *SOPHISTICAL REFUTATIONS*
34, 183^a27–184^b8

Now, as for the number and variety of premisses from which fallacies arise for those arguing, and how we can both show someone is
at fault and make someone state a paradox; and next, what

30 premisses the deduction results from, how it is to be presented in
questions, and what the arrangement of questions is; and next,
what all such arguments are useful for; and about the whole business of answering, and how to find solutions to arguments and
deductions—let this be what we have to say about all these sub-
35 jects. What remains, concerning our initial project, is to offer something brief by way of summary and add the finishing touch to our
remarks.

Now, we undertook to discover a certain power of producing
deductions about any problem presented, from the most acceptable
premisses available: for that is the function of dialectic in itself and
183ᵇ of the art of making trial. But since there is ascribed to this art the
additional power, because of its nearness to sophistry, that it is able
to make trial not only dialectically but also as if possessing knowledge—for this reason, we assumed for our method not only the
5 purpose we mentioned of being able to *give* arguments, but also
how, when *undergoing* argument, we may in like fashion defend
our position through the most acceptable premisses. We have said
what the cause of this is, since it was also for this reason that
Socrates used to ask questions but would not answer: for he would
not agree that he knew.

It has been spelt out in the preceding remarks what problems
10 this is possible against, and from what premisses, and how we are
to be prepared with these, and moreover how they should be
put as questions and how the whole interrogation should be
arranged, as well as the matters of answering and giving solutions
for deductions. Everything else pertaining to the same method
of arguments has also been spelt out. In addition to these things,
we have completed a treatment of fallacies, as indeed we said
above.

15   So then, it is evident that what we undertook to do has been
sufficiently accomplished. But we must not overlook what has happened concerning this present treatise. For in the case of all discoveries, materials acquired from others and already worked up earlier
have advanced bit by bit under those who inherited them subse-
20 quently, whereas initial discoveries usually attain at first only a
limited state of advancement, although a much more valuable one
than the growth that later comes from them. For the beginning of
anything is perhaps the greatest part, as they say, which is why it is
also the most difficult: for since it is smallest in size to the extent
25 that it is greatest in power, it is most difficult to discern. But once

this beginning has been found, it is an easier matter to add to it and
to assist in the development of the rest.

This is just what has happened in connection with rhetorical
treatises (and probably all the other 'arts' too). For those who
discovered the starting-points advanced only a little way; but the
famous practitioners of our day, inheriting through a kind of line of 30
succession from many others who made progress, bit by bit, have
enlarged the art in this way—Teisias after the earliest of them,
Thrasymachus after Teisias, Theodorus after him—and many have
contributed many parts. This is why it is nothing remarkable for the
art to possess a certain magnitude.

But as for this study of ours, it is not the case that part had been 35
previously worked up and part had not: rather, nothing existed at
all. Indeed, the art of those who taught contentious arguments for
a fee was rather like the education in Gorgias' system: they would
each give arguments—rhetorical and interrogative, respectively—
to be committed to memory, into which they thought arguments of
their respective kinds could most often be fitted. That is why the 184[a]
instruction they imparted to those who learned from them was
quick but without art: for they believed they could educate by
giving, not an art, but the products of the art—as if someone who
claimed he was going to impart a science for keeping feet from 5
hurting were then not to teach shoemaking, nor even where one
would be able to buy such things, but instead were to give people
many kinds of shoes of every description: this fellow has assisted
with a need, but he has not imparted an art. In the case of rhetoric,
there were also available the many older accounts that we mention, 184[b]
but when it came to deduction we had absolutely no other previous
work to mention—even though we devoted much time to a labori-
ous search. And if it seems to you who have studied it that our
method, arising from these circumstances as from its beginning, is
in an adequate condition by comparison with those other systems
which have been built up from a tradition, then the task would
remain for all of you, or our audience, to show indulgence for
the deficiencies of our method and to be most grateful for its
discoveries.

NOTES ON THE TEXT

BOOK ONE

100ª30–ᵇ19: The language of the phrase is unusual, although not without parallel (*Cat.* 9ᵇ19–21 is very similar; cf. also *GA* 751ᵇ5). Other translators (except Colli) try instead to make 'knowledge' the subject of εἴληφεν (e.g. Pickard-Cambridge: 'our knowledge of them has originally come through premisses which are primary and true'), but this is grammatically impossible since τῆς γνώσεως is genitive.

101ᵇ3–4: I punctuate ἐξεταστικὴ γὰρ οὖσα πρὸς τὰς ἁπασῶν τῶν μεθόδων ἀρχάς, ὁδὸν ἔχει; other translators punctuate after οὖσα instead of ἀρχάς. For ὁδὸν ἔχει as 'has a way to proceed' cf. *HA* 625ª13, where ὁδὸν μὴ ἔχουσιν means 'they have no way to get through'. At *EN* 1095ª33 Aristotle does speak of *the* 'road to (ἐπὶ) the starting-points', contrasted with the 'road from' them (i.e. demonstration), but the present passage differs from this in using the preposition πρὸς rather than ἐπὶ and in lacking a definite article with 'way'. These are small differences, but I believe they are significant.

101ᵇ7: 'And that is': following Brunschwig in bracketing τοῦτο δ' ἐστὶ . . . προαιρούμεθα.

101ᵇ8: 'under all circumstances' (ἐκ παντὸς τρόπου): not 'in every way' (as some translators think). Aristotle is not saying that there are some types of persuasion that are beneath the orator's proper business or some types of healing that are not part of the medical art, only that there are limits to what skill can accomplish.

102ª31–2: 'which differ in species' (καὶ διαφερόντων τῷ εἴδει): καὶ epexegetical.

103ª15–16: ἔχειν τινὰ διαφοράν: for a parallel use of ἔχειν διαφορὰν as 'has a differentia' see *Pol.* IV. 4, 1290ᵇ29–34.

103ª34: 'some person who is seated' (τινὰ τῶν καθημένων): literally 'one of those who are seated'. Brunschwig, noting that it will not help clarify the order to say 'the one sitting' if several people are seated, proposes to read 'someone, the one seated' (τινὰ τὸν καθήμενον) on the basis of rather slender manuscript evidence. But Aristotle often uses this sort of construction with a genitive plural as a periphrastic form of predication: 'some one of the Xs' for 'some X'.

179

103ᵇ27–8: 'an expression signifying the what-it-is' (ὁ τὸ τί ἐστι σημαίνων): translators and commentators usually take the masculine gender to indicate that it is a person that 'signifies' here. But Aristotle frequently refers to a definition as λόγος ὁ τὸ τί ἐστι σημαίνων; therefore, since it is clearly an expression that 'signifies' in 103ᵇ35–9, I have taken the entire passage this way.

103ᵇ33–4: Brunschwig, following Prantl, reads the text as 'if he says the example is a foot long or a length' (φῇ τὸ ἐκκείμενον πηχυαῖον εἶναι ἢ μέγεθος), thus making this third example parallel to the preceding two ('length' is the genus of 'foot-long'). But though this would improve the sense, the authority for it is weak and it is really a conjecture: let the reader choose.

104ᵃ10–11: The force of μὴ is to qualify the whole phrase καὶ τούτοις … γνωρίμοις. (Cf. the following sentence, which makes this point quite explicitly.)

104ᵇ4: Ross needlessly deletes 'the public think the opposite of the wise' (οἱ πολλοὶ τοῖς σοφοῖς) as redundant: the phrase may indeed be redundant, but so sometimes is Aristotle.

104ᵇ6: 'only for the sake of choosing': 'only' (μόνον) is found in almost all manuscripts, but editors (except for Brunschwig) reject it as ruining a contrast between what it is valuable to know for some other purpose and what it is valuable to know for no further purpose than knowing it. But this supposes that what we want to know for choice and avoidance is *also* something we want to know for the sake of knowing it, which Aristotle probably would deny: he regards theoretical and practical wisdom as having separate and non-overlapping subject-matters.

104ᵇ24: 'something about which we possess an argument contrary to our opinions': I follow the text of most manuscripts (περὶ ὧν λόγον ἔχομεν ἐναντίον ταῖς δόξαις), according to which it is the *argument* that is contrary to our opinions. That is, the thesis itself takes that side of the problem which is 'contrary to opinion' on the basis of an argument. Brunschwig instead reads ἐναντίων, giving the sense 'something contrary to our opinions about which we possess an argument'. Though the difference is small, this reading does fit the remainder of Aristotle's remarks somewhat better: a thesis is, to begin with, something 'contrary to opinion' which is worth discussing *either* because it has the support of some authority *or* because it has the support of an argument. However, as Brunschwig concedes, his reading does lead to very difficult syntax, and I have been reluctant to follow it.

104ᵇ35:   'In practice' (νῦν): see Verdenius, (1968), 24.

105ᵃ17:   'in the manner of perception': one of several possible renderings of κατὰ τὴν αἴσθησιν.

105ᵃ27–8:   Translators generally supply a definite article with 'choiceworthy' (αἱρετὸν) and make it the subject of the sentence. But 106ᵃ4–6 is a close parallel: Aristotle's point is that the noble, the pleasant, and the useful are all said to be choiceworthy *but in different ways*.

105ᵃ30–1:   'training program . . . in training' (εὐεκτικός, εὐεξία): εὐεξία is the state of being in good athletic condition ('in shape', 'in training'); what is εὐεκτικὸν is what produces such a state (i.e. a training diet, exercises). Reproducing the parallel with 'healthful/health' (ὑγιεινὸν/ὑγίεια) is difficult in English.

105ᵃ37:   'or the contraries' (ἢ τὰς ἐναντίας): Waitz, Ross, and Brunschwig all find some way to add 'not' (μὴ) before 'contraries', thus giving a sense parallel to the μὴ παράδοξος of 104ᵃ10–11. But this is unnecessary (see the Commentary).

105ᵇ11:   I have rendered θέσις as 'concession' to capture its connection with its cognate verb τιθέασι that follows at once. To translate it as 'thesis' would call to mind the technical term defined in I. 11, 104ᵇ18–28, which would be absurd here.

106ᵇ1–4:   As Verdenius (1968) notes, the ambiguity in question here is that the verb φιλεῖν means both 'feel love towards' and 'kiss'.

106ᵇ4–12:   I switch to 'bright' and 'dark' here for λευκός and μέλας, since 'white' and 'black' have no standard senses in application to sounds. The word I translate 'nasal' (σομφός) is not very common, especially in application to sounds (applied to objects it means 'spongy'). In the Hippocratic treatise *On Diseases* it is used of the voice of a person with nasal polyps (2. 33).

107ᵃ9:   'is good': we find 'good' twice in succession in the manuscripts. (τὸ ἐν τῷ καιρῷ ἀγαθόν· ἀγαθόν γάρ). Brunschwig, following W. S. Maguinness, deletes one of these to bring this case into parallel with the one following.

107ᵃ32–5:   Here alone in the latter part of I. 15, Aristotle reverts to the idiom πολλαχῶς λέγεται.

107ᵇ9–12:   The text is uncertain. I have kept 107ᵇ11 τοσοῦτον ('of such an amount'), with most manuscripts and editors; Ross reads τοιοῦτον ('of such a sort'). In 'what indicates and what produces health' (τὸ σημαντικὸν καὶ τὸ ποιητικὸν ὑγιείας), many manuscripts omit the second τὸ, and Barnes follows this ('what indicates and produces'). Brunschwig deletes 'to health' (πρὸς ὑγίειαν) in 107ᵇ9, though it is well attested (see his notes).

108ª26–7:   The verb παραλογίζειν corresponds to παραλογισμός, 'fallacy', and would mean 'use a fallacy', or more accurately 'deceive someone with a fallacy' (see 101ª5–17 and Commentary); I translate the passive μὴ παραλογισθῆναι as 'resisting fallacies'.

BOOK EIGHT

156ª3–10:   I take τὰς δὲ παρὰ ταύτας εἰρημένας to allude to 155ᵇ36 τὰς ἀναγκαίας ληπτέον: Aristotle is now talking about *additional* types of necessary premiss. 156ª4 τούτων χάριν means 'for the sake of standing off or induction'; 156ª2 ἐκείνως means 'by either of these two ways'.

156ª19:   With Brunschwig, I read 'previously' (πρότερον) rather than 'the previous deductions' (προτέρων), but both readings are well attested and either may be correct.

156ª21:   Though some other translators (e.g. Pickard-Cambridge, Colli) agree that the sentence has the meaning I give it, the grammar is difficult. I take ἐκεῖνα ὑφ' ὧν ὁ συλλογισμὸς γίνεται as elliptical for something like ἐκεῖνα τὰ λήμματα τὰ τῶν ὑφ' ὧν ὁ συλλογισμὸς γίνεται (so that ἐκεῖνα contrasts with τὰ τούτου λήμματα): double-duty ὧν after a preposition is common in Aristotle. Barnes's more literal 'not the assumptions on which it is based, but only those by which the deduction proceeds' does not seem intelligible to me.

156ª38–ᵇ3:   'not correct' (οὐκ ἀληθής): some manuscripts read 'not sufficient' (οὐκ ἱκανή), but Aristotle proceeds to argue that the counter-example is erroneous.

157ᵇ16:   'because he has forgotten' (διότι ἐπιλέλησται): this is the text of most manuscripts, but Ross follows a minority in reading ὅτι ('that he has forgotten').

157ᵇ17–18:   'Why is it' (διὰ τί): most manuscripts read διότι, which usually means 'because' in Aristotle. Ross, following Boethius' translation, emends the text to ὅτι ('that'). But he is then forced to add a 'not' to get a good sense ('those objecting that the greater evil is not opposed to the greater good').

157ᵇ32–3: 'holds of many cases': οὕτως ἐπὶ πολλῶν ἔχουσαν is equivalent to οὕτως ἔχει ἐπὶ πολλῶν (cf. 158ᵃ3); 'holds in this way of many cases' is wrong.

158ᵃ4: 'it is not a simple matter to discern it': with Brunschwig, I read μὴ ἐπιπολῆς ἢ τὸ συνιδεῖν. Ross omits ἢ; the manuscripts vary.

159ᵇ10: 'what does not seem so': in this section, Aristotle uses τὸ δοκοῦν, 'what seems' (or perhaps even 'what is thought'), as an equivalent of 'acceptable'. So also at 159ᵇ21 'apparent' (φαινόμενα).

159ᵇ23–4: 'Now if' (εἰ μὲν οὖν): μὲν οὖν marks the transition to a new point (in this case resuming the distinction made at 159ᵃ39–ᵇ1 of varieties of ἔνδοξα).

160ᵃ3: I follow Brunschwig in reading δοκοῦν with the manuscripts, instead of Wallies's δοκεῖν. Aristotle is saying that the answerer should add 'But that is not acceptable' (in the relevant way), not 'But that is not what I think'.

161ᵇ4: For the meaning of ἐκδεχόμενος see EN IV. 1, 1120ᵃ3.

161ᵇ22: 'the premisses used to get the conclusion' (ἐν οἷς τὸ συμπέρασμα): the common alternative translation 'the premisses on which the conclusion rests' implies that there is a valid argument, which in this case there is not.

162ᵃ15–18: 'A philosopheme': with Brunschwig, I bracket 162ᵃ15–18 ἔστι δὲ φιλοσόφημα ... ἀντιφάσεως (see the Commentary).

162ᵃ32: 'this opinion is a more precise opinion' (αὕτη δόξα ἀκριβεστέρα ἐστίν): there is considerable variation among the manuscripts here: besides αὕτη δόξα ἀκριβεστέρα, we find αὐτὴ δόξα ἀληθὴς ἀκριβεστέρα | ἡ αὐτοδόξα ἀληθὴς ἀκριβεστέρα | ἡ αὐτὴ δόξα ἀληθὴς ἀκριβεστέρα | αὕτη δόξα μάλιστα ἀληθὴς ἀκριβεστέρα.

162ᵇ17–18: The text at this point is uncertain, though the sense does not seem to be affected. Some good manuscripts add ὅτι ψευδῆ λόγον εἶπέ τινα after λανθάνει αὐτὸν ('he is not aware that he stated a false argument'). I translate 'not even a fault of the speaker in every case' in l. 17; this second occurrence of 'fault' is present in some manuscripts (which add τὸ ἁμάρτημα after ἀεί), but it may be supplied as the implicit subject even if absent.

163ᵃ23: 'two sets of premisses': the phrase τοιαῦτα ... δύο ἐξ ὧν ἔσται ἡ ἀντικειμένη ἀντίφασις might, as Alexander thought, mean 'two premisses such that from them . . . ', but Aristotle makes little use elsewhere of the *Analytics'* claim that every deduction has exactly two premises. It is awkward but possible to take δύο to mean 'two sets of premises' (in this case, we should probably also take 'contradiction' to mean 'pair consisting of a proposition and its denial', as it often does in Aristotle).

163ᵇ13: 'naturally gifted with respect to truth' (ἡ κατ᾽ ἀλήθειαν εὐφυΐα): other translators make this 'true natural ability'.

163ᵇ17: 'Arise to deal with' is a rather expansive translation of ἐμπίπτοντα; other translators prefer 'encountered'. But we do not find this sense elsewhere in Aristotle. The verb ἐμπίπτειν means 'fall into' (in spatial senses), 'fall on' (i.e. attack), 'fall among' (i.e. be attacked by), or even 'afflict' (of diseases). All these senses are found in Aristotle. He also uses it frequently in connection with definitions, Platonic divisions, etc., with the meaning 'fall under' (e.g. a few lines later at 163ᵇ22), though that sense does not seem to be involved here. The term πρόβλημα itself indicates that a dialectical problem is a challenge to the questioner, who must deal with it, and this is easily extended to 'problems' arising as components of larger deductions.

163ᵇ20–1: I take 'at your fingertips' (προχείρους) to be feminine, modifying either an understood 'theses' (θέσεις) suggested by the previous line, or perhaps 'premises' (προτάσεις). Other translators suppose it is masculine, in agreement with 'definitions' (ὅρων) in l. 20.

163ᵇ23: 'other arguments': this follows the emendation adopted by Barnes and Brunschwig (οἱ ἄλλοι λόγοι). The manuscripts appear to be corrupt: the best sources are divided between 'another argument' (ἄλλος λόγος) and 'the dialogues' (οἱ διάλογοι); Alexander's citation, adopted by Ross, is 'the arguments' (οἱ λόγοι).

163ᵇ25: 'at your fingertips': here the adverb προχείρως, not the adjective (as elsewhere in this passage). In Aristotle this almost always means 'off-handedly', 'without needing thought', whether in a positive sense (implying easy familiarity with a subject) or a negative one (implying triviality, lack of deep thought). For negative senses, see *EE* II. 4 1222ᵃ3, *Mete.* 369ᵇ24–5, and the remark about people who think they are good at deduction in VIII. 1, 156ᵇ39: 'they concede things off-handedly, trusting in their talent and believing that they cannot be convinced of anything'.

163ᵇ37: 'That can undergo this to the most universal degree': I retain 'can' (δύνανται), with the best manuscripts, which Ross omits.

164ᵃ12 ff: 'Beginner' is a better sense for *νέον* than 'young', given the contrast with 'experienced' (*ἔμπειρον*). 'assigned' (*ἀποδοτέον*): others take this to mean 'display', but that is not appropriate here: the purpose of the section is to explain how to go about improving one's dialectical skill, not how to make the best showing. The verb *ἀποδιδόναι* is ubiquitous in the *Topics* in the sense 'give as a response' (e.g. give a definition, give a reply, offer a distinction). We might so take it here (e.g. 'people apt at inductive arguments should give answers to a beginner'), but not very naturally. I take it instead to mean 'assign': cf. *Pol.* 1316ᵇ39 for this use of *ἀποδοτέον πρός*. Since *ἐπακτικῶν* and *συλλογιστικῶν* must refer to persons in the next sentence, it is likely that they also do so here.

164ᵇ5: 'In general' (*ὅλως*): though Aristotle almost always uses this word in this sense, it is strictly speaking an adverbial form of *ὅλος* ('whole'), and other translators undertake so to render it ('one thing must be taken as a whole')—implausibly, in my opinion.

164ᵇ13: 'the level of argument is bound to degenerate': a free translation of *ἀνάγκη γὰρ πονηρολογίαν συμβαίνειν*. The word *πονηρολογία* is a *hapax*; the closely related *κακολογία* commonly meant 'verbal abuse' or even 'slander', but Plato uses it in the sense 'bad writing-style' (see *Rep.* 401ᵃ5–7). I take *πονηρολογία* to have an analogous sense ('bad argumentative form', 'degenerate argumentation'). The problem is not so much that arguments with the untutored may become abusive as that they may encourage bad practices.

164ᵇ19: I follow here the text of the manuscripts (*καὶ πρὸς οὓς πορίζεσθαι* instead of Ross's *καὶ οὓς προσπορίζεσθαι*). However, I punctuate after 'universal arguments' (*οἱ καθόλου*) in l. 18 and treat *πρός* as adverbial ('in addition'). Adverbial *πρός* is not unknown in Aristotle (cf. *SE* 4, 166ᵃ35), but the only other occurrence of *προσπορίζεσθαι* (*Mete.* III. 5, 376ᵃ14) has a technical mathematical sense that cannot fit here.

EXCERPT A

113ᵇ15: 'from the negations': *ἐκ* (MSS), not *ἐπὶ* (Wallies).

114ᵇ36–7: 'and all those': *σύστοιχα δὲ* with the manuscripts rather than *σύστοιχα δὴ* (Wallies).

114ᵇ3: 'And "justly"': retaining *δικαίως καὶ*, which Wallies deletes.

114ᵇ10: 'skilfully' (*ἐμπείρως*): lit. 'in an experienced manner'.

114^{b}19–20: 'themselves evils': Ross follows Wallies in adding 'and if they are themselves evils, then their generations are evils' (καὶ εἰ αὐτὰ τῶν κακῶν, καὶ αἱ γενέσεις τῶν κακῶν).

114^{b}37: 'from more': I omit 'and less' (καὶ ἧττον) with ABD and Boethius.

EXCERPT B

119^{b}17–18: 'or what it belongs to': reading ἢ ᾧ ἂν ὑπάρχῃ. Ross deletes 'or' (ἤ).

119^{b}4–5: 'if something done unjustly is a good, then something unjust {4–5} is a good': I follow Brunschwig, who adopts the text of his VP (πάλιν εἴ τι τῶν ἀδίκως ἀγαθόν, καὶ τῶν ἀδίκων τι ἀγαθόν). The other manuscripts give many variants: Ross combines sources to read πάλιν εἴ τι τῶν ἀδίκων ἀγαθόν, καὶ τῶν δικαίων τι κακόν. πάλιν εἴ τι τῶν δικαίως κακόν, καὶ τῶν ἀδίκως τι ἀγαθόν. Cf. 114^{a}37–^{b}3.

119^{b}6: 'something done pleasantly' (τι τῶν ἡδέως): Ross instead reads 'something pleasant' (τι τῶν ἡδέων), but that destroys the parallel.

120^{a}33: '⟨species⟩ of that which something is said to belong or not belong to' (ἐν οἷς ὑπάρχειν τι ἢ μὴ εἴρηται): compare I. 9, 103^{b}21 ἐν οἷς ὑπάρχουσιν and II. 2, 109^{b}13–14 τὸ ἐπιβλέπειν οἷς ὑπάρχειν ... εἴρηται.

120^{a}35: 'as was said earlier': II. 2, 109^{b}13–29.

EXCERPT C

171^{b}36–7: 'same premisses as dialectic': reading τῇ διαλεκτικῇ, with the manuscripts, rather than τῷ διαλεκτικῷ ('as the dialectician').

171^{b}37: 'the geometer': reading τὸν γεωμέτρην rather than Ross's τῷ γεωμέτρῃ, which would give the sense 'just as the fake-diagrammer leads into fallacies from the same premisses as the geometer'. The point is that the fake-diagrammer does the same thing *to the geometer*—i.e. leads him into a fallacy using his own principles—that the contentious reasoner does to those who use dialectic.

172^{a}1: 'Now ... applied to other subjects': reading περὶ μὲν τἆλλα (Ross deletes μὲν).

172ª11: 'The former subjects' (ἐκείνων): i.e. the (putative) subjects of dialectic, in contrast to the 'other subjects' mentioned at 172ª2. If contentious argument were fully analogous to fake-diagramming, we could say: 'Just as the fake-diagrammer's argument is not contentious about the subjects of geometry, so the contentious argument is not contentious about the subjects of dialectic'. The point of disanalogy is that dialectic does not have a subject-matter in the way geometry does.

172ª36: 'these premisses' (ταῦτα): Ross reads ταὐτά ('the same premisses').

EXCERPT D

183ᵇ1: 'ascribed ... the additional power': reading προσκατασκενάζεται instead of Ross's conjecture προσκατασκευαστέον ('there should be ascribed in addition').

183ᵇ15: 'said above': the reference is to 183ª27–30.

183ᵇ27–8: 'the other "arts" ': the word 'art' (τέχνη) can mean a systematic treatise, especially an 'art of rhetoric'.

184ᵇ2: 'other previous work to mention—even though': reading πρότερον ἄλλο λέγειν ἀλλ' ἤ (Ross gives πρότερον λέγειν ἤ).

184ᵇ6: 'or' (ἤ) is in all the manuscripts, but Ross deletes it.

BIBLIOGRAPHY

TEXTS, TRANSLATIONS, AND COMMENTARIES

ACKRILL, J. L. (1963), *Aristotle, Categories and De Interpretatione* (Clarendon Aristotle Series).

Alexander of Aphrodisias (1891), *In Aristotelis Topicorum Libri Octo Commentaria*, ed. Max Wallies (Commentaria in Aristotelem Graeca II. 2; Berlin: G. Reimer).

BARNES, JONATHAN (ed.) (1984), *The Complete Works of Aristotle* (the 'Revised Oxford' translation), 2 vols. (Princeton: Princeton University Press), i. 167–277.

BOETHIUS (1969), *Topica: Translatio Boethii, fragmentum recensionis alterius, et translatio anonyma*, ed. L. Minio-Paluello and E. G. Dod (Aristoteles Latinus v/1–3; Brussels: Desclée de Brouwer).

BRUNSCHWIG, JACQUES (1967), *Aristote, Topiques I–IV* (Paris: Éditions 'Les Belles Lettres').

COLLI, GIORGIO (1955), *Aristotele, Organon* (Turin: G. Einaudi).

FORSTER, G. (1960), *Aristotle, Posterior Analytics, Topica*, trans. Hugh Tredennick (*Posterior Analytics*) and G. Forster (*Topica*) (Loeb Classical Library; Cambridge, Mass.: Harvard University Press).

KIRWAN, CHRISTOPHER (1973), *Aristotle, Metaphysics Γ, Δ, and E* (Clarendon Aristotle Series).

PACIUS, JULIUS (Giulio Pace) (1623), *Aristotelis Stagiritae Peripateticorum Principis Organon* (repr. Frankfurt am Main: Minerva, 1967).

PICKARD-CAMBRIDGE, W. A. (1928), translation in W. D. Ross (ed.), *The Works of Aristotle Translated into English* (the 'Oxford Translation'), i (Oxford: Clarendon Press).

ROLFES, EUGEN (1922), *Aristoteles, Topik (Organon V)*, trans. Eugen Rolfes (2nd edn., Hamburg: Verlag von Felix Meiner).

ROSS, W. D. (ed.) (1958), *Aristotelis Topica et Sophistici Elenchi* (Oxford Classical Texts; Oxford: Clarendon Press).

TRICOT, J. (1984), *Organon V: Les Topiques* (Paris: Librairie Philosophique J. Vrin).

WAITZ, THEODOR (ed.) (1844–6), *Aristotelis Organon Graece* (Leipzig: Hahn; repr. Aalen: Scientia Verlag, 1965).

WALLIES, MAXIMILIANUS (ed.) (1923), *Aristotelis Topica cum libro de Sophisticis Elenchis* (Leipzig: Teubner).

TOPICS

BOOKS AND ARTICLES

BARNES, JONATHAN (1986), 'Aristotle on the Methods of Ethics', *Revue Internationale de Philosophie*, 34: 490–511.

BOLTON, ROBERT (1990), 'The Epistemological Basis of Aristotelian Dialectic', in D. Devereux and P. Pellegrin (eds.), *Biologie, logique, et métaphysique chez Aristote* (Paris: Éditions du CNRS), 185–236.

BRUNSCHWIG, JACQUES (1986), 'Aristotle on Arguments without Winners or Losers', *Wissenschaftskolleg Jahrbuch* 1984/5 (Berlin), 31–40.

BURNYEAT, MILES (1980), 'Aristotle on Learning to Be Good', in A. Rorty (ed.), *Essays on Aristotle's Ethics* (Berkeley and Los Angeles: University of California Press), 69–92.

——(1981), 'Aristotle on Understanding Knowledge', in E. Berti (ed.), *Aristotle on Science: The 'Posterior Analytics'* (Padua: Antenore), 97–139.

CODE, ALAN (1986), 'Aristotle's Investigation of a Basic Logical Principle: Which Science Investigates the Principle of Non-Contradiction?', *Canadian Journal of Philosophy*, 16: 341–58.

COOPER, JOHN (1975), *Reason and Human Good in Aristotle* (Cambridge, Mass.: Harvard University Press).

EVANS, J. D. G. (1977), *Aristotle's Concept of Dialectic* (Cambridge: Cambridge University Press).

GEACH, PETER (1972), 'History of the Corruptions of Logic', in his *Logic Matters* (Oxford: Blackwell), 44–61.

HAMLYN, D. J. (1990), 'Aristotle on Dialectic', *Philosophy*, 65: 465–76.

IRWIN, TERENCE (1978), 'Aristotle's Discovery of Metaphysics', *Review of Metaphysics*, 31: 210–29.

——(1981), 'Homonymy in Aristotle', *Review of Metaphysics*, 34: 523–44.

——(1988), *Aristotle's First Principles* (Oxford: Clarendon Press).

KNEALE, WILLIAM, and KNEALE, MARTHA (1962), *The Development of Logic* (Oxford: Clarendon Press).

KNORR, WILBUR (1975), *The Evolution of the Euclidean Elements* (Dordrecht: D. Reidel).

KOSMAN, ARYEH (1973), 'Understanding, Explanation, and Insight in the *Posterior Analytics*', in H. D. P. Lee, A. P. D. Mourelatos, and R. Rorty (eds.), *Exegesis and Argument: Studies in Greek Philosophy Presented to Gregory Vlastos* (*Phronesis*, Supp. Vol. 1), 374–92.

MAGUINNESS, W. S. (1946), 'Aristotle, Topica 107a8–10', *Classical Review*, 60: 19.

MORAUX, PAUL (1968), 'La Joute dialectique d'après le huitième livre des *Topiques*', in Owen (1968a), 277–311.

NUSSBAUM, MARTHA (1986), *The Fragility of Goodness* (Cambridge: Cambridge University Press).

OWEN, G. E. L. (1960), 'Logic and Metaphysics in Some Earlier Works of Aristotle', in I. Düring and G. E. L. Owen (eds.), *Aristotle and Plato in the mid-Fourth Century* (Proceedings of the Second Symposium Aristotelicum; Göteborg: Elanders), 163–90.

——(1961), '*Tithenai ta Phainomena*', in S. Mansion (ed.), *Aristote et les problèmes de méthode* (Louvain: Publications Universitaires de Louvain), 83–103.

——(1968), 'Dialectic and Eristic in the Treatment of the Forms', in Owen (1968*a*), 103–25.

——(ed.) (1968*a*), *Aristotle on Dialectic: The Topics*, (Proceedings of the Third Symposium Aristotelicum; Oxford: Clarendon Press).

OWENS, JOSEPH (1963), *The Doctrine of Being in the Aristotelian Metaphysics*, 2nd edn. (Toronto: Pontifical Institute of Medieval Studies).

PRANTL, CARL (1855–67), *Geschichte der Logik im Abendlande* (Leipzig: Hirzel; repr. Graz: Akademische Druck- und Verlagsanstalt, 1955).

RYLE, GILBERT (1968), 'Dialectic in the Academy', in Owen (1968*a*), 69–79.

SMITH, ROBIN (1982), 'The Syllogism in *Posterior Analytics I*', *Archiv für Geschichte der Philosophie*, 64: 113–35.

——(1986), 'Immediate Propositions and Aristotle's Theory of Proof', *Ancient Philosophy*, 6: 47–68.

——(1993), 'Aristotle on the Uses of Dialectic', *Synthèse*, 96: 335–58.

——(1994), 'Logic', in Jonathan Barnes (ed.), *The Cambridge Companion to Aristotle* (Cambridge: Cambridge University Press), 27–65.

SOLMSEN, FRIEDRICH (1929), *Die Entwicklung der aristotelischen Logik und Rhetorik* (Berlin: Weidmann).

SORABJI, RICHARD (1972), *Aristotle on Memory* (Providence: Brown University Press).

STUMP, ELEONORE (1978), *Boethius's De topicis differentiis* (Ithaca, NY: Cornell University Press).

VERDENIUS, J. (1968), 'Notes on the *Topics*', in Owen (1968*a*), 3–21.

GLOSSARY

This list is for the most part limited to terms with technical senses. Grammar and construction occasionally require deviations from these renderings; I have noted some, but not all, variations here. Some terms are included which occur in the Excerpts but not in Topics I or VIII.

ἀγωνιστικός	combative
ἀδικομαχία	dirty fighting (171ᵇ23)
ἀδολέσχειν	ramble
ἄδοξος	unacceptable; disgraceful (160ᵇ18–22)
ἀδύνατον	impossible
διὰ τοῦ ἀδυνάτου	through the impossible (of arguments)
αἰτεῖν	ask (for)
τὸ ἐν ἀρχῇ αἰτεῖν	ask for the initial thing (162ᵇ31 ff.)
ἀκολούθησις	consequence (113ᵇ19ff.)
ἀκριβής	exact
ἀμφισβητεῖν, ἀμφισβήτησις	dispute (verb, noun)
ἀνάγκη	necessity; necessarily
ἀναγκαῖος	(premiss) needed for a conclusion (155ᵇ19)
ἀναιρεῖν	reject
ἀνασκευάζειν	reject
ἀντεπιχειρεῖν	counterattack
ἀντίθεσις	opposition
ἀντικατηγορεῖσθαι	counterpredicate (with)
ἀντικεῖσθαι, ἀντιτιθέναι	(be) opposed to
ἀντικείμενον	opposite
ἀντιλογία	disputation (171ᵇ23)
ἀντιλογικός	skilled in contradiction
ἀντιστρέφειν	convert
ἀντίφασις	negation
ἀξιοῦν	claim; claim a right; expect
ἀξίωμα	claim (noun)
ἁπλῶς	without qualification
ἀποδεικνύναι	demonstrate
ἀπόδειξις	demonstration
ἀποκρίνεσθαι	answer (verb)
ἀποκρινόμενος	answerer
ἀπόκρισις	answer (noun)
ἀπόστασις, ἀφιστάναι	standing off, stand off
ἀποφάναι	deny

193

ἀπόρημα, ἀπορία	puzzle
ἀρχή	starting-point; beginning
γενικός	genus-like
γένος	genus
γνώριμος	familiar; intelligible
γνωρίζειν	recognize
γνῶσις	knowledge
γραμματικός	literate
γραμματική	literacy (ability to read and write)
γράφειν	draw; prove (in geometry)
γυμνάζεσθαι	(to) exercise
γυμνασία	exercise (noun)
διαλέγεσθαι	argue
διαλεκτική	dialectical art
διαλεκτικός	dialectical, dialectician
διαφορά	differentia; different varieties (100ᵃ22)
διαπορεῖν	go through the puzzles
δόγμα	belief
δοκεῖν	seem (τινι); think
τὰ δοκοῦντα	what people think
δόξα	opinion
δοξάζειν	think
δυσκολαίνειν	be cantankerous
δύσκολος	cantankerous
εἶδος	species
ἐκλέγειν	collect (premisses) (105ᵃ34ff.)
ἐλέγχειν	refute
ἐναντίος	contrary
ἔνδοξος	acceptable; esteemed (100ᵇ23)
ἐνίστασθαι	object (bring an objection)
ἔνστασις	objection
ἕξις	state (opp. στέρησις)
ἐπάγειν	argue by induction; bring in (159ᵃ18–19)
ἐπαγωγή	induction
ἐπὶ μέρους	partial (120ᵃ3, 120ᵃ20)
ἐπιχειρεῖν	attack
ἐπισκέψασθαι	inquire
ἐπιζητεῖν	inquire
ἐπιστήμη	science
ἐπιτιμᾶν, ἐπιτίμησις	criticize, criticism
ἐριστικός	contentious
ἐρωτᾶν	ask, question

ἐρώτησις	asking
ἐρωτῶν	questioner
ἐρωτηματίζειν	devise questions
εὐήθης	silly
εὐπορεῖν	be equipped to deal with
ζήτησις	search
ἠθικός	ethical
θέσις	thesis; concession
θεώρημα	point of speculation
θεωρία	study
ἴδιον	unique property
ἴδιος	unique
καθόλου	universal
καταριθμεῖσθαι	enumerate
κατασκευάζειν	establish
κατηγορεῖσθαι	predicate (verb)
κατηγορία	category
κόσμος	embellishment
κρύπτεσθαι, κρύψις	conceal, concealment
κύριος	literal, strict
λῆμμα	premiss
λογικός	logical
λόγος	argument; phrase; account
λύειν	solve (a fallacy or contrary argument)
λύσις	solution
μεταβιβάζειν	change (someone else's) mind
οἱ πολλοί	the public
οἱ πλεῖστοι	the majority
οἰκεῖος	appropriate
ὁμώνυμος	equivocal
ὄνομα	word; name
ὁρισμός, ὅρος	definition
ὁρίζεσθαι	define
ὁρικός	definitory
οὐσία	being; substance
παράδοξος	contrary to opinion
παραλογίζεσθαι	conclude fallaciously; produce a fallacy
παραλογισμός	fallacy
πεῖρα	testing; trial (171^b4)
πεῖραν λαμβάνειν	make trial (171^b4)
πειραστική	art of making trial (171^b4, 172^a21, 172^a31)
πίστις	conviction; trustworthiness; proof (103^b3)

πιθανός	convincing
πραγματεία	study; treatise
πρόβλημα	problem
προβάλλειν	make a problem of
πρότασις	premiss
προτείνειν	hold out [a premiss]
πρόθεσις	goal (100)
πτῶσις	case; inflected form (see 114ᵃ33 ff.)
πυνθάνεσθαι	get answers
σημαίνειν	signify
σκέψις	examination
στέρησις	privation (cf. ἕξις)
στοιχεῖον	element
συλλογισμός	deduction
συλλογίζεσθαι	deduce
συμβαίνειν	result; happen; accompany
συμβεβηκός	accident
συμπέρασμα	conclusion
συνώνυμος	univocal
σύστοιχος	co-ordinate (see 114ᵃ27 ff.)
τάξις	arrangement
τάττεσθαι	arrange
τί ἐστι	what it is
ἐν τῷ τί ἐστι	in the what-it-is (of predication)
τί ἦν εἶναι	what-it-is (essence)
τιθέναι	concede; suppose
τόπος	location (of an argument)
τρόπος	form; way
τύπος	outline
τύπῳ	in outline
ὑπέχειν λόγον	submit to argument (i.e. play the answerer)
ὑπόθεσις	assumption
φιλοσόφημα	(see 162ᵃ15)
φιλοσοφία	philosophy
φυσικός	scientific (105ᵇ24)
ψευδογραφεῖν	draw fake diagrams (101ᵃ10, 157ᵃ2, 160ᵇ36)
ψευδογράφημα	fake diagram (171ᵇ12, 14)
ψευδογράφος	fake-diagrammer (171ᵇ37, 172ᵃ10, ᵇ2)

INDEX LOCORUM

197

INDEX LOCORUM

GENERAL INDEX

Boldface numbers indicate pages in the translation, including the translated excerpts. All other arabic numbers indicate pages in the commentary.

education (moral vs.
  scientific) 154–5
elements (geometrical) 124, 157,
  158
embellishment (*kosmos*) 107, 115
Empedocles **12**
encounters **2**, 51
enthymemes **40**
enumeration 161
equipped to deal with
  (*euporein*) 77
equivocal 94–5
eristic xiii–xiv, 101; *see
  also* contentious
essence 60; *see* what-it-is-to-be
essential, *see* what-it-is
ethical (premises) **12–13**, 81, 90–1
example, argument from 113
exercise **2**, **28**, **38**

fake diagrammer
  (*pseudographos*) **2**, **23**, **32**, 50,
  114, 138, **174**, **175**
fallacies **2**, **18**, 48, 137, **175**
fallaciously conclude
  (*paralogizesthai*) 49, 112
false (of arguments) 147–9
false cause 136, 150
false-drawer, *see* fake-diagrammer
fault (*hamartēma*) 149
fine (*kalon*) 94–5
first philosophy 91
first principles 109
focal meaning 99, 95

Geach, Peter 58
genus (*genos*) **3**, **5**, **16**, 57, 73, 74,
  102
genus-like (*genikon*) **6**, 64
geometers, geometry **2**, **34**, **39**, 80,
  123, **174**
geometrical proof 49
geometrical theorems 124
get answers (*punthanesthai*) 114
Gorgias **177**
gymnastic xx–xxiii, 105, 139

habituation xiv, 83–4,
Hamlyn, D. M. 82
happiness, definition 156
hard to deal with
  (*dusepicheirētos*) 123, 126
harmonics, numerical **15**
Heraclitus xxiv, **10**, **30**, 132
Herminus 142
Hippocrates **173**
Homer **23**, 115, 116
homonyny 95
hoodwink (*parakrouesthai*) 117

Ideas, Platonic 95, 97, 145

immediate (*amesos*) 45–7
impossible, argument through
  the 150
initial thing (*thesis*) 105, 111
indefinite (statements) 119, **172**
index locations 157
induction, inductive arguments
  xxii, **7**, **11**, **19**, **20**, **21**, **22**, **23**,
  24, **40**, 43, 72, 84–7, 92, 101–2,
  106, 109–10, 115, 116–17, 163,
  165
inference, common 155
inference, rules of 156–7
inference, specific 155
infinite regress 46
inflection, inflected form
  (*ptōsis*) **15**, 93, 97
inquiry (and dialectic) **29**, 81–2
insensible (*anaisthētos*) 96
instruction and dialectical
  arguments 127–8
instruments (of dialectic) 92
Irwin, Terence xviii, 52, 53, 82

judges (of dialectical
  exchanges) 113, 122
Judson, Lindsay vii

Kansas State University vii
Kirwan, Christopher 83
Kneale, Martha and William 58

DATE DUE